To Rev. A. J. Billings
With Kindest regards
of Geo. B. Loring

A. B. Mead.
from A. Billings,
[illegible] 1890

WESLEY, HIS OWN HISTORIAN.

ILLUSTRATIONS OF HIS CHARACTER, LABORS, AND ACHIEVEMENTS.

FROM HIS OWN DIARIES.

By Rev. EDWIN L. JANES,
OF THE NEW YORK EAST ANNUAL CONFERENCE

New York:
CARLTON & LANAHAN.
SAN FRANCISCO: E. THOMAS.
CINCINNATI: HITCHCOCK & WALDEN.
1870.

PREFACE.

THE volume now offered to the Christian public has this peculiarity: it allows Mr. Wesley to speak for himself. The entire volume, with the exception of a few preliminary and closing pages, consists of selections from the third and fourth volumes of his Works, American edition, comprising his journal from Oct. 14, 1735, to Oct 24, 1790, a period of more than half a century.

I have endeavored to make such selections as point directly to some event in Mr. Wesley's life, some trait in his character, some expression of his views, or some achievement in his work. No one, we think, can open this casket of jewels without being attracted by their luster, and charmed with their beauty.

As the reader peruses these pages he will find the extracts as so many index fingers pointing to the faith, patience, charity, humility, gentleness, sympathy, sincerity, and devotion of this wonderful man.

His account of his marvelous labors, sufferings, and successes, as presented in his own artless but nervous and comprehensive style, will bring him before the reader in his diversified work of preaching, visiting the sick and dying, burying the dead, praying with penitents, visiting the classes, examining and sifting the societies, adjusting difficulties, harmonizing discordant elements, instructing his "assistants," abbreviating and translating useful books, preparing sermons for the press, and explaining and defending the truths he taught: for although Mr. Wesley did not love controversy, and sought to avoid it, yet when the interests of evangelical truth required it he gathered up the broken shafts that fell at his feet, and re-sharpened by his logical skill, hurled them against his enemies with fatal precision and force.

Probably no man ever had as many preaching places, or as great a variety of hearers, as John Wesley; but it made little difference to him whether he preached on moor or mountain, in street or market-place, in church or barn, in cathedral or cottage, in parlor or poor-house, in jail or hospital, so long as he could proclaim a free and full salvation to perishing sinners.

The fires of his love and zeal burned as intensely, and glowed as brightly when preaching to "a people dead as stones," "a lifeless, noisy, glittering people," "a dull, rude, senseless multitude," "a wild, unbroken herd," as when preaching to a "willing multitude," "a people all alive and ready to devour the word," "a brilliant congregation."

Whether proclaiming Christ to the learned or illiterate, rich or poor, Protestant or Papist, keelmen or colliers—to a score of hearers or a score of thousands—this great evangelist seems to have been actuated by the purest motives and most ardent zeal that can possibly inspire the heart, or govern the life, of a mortal.

These pages will show that the immediate effects of Mr. Wesley's preaching were often surprising. On some occasions "It was as though we were standing before the great white throne;" at other times, "The hearts of the hearers were as melting wax."

The reader's attention will also be arrested by his remarkable power with God in prayer, especially when pleading for the penitent and for despairing souls, for the sick and afflicted, and for himself, when needing physical strength for the hour.

In the perusal of this volume the reader will not fail to observe the many escapes of Mr. Wesley from fire and flood, and from the dangers incident to traveling, as well as from the plots and power of his persecutors. His wonder will be excited by the powers of endurance he exhibited in his unparalleled labors, as also by his sudden recovery to health and strength, his recuperative energies acting with almost miraculous quickness.

He will be amazed at the magic influence this great organizer and leader in the Church of God wielded over his preachers and hearers, and over infuriated mobs, and he will be led to admire the courage and wisdom displayed in the use of this power.

He will reach the conclusion that Mr. Wesley never lost his self-possession or fortitude amid the exciting and dangerous scenes through which he passed; and that he literally carried out his inflexible purpose, that, in spite of opposition and obstacles, he would make no compromise with earthly powers or policy, nor pause in his career, nor rest from his labors, till dismissed from the field by his Divine Master.

All through the volume the reader will meet with Mr. Wesley's pithy sayings, replete with truth and common sense; with sharp criticisms on men and books; and with many sentences marked with sprightliness, and at times with playfulness.

So vivid are the descriptions of the scenes through

which he passes in his travels and labors, that the reader will seem to be one of his traveling companions, listening to his pathetic and persuasive discourses, rejoicing with him when "the power" descends upon his congregations or pervades the love-feast, and sharing in his triumph of soul when in some hard-fought battle the enemy is conquered, and the standard of the cross planted.

We will only add, that where we have made one or two selections as illustrating some fact in the history or trait in the character of Mr. Wesley a score might have been added, but this would have extended the work to an undue size. We do not claim for this volume that it gives a full and connected history of this great reformer, but we think its contents will impart much useful information, and lead the reader to the resolve to be a more spiritual and active Christian.

We trust that many will be so profited by this stream from the fountain as to give the entire journals a thorough and prayerful perusal; and in doing so they will doubtless coincide with the sentiment of our great historian of Methodism, that "Wesley's Journals are the most interesting productions of his pen. They are the history of the man and of his cause." May we not also hope that this volume may prove timely as affording a practical answer to the great question of the day, "How shall we reach and evangelize the masses?"

The contents of this book are placed in the chronological order in which they are found in the third and fourth volumes of his Works, which will be a sufficient guide for purposes of reference. E. L. J.

WESLEY HIS OWN HISTORIAN.

Wesley's Parentage.

JOHN WESLEY was born in Epworth, Lincolnshire, England, on the 14th of June, 1703. His father, Rev. Samuel Wesley, was a minister of the Church of England, and was a man of superior learning and of stern integrity. His mother, Mrs. Susanna Wesley, was the daughter of Dr. Samuel Annesley, and was a woman "of extraordinary sense and piety." "The firm and manly character, the practical sense, the active and unwearied habits of the father, with the calm, reflecting, and stable qualities of the mother, were in particular inherited by John Wesley, and in him were most happily blended."—*Watson's Wesley*, chap. i.

His Early Education.

"Mrs. Wesley was the instructress of her children in their early years. She was particularly led to interest herself in John, who, when about six years old, had a providential and singular escape from being burned to death upon the parsonage being consumed." She considered this event as laying her under special obligation "to be more particularly careful of the soul of a child whom God had so mercifully provided for." "The effect of this special care was, that, under the Divine blessing, he became early serious, for at the age of eight years he was admitted by his father to partake of the sacrament."

"In 1714 Wesley was placed at the Charter House, where he was noticed for his diligence and progress in learning, and he became a favorite with his master, Dr. Walker, on account of his quietness, regularity, and application."

Wesley Elected to Christ Church, Oxford.

"When he had attained his seventeeth year he was elected to Christ Church, Oxford, where he pursued his studies to great advantage, under the direction of Dr. Wigham, a gentleman eminent for his classical knowledge."

Mr. Wesley's natural temperament in his youth was gay and sprightly, with a turn for wit and humor. When he was about twenty-one years of age he appeared, as Mr. Babcock has observed, "the very sensible and acute collegian, of the finest classical taste, and of the most liberal and manly sentiments." His perfect knowledge of the classics gave a smooth polish to his wit, and an air of superior elegance to all his compositions.

His Ordination, and Election as Fellow of Lincoln College.

Wesley was ordained Deacon in Sept., 1725, and the year following was elected Fellow of Lincoln College. His previous seriousness had been the subject of much banter and ridicule, and appears to have been urged against him in his election by his opponents; but his reputation for learning and diligence, and the excellence of his character, triumphed,

Wesley's Literary Character Established in the University.

The following summer he spent in Lincolnshire with his parents, and in September returned to Oxford and resumed his usual studies. His literary character was now established in the University; he was acknowledged by all parties to be a man of talent, and an excellent critic in the learned languages. His compositions were distinguished by an elegant simplicity of style, and justness of thought, that strongly marked the excellence of his classical taste.

Wesley's skill in logic, or the art of reasoning, was universally known and admired. The high opinion that was entertained of him in these respects was soon publicly expressed by choosing him Greek Lecturer and Moderator of the classes, on the seventh of November, though he had only been elected Fellow of the College in March, when he was little more than twenty-three years of age, and had not proceeded Master of Arts. He took the degree in February, 1727; became his father's curate in August the same year; returned to Oxford in 1728 to obtain Priests' Orders, and paid another visit to Oxford in 1729, but returned in about a month to Epworth.

Becomes Tutor in the College.

At the instance of Dr. Morley, the rector of his college, he left his father's curacy, and in November again settled in Oxford. He now obtained pupils and became tutor in the college, presided as Moderator in the disputations six times a week, and had the chief direction of a religious society. From this time he stood more prominently forward in his religious character, and began more fully to prove that they that will live godly in Christ Jesus must suffer persecution.—*Watson's Wesley*, chap. i.

Wesley's First Efforts at Religious Usefulness.

In a letter addressed to Mr. Morgan, Sen., and written in October, 1730, Mr. Wesley says: "In November, 1729, at which time I came to reside at Oxford, your son, my brother, myself, and one more, agreed to spend three or four evenings in a week together. Our design was to read over the classics, which we had before read in private on common nights, and on Sunday some book in divinity. In the summer following Mr. M. told me he had called at the jail, to see a man who was condemned for killing his wife; and that, from the talk he had with one of the debtors, he verily believed it would do much good, if any one would be at the pains of now and then speaking with them. This he so frequently repeated, that on the 24th of August, 1730, my brother and I walked with him to the castle. We were so well satisfied with our conversation there that we agreed to go thither once or twice a week, which we had not done long before he desired me to go with him to see a poor woman in the town who was sick. In this employment too, when we came to reflect upon it, we believed it would be worth while to spend an hour or two in a week, provided the minister of the parish, in which any such person was, were not against it."

Wesley Consults his Father.

"But, that we might not depend wholly on our own judgments, I wrote an account to my father of our whole design; withal begging that he, who had lived seventy years in the world, and seen as much of it as most private men have ever done, would advise us whether we had yet gone too far, and whether we should now stand still or go forward."

Part of his father's answer, dated Sept. 21, 1730, was this: "And now as to your own designs and employments, what can I say less of them than *Valde probo*;* and that I have the highest reason to bless God that he has given me two sons together at Oxford, to whom he has given grace and courage to turn the war against the world and the devil, which is the best way to conquer them. They have but one more enemy to combat with, the flesh; which, if they take care to subdue by fasting and prayer, there will be no more for them to do, but to proceed steadily in the same course, and expect 'the crown which fadeth not away.' You have reason to bless God, as I do, that you have so fast a friend as Mr. M., who, I see, in the most difficult service, is ready to break the ice for you. You do not know of how much good that poor wretch who killed his wife has been the providential occasion. I think I must adopt Mr. M. to be my son, together with you and your brother Charles; and when I have such a ternion to prosecute that war, wherein I am now *miles emeritus*,† I shall not be ashamed when they speak with their enemies in the gate."

The Holy Club.

In a letter to "a clergyman of known wisdom and integrity," after describing the plans of usefulness and piety he and his friends had formed, Mr. Wesley says: "Almost as soon as we had made our first attempts this way, some of the men of wit in Christ Church

* I greatly approve. † A soldier past service.

entered the lists against us; and, between mirth and anger, made a pretty many reflections upon the Sacramentarians, as they were pleased to call us. Soon after their allies at Merton changed our title, and did us the honor of styling us, The Holy Club."

Wesley Sails to America—Motive.

Tuesday, Oct. 14, 1735. Mr. Benjamin Ingham, of Queen's College, Oxford, Mr. Charles Delamotte, son of a merchant in London, who had offered himself some days before, my brother Charles Wesley, and myself, took boat for Gravesend, in order to embark for Georgia. Our end in leaving our native country was not to avoid want, (God having given us plenty of temporal blessings,) nor to gain the dung or dross of riches or honor; but singly this—to save our souls; to live wholly to the glory of God. In the afternoon we found the Simmons off Gravesend, and immediately went on board.

How Employed on Shipboard.

Tuesday, Oct. 21. We sailed from Gravesend. When we were past about half the Goodwin Sands the wind suddenly failed. Had the calm continued till ebb, the ship had probably been lost. But the gale sprung up again in an hour, and carried us into the Downs.

We now began to be a little regular. Our common way of living was this: From four in the morning till five, each of us used private prayer. From five to seven we read the Bible together, carefully comparing it (that we might not lean to our own understandings) with the writings of the earliest ages. At seven we breakfasted. At eight were the public prayers. From nine to twelve I usually learned German, and Mr. Delamotte, Greek. My brother writ sermons, and Mr. Ingham instructed the children. At twelve we met to give an account to one another of what we had done since our last meeting, and what we designed to do before our next. About one we dined. The time from dinner to four we spent in reading to those whom each of us had taken in charge, or in speaking to them severally, as need required. At four were the evening prayers; when either the Second Lesson was explained, (as it was always in the morning,) or the children were catechised, and instructed before the congregation. From five to six we again used private prayer. From six to seven I read in our cabin to two or three of the passengers, (of whom there were about eighty English on board,) and each of my brethren to a few more in theirs. At seven I joined with the Germans in their public service; while Mr. Ingham was reading between the decks to as many as desired to hear. At eight we met again, to exhort and instruct one another. Between nine and ten we went to bed, where neither the roaring of the sea nor the motion of the ship could take away the refreshing sleep which God gave us.

Wesley Unwilling to Die.

Sunday, Nov. 23. At night I was waked by the tossing of the ship and roaring of the wind, and plainly showed I was unfit, for I was unwilling, to die.

Storms at Sea.

Saturday, Jan. 17, 1736. Many people were very impatient at the contrary wind. At seven in the evening they were quieted by a storm. It rose higher and higher till nine. About nine the sea broke over us from stem to stern; burst through the windows of the state cabin, where three or four of us were, and covered us all over, though a bureau sheltered me from the main shock. About eleven I lay down in the great cabin, and in a short time fell asleep, though very uncertain whether I should wake alive, and much ashamed of my unwillingness to die. O how pure in heart must he be who would rejoice to appear before God at a moment's warning! Toward morning, "He rebuked the winds and the sea, and there was a great calm."

Friday, Jan. 23. In the evening another storm began. In the morning it increased, so that they were forced to let the ship drive. I could not but say to myself, "How is it that thou hast no faith?" being still unwilling to die. About one in the afternoon, almost as soon as I had stepped out of the great cabin door, the sea did not break as usual, but came with a full smooth tide over the side of the ship. I was vaulted over with water in a moment, and so stunned that I scarce expected to lift my head again till the sea should give up her dead. But, thanks be to God! I received no hurt at all. About midnight the storm ceased.

Sunday, Jan. 25. At noon our third storm began. At four it was more violent than before. Now, indeed, we could say, "The waves of the sea" were mighty, and raged "horribly." They rose up to the heavens above, and" clave "down to hell beneath." The winds roared round about us, and (what I never heard before) whistled as distinctly as if it had been a human voice. The ship not only rocked to and fro with the utmost violence, but shook and jarred with so unequal, grating a motion, that one could not but with great difficulty keep one's hold of any thing, nor stand a moment without it. Every ten minutes came a shock against the stern or side of the ship, which one would think should dash the planks in pieces. At this time a child, privately baptized before, was brought to be received into the Church. It put me in mind of Jeremiah's buying the field, when the Chaldeans were on the point of destroying Jerusalem, and seemed a pledge of the mercy God designed to show us, even in the land of the living.

We spent two or three hours after prayers in conversing suitably to the occasion, confirming one another in a calm submission to the wise, holy, gracious will of God. And now a storm did not appear so terrible as before. Blessed be the God of all consolation!

At seven I went to the Germans. I had long before observed the great seriousness of their behavior. Of their humility they had given a continual proof, by performing those servile offices for the other passengers which none of the English would undertake; for which they desired, and would receive, no pay, saying, "It was good for their proud hearts," and "their loving Saviour had done more for them." And every day had given them occasion of showing a meekness which no injury could move. If they were pushed, struck, or thrown down, they rose again and went away; but no complaint was found in their mouth.

There was now an opportunity of trying whether they were delivered from the spirit of fear, as well as from that of pride, anger, and revenge. In the midst of the psalm wherewith their service began, the sea broke over, split the mainsail in pieces, covered the ship, and poured in between the decks, as if the great deep had already swallowed us up. A terrible screaming began among the English. The Germans calmly sung on. I asked one of them afterward, "Was you not afraid?" He answered, "I thank God, no." I asked, "But were not your women and children afraid?" He replied mildly, "No; our women and children are not afraid to die."

Devotions on the American Shore.

Friday, Feb. 6. About eight in the morning, we first set foot on American ground. It was a small uninhabited island over against Tybee. Mr. Oglethorpe led us to a rising ground, where we all kneeled down to give thanks. He then took boat for Savannah. When the rest of the people were come on shore, we called our little flock together to prayers. Several parts of the Second Lesson (Mark vi,) were wonderfully suited to the occasion; in particular, our Lord's directions to the first preachers of his Gospel, and their toiling at sea, and deliverance; with these comfortable words, "It is I, be not afraid."

Wesley's Interview with Mr. Spangenberg.

Saturday, Feb. 7. Mr. Oglethorpe returned from Savannah with Mr. Spangenberg, one of the pastors of the Germans. I soon found what spirit he was of, and asked his advice with regard to my own conduct. He said, "My brother, I must first ask you one or two questions. Have you the witness within yourself? Does the Spirit of God bear witness with your spirit that you are a child of God?" I was surprised, and knew not what to answer. He observed it, and asked, "Do you know Jesus Christ?" I paused, and said, "I know he is the Saviour of the world." "True," replied he; "but do you know he has saved you?" I answered, "I hope he has died to save me." He only added, "Do you know yourself?" I said, "I do." But I fear they were vain words.

Disappointed that he cannot Preach to the Indians.

Tuesday, Nov. 23. Mr. Oglethorpe sailed for England, leaving Mr. Ingham, Mr. Delamotte, and me, at Savannah, but with less prospect of preaching to the Indians than we had the first day we set foot in America. Whenever I mentioned it, it was immediately replied, "You cannot leave Savannah without a minister." To this, indeed, my plain answer was, "I know not that I am under any obligation to the contrary. I never promised to stay here one month. I openly declared both before, at, and ever since my coming hither, that I neither would nor could take charge of the English any longer than till I could go among the Indians." If it was said, "But did not the Trustees of Georgia appoint you to be minister at Savannah?" I replied, "They did, but it was not done by my solicitation; it was done without either my desire or knowledge. Therefore, I cannot conceive that appointment to lay me under any obligation of continuing there any longer than till a door is opened to the heathens, and this I expressly declared at the time I consented to accept of that appointment." But though I had no other obligation not to leave Savannah now, yet that of love I could not break through; I could not resist the importunate request of the more serious parishioners "to watch over their souls yet a little longer, till some one came who might supply my place." And this I the more willingly did, because the time was not come to preach the Gospel of peace to the heathens; all their nations being in a ferment; and Paustoobee and Mingo Mattaw having told me, in terms, in my own house, "Now our enemies are all about us, and we can do nothing but fight; but if the beloved ones should ever give us to be at peace, then we would hear the great word."

Reasons for Wesley's Return to England.

Oct. 7. I consulted my friends, whether God did not call me to return to England? The reason for which I left it had now no force, there being no possibility as yet of instructing the Indians; neither had I as yet found or heard of any Indians on the continent of America who had the least desire of being instructed.

Wesley takes Leave of America.

Thursday, Jan. 22, 1738. I took leave of America, (though, if it please God, not forever,) going on board the Samuel, Captain Percy, with a young gentleman who had been a few months in Carolina, one of my parishioners of Savannah, and a Frenchman, late of Purrysburgh, who was escaped thence with the skin of his teeth.

Reflections on Landing in England.

Feb. 17. It is now two years and almost four months since I left my native country, in order to teach the Georgian Indians the nature of Christianity; but what have I learned myself in the meantime? Why, (what I the least of all suspected,) that I, who went to America to convert others, was never myself converted to God. (I am not sure of this.) "I am not mad," though I thus speak; but "I speak the words of truth and soberness;" if haply some of those who still dream may awake, and see that as I am so are they.

Are they read in philosophy? So was I. In ancient or modern tongues? So was I also. Are they versed in the science of divinity? I too have studied it many years. Can they talk fluently upon spiritual things? The very same could I do. Are they plenteous in alms? Behold, I gave all my goods to feed the poor. Do they give of their labor as well as of their substance? I have labored more abundantly than they all. Are they willing to suffer for their brethren? I have thrown up my friends, reputation, ease, country; I have put my life in my hand, wandering into strange lands; I have given my body to be devoured by the deep, parched up with heat, consumed by toil and weariness, or whatsoever God should please to bring upon me. But does all this (be it more or less, it matters not) make me acceptable to God? Does all I ever did or can know, say, give, do, or suffer, justify me in his sight? Yea, or the constant use of all the means of grace? (which, nevertheless, is meet, right, and our bounden duty.) Or that I know nothing of myself; that I am, as touching outward, moral righteousness, blameless? Or (to come closer yet) the having a rational conviction of all the truths of Christianity? Does all this give me a claim to the holy, heavenly, divine character of a Christian? By no means. If the oracles of God are true, if we are still to abide by "the law and the testimony," all these things, though, when ennobled by faith in Christ,* they are holy and just and good, yet without it are "dung and dross," meet only to be purged away by "the fire that never shall be quenched."

This, then, have I learned in the ends of the earth—that I "am fallen short of the glory of God;" that my whole heart is "altogether corrupt and abominable, and, consequently, my whole life; (seeing it cannot be that an "evil tree" should "bring forth good fruit;") that "alienated" as I am "from the life of God," I am "a child of wrath,"† an heir of hell; that my own works, my own sufferings, my own righteousness, are so far from reconciling me to an offended God—so far from making any atonement for the least of those sins which are more in number than the hairs of my head—that the most specious of them need an atonement themselves, or they cannot abide his righteous judgment; that having "the sentence of death" in my heart, and having nothing in or of myself to plead, I have no hope but that of being justified freely, "through the redemption that is in Jesus." I have no hope but that if I seek I shall find Christ, and "be found in him, not having my

* I had even then the faith of a servant, though not of a son.

† I believe not.

own righteousness, but that which is through the faith of Christ, the righteousness which is of God by faith." Phil. iii, 9.

Results to Wesley of his Visit to America.

Feb. In the evening I came once more to London, whence I had been absent two years and near four months. Many reasons I have to bless God, though the design I went upon did not take effect, for my having been carried into that strange land, contrary to all my preceding resolutions. Hereby I trust he hath in some measure "humbled me, and proved me, and shown me what was in my heart." Hereby I have been taught to "beware of men;" hereby I am come to know assuredly that if "in all our ways we acknowledge God" he will, where reason fails, "direct our path" by lot, or by the other means which he knoweth. Hereby I am delivered from the fear of the sea, which I had both dreaded and abhorred from my youth.

Hereby God has given me to know many of his servants, particularly those of the Church of Hernhuth. Hereby my passage is opened to the writings of holy men in the German, Spanish, and Italian tongues. I hope, too, some good may come to others hereby. All in Georgia have heard the word of God. Some have believed, and began to run well. A few steps have been taken toward publishing the glad tidings both to the African and American heathens. Many children have learned "how they ought to serve God," and to be useful to their neighbor. And those whom it most concerns have an opportunity of knowing the true state of their infant colony, and laying a firmer foundation of peace and happiness to many generations.

Wesley's first Interview with Peter Bohler.

Tuesday, Feb. 7. (A day much to be remembered.) At the house of Mr. Weinantz, a Dutch merchant, I met Peter Bohler, Schulius Richter, and Wensel Neiser, just then landed from Germany. Finding they had no acquaintance in England, I offered to procure them a lodging, and did so, near Mr. Hutton's, where I then was. And from this time I did not willingly lose any opportunity of conversing with them while I stayed in London.

Impressed to leave off Preaching.

Saturday, March 4. I found my brother at Oxford, recovering from his pleurisy, and with him Peter Bohler, by whom (in the hand of the great God) I was, on *Sunday* the 5th, clearly convinced of unbelief—of the want of that faith whereby alone we are saved. (With the full Christian salvation.) Immediately it struck into my mind, "Leave off preaching. How can you preach to others, who have not faith yourself?" I asked Bohler whether he thought I should leave it off or not. He answered, "By no means." I asked, "But what can I preach?" He said, "Preach faith *till* you have it, and then, *because* you have it, you *will* preach faith."

Monday, March 6. I began preaching this new doctrine, though my soul started back from the work. The first person to whom I offered salvation by faith alone was a prisoner under sentence of death. His name was Clifford. Peter Bohler had many times desired me to speak to him before; but I could not prevail on myself so to do, being still (as I had been many years) a zealous assertor of the impossibility of a death-bed repentance.

The Fruits of Living Faith.

Thursday, March 23. I met Peter Bohler again, who now amazed me more and more by the account he gave of the fruits of living faith, the holiness and happiness which he affirmed to attend it. The next morning I began the Greek Testament again, resolving to abide by "the law and the testimony;" and being confident that God would hereby show me whether this doctrine was of God.

Conversion of a Condemned Criminal.

Monday, March 27. Mr. Kinchin went with me to the Castle, where, after reading prayers, and preaching on "It is appointed unto men once to die," we prayed with the condemned man, first in several forms of prayer, and then in such words as were given us in that hour. He kneeled down in much heaviness and confusion, having "no rest in" his "bones, by reason of" his "sins." After a space he rose up, and eagerly said, "I am now ready to die. I know Christ has taken away my sins, and there is no more condemnation for me." The same composed cheerfulness he showed when he was carried to execution; and in his last moments he was the same, enjoying a perfect peace, in confidence that he was "accepted in the Beloved."

Wesley breaks away from Forms of Prayer.

Saturday, April 1. Being at Mr. Fox's society, my heart was so full that I could not confine myself to the forms of prayer which we were accustomed to use there. Neither do I propose to be confined to them any more; but to pray indifferently, with a form or without, as I may find suitable to particular occasions.

Ten Years' Struggle between Nature and Grace.

May. All the time I was at Savannah I was beating the air. Being ignorant of the righteousness of Christ, which, by a living faith in him, bringeth salvation "to every one that believeth," I sought to establish my own righteousness, and so labored in the fire all my days. I was now properly "under the law;" I knew that "the law" of God was "spiritual; I consented to it, that it was good." Yea, "I delighted in it, after the inner man." Yet was I "carnal, sold under sin." Every day was I constrained to cry out, "What I do, I allow not: for what I would, I do not; but what I hate that I do. To will is" indeed "present with me; but how to perform that which is good I find not. For the good which I would, I do not; but the evil which I would not, that I do. I find a law, that when I would do good, evil is present with me:" even "the law in my members, warring against the law of my mind," and still "bringing me into captivity to the law of sin."

In this vile, abject state of bondage to sin I was indeed fighting continually, but not conquering. Before, I had willingly served sin; now it was unwillingly; but still I served it. I fell, and rose, and fell again. Sometimes I was overcome, and in heaviness: sometimes I overcame, and was in joy. For as in the former state I had some foretastes of the terrors of the law, so had I in this of the comforts of the Gospel. During this whole struggle between nature and grace, which had now continued above ten years, I had many remarkable returns to prayer, especially when I was in trouble; I had many sensible comforts; which are indeed no other than short anticipations of the life of faith. But I was still "under the law," not "under grace:" (the state most who are called Christians are content to live and die in:) for I was only striving with, not freed from, sin; neither had I the witness of the Spirit with my spirit, and indeed could not; for I "sought it not by faith, but, as it were, by the works of the law."

On my return to England, January, 1738, being in imminent danger of death, and very uneasy on that account, I was strongly convinced that the cause of that uneasiness was unbelief, and that the gaining a true living faith was the "one thing needful" for me. But still I fixed not this faith on its right object: I meant only faith in God, and faith in or through Christ. Again, I knew not that I was wholly void of this faith; but only thought I had not enough of it. So that when Peter Bohler, whom God prepared for me as soon as I came to London, affirmed of true faith in Christ, (which is but one,) that it had those two fruits inseparably attending it, "Dominion over sin, and constant peace from a sense of forgiveness," I was quite amazed, and looked upon it as a new Gospel. If this was so, it was clear I had not faith.

But I was not willing to be convinced of this. Therefore, I disputed with all my might, and labored to prove that faith might be where these were not; especially where the sense of forgiveness was not; for all the Scriptures relating to this I had been long since taught to construe away; and to call all Presbyterians who spoke otherwise. Besides, I well saw no one could, in the nature of things, have such a sense of forgiveness and not *feel* it. But I felt it not. If, then, there was no faith without this, all my pretensions to faith dropped at once.

When I met Peter Bohler again, he consented to put the dispute upon the issue which I desired, namely, Scripture and experience. I first consulted the Scripture. But when I set aside the glosses of men, and simply considered the words of God, comparing them together, endeavoring to illustrate the obscure by the plainer passages, I found they all made against me, and was forced to retreat to my last hold, "that experience would never agree with the *literal interpretation* of those Scriptures. Nor could I therefore allow it to be true, till I found some living witnesses of it." He replied, he could show me such at any time; if I desired it, the next day. And accordingly, the next day he came again with three others, all of whom testified, of their own personal experience, that a true living faith in Christ is inseparable from a sense of pardon for all past, and freedom from all present, sins. They added with one mouth, that this faith was the gift, the free gift of God; and that he would surely bestow it upon every soul who earnestly and perseveringly sought it. I was now thoroughly convinced; and by the grace of God I resolved to seek it unto the end, 1. By absolutely renouncing all dependence, in whole or in part, upon *my own* works or righteousness; on which I had really grounded my hope of salvation, though I knew it not, from my youth up. 2. By adding to the constant use of all the other means of grace continual prayer for this very thing, justifying, saving faith, a full reliance on the blood of Christ shed for *me;* a trust in him, as *my* Christ, as *my* sole justification, sanctification, and redemption.

His Conversion.

May. I continued thus to seek it, (though with strange indifference, dullness, and coldness, and unusually frequent relapses into sin,) till Wednesday, May 24. I think it was about five this morning that I opened my Testament on those words, *Τα μεγιϛα ἡμιν και τιμια επαγγελματα δεδωρηται, ινα γενησθε θειας κοινωνοι φυσεως*: "There are given unto us exceeding great and precious promises, even that ye should be partakers of the Divine nature." 2 Pet. i, 4. Just as I went out, I opened it again on those words, "Thou art not far from the kingdom of God." In the afternoon I was asked to go to St. Paul's. The anthem was, "Out of the deep have I called unto thee, O Lord: Lord, hear my voice. O let thine ears consider well the voice of my complaint. If thou, Lord, wilt be extreme to mark what is done amiss, O Lord, who may abide it? For there is mercy with thee; therefore shalt thou be feared. O Israel, trust in the Lord: for with the Lord there is mercy, and with him is plenteous redemption. And he shall redeem Israel from all his sins."

In the evening I went, very unwillingly, to a society in Aldersgate-street, where one was reading Luther's preface to the Epistle to the Romans. About a quarter before nine, while he was describing the change which God works in the heart through faith in Christ, I felt my heart strangely warmed. I felt I did trust in Christ, Christ alone, for salvation; and an assurance was given me that he had taken away *my* sins, even *mine*, and saved *me* from the law of sin and death.

Wesley Visits Germany.

Wednesday, June 7. I determined, if God should permit, to retire for a short time into Germany. I had fully proposed, before I left Georgia, so to do if it should please God to bring me back to Europe. And I now clearly saw the time was come. My weak mind could not bear to be thus sawn asunder. And I hoped the conversing with those holy men who were themselves living witnesses of the full power of faith, and yet able to bear with those that are weak, would be a means, under God, of so establishing my soul that I might go on from faith to faith, and "from strength to strength."

Meets with Living Proofs of the Power of Faith.

July 6. I lodged with one of the brethren at Eckershausen, an English mile from Marienborn, where I usually spent the day, chiefly in conversing with those who could speak either Latin or English; not being able, for want of more practice, to speak German readily. And here I continually met with what I sought for, namely, living proofs of the power of faith; persons saved from inward as well as outward sin, by "the love of God shed abroad in their hearts;" and from all doubt and fear, by the abiding witness of "the Holy Ghost given unto them."

Count Zinzendorf's and Bohler's Views of Justification.

Sunday, July 9. The Count preached in the old castle at Runneberg, (about three English miles from Marienborn,) where is also a small company of those who seek the Lord Jesus in sincerity. *Wednesday*, 12, was one of the conferences for strangers; where one of Frankfort proposing the question, Can a man be justified and not know it? the Count spoke largely and scripturally upon it, to this effect:

1. Justification is the forgiveness of sins.

2. The moment a man flies to Christ he is justified;

3. And has peace with God; but not always joy:

4. Nor perhaps may he know he is justified till long after.

5. For the assurance of it is distinct from justification itself.

6. But others may know he is justified by his power over sin, by his seriousness, his love of the brethren, and his "hunger and thirst after righteousness," which alone prove the spiritual life to be begun.

7. To be justified is the same thing as to be born of God. (Not so.)

8. When a man is awakened, he is begotten of God, and his fear and sorrow, and sense of the wrath of God, are the pangs of the new birth.

I then recollected what Peter Bohler had often said upon this head, which was to this effect:

1. When a man has living faith in Christ, then is he justified:

2. This is always given in a moment;
3. And in that moment he has peace with God;
4. Which he cannot have without knowing that he has it:
5. And being born of God, he sinneth not:
6. Which deliverance from sin he cannot have without knowing that he has it.

Wesley's description of Hernhuth, the Home of the Moravians.

Tuesday, Aug. 1. At three in the afternoon I came to Hernhuth, about thirty English miles from Dresden. It lies in Upper Lusatia, on the border of Bohemia, and contains about a hundred houses, built on a rising ground, with evergreen woods on two sides, gardens and cornfields on the others, and high hills at a small distance. It has one long street, through which the great road from Zittau to Löbau goes. Fronting the middle of this street is the Orphan House; in the lower part of which is the apothecary's shop, in the upper, the chapel, capable of containing six or seven hundred people. Another row of houses runs at a small distance from either end of the Orphan House, which accordingly divides the rest of the town (besides the long street) into two squares. At the east end of it is the Count's house; a small, plain building like the rest; having a large garden behind it, well laid out, not for show, but for the use of the community.

Mode of Worship in a Lutheran Church.

Sunday, Aug. 6. We went to church at Bertholdsdorf, a Lutheran village about an English mile from Hernhuth. Two large candles stood lighted upon the altar: the last supper was painted behind it; the pulpit was placed over it; and over that a brass image of Christ on the cross.

The minister had on a sort of pudding sleeve gown, which covered him all round. At nine began a long voluntary on the organ, closed with a hymn, which was sung by all the people sitting; in which posture, as is the German custom, they sung all that followed. Then the minister walked up to the altar, bowed, sung these Latin words, "*Gloria in excelsis Deo,*" bowed again, and went away. This was followed by another hymn, sung, as before, to the organ, by all the people. Then the minister went to the altar again, bowed, sung a prayer, read the epistle, and went away. After a third hymn was sung, he went a third time to the altar, sung a versicle, (to which all the people sung a response,) read the third chapter to the Romans, and went away. The people having then sung the creed in rhyme, he came and read the gospel, all standing. Another hymn followed, which being ended, the minister in the pulpit used a long extemporary prayer, and afterward preached an hour and a quarter on a verse of the gospel. Then he read a long intercession and general thanksgiving, which, before twelve, concluded the service.

After the evening service at Hernhuth was ended all the unmarried men (as is their custom) walked quite round the town, singing praise with instruments of music; and then, on a small hill at a little distance from it, casting themselves into a ring, joined in prayer. Thence they returned into the great Square, and a little after eleven, commended each other to God.

Wesley's return to England.

September. The ship lingering still, I had time to exhort several English, whom we met with at our inn, to pursue inward religion; the renewal of their souls in righteousness and true holiness. In the morning a daughter of affliction came to see me, who teaches a school at Rotterdam. She had been for some time under deep convictions, but could find none to instruct or comfort her. After much conversation we joined in prayer, and her spirit a little revived. Between nine and ten we went on board. In the afternoon I read prayers, and preached in the great cabin. The wind being contrary, we did not get out of the river till *Wednesday*, nor to London till *Saturday* night.

He Renews his Labors.

Sunday, Sept. 17. I began again to declare in my own country the glad tidings of salvation, preaching three times, and afterward expounding the Holy Scripture to a large company in the Minories. On *Monday* I rejoiced to meet with our little society, which now consisted of thirty-two persons. The next day I went to the condemned felons, in Newgate, and offered them free salvation. In the evening I went to a society in Bear-yard, and preached repentance and remission of sins. The next evening I spoke the truth in love at a society in Aldersgate-street: some contradicted at first, but not long; so that nothing but love appeared at our parting.

Thursday, Sept. 21. I went to a society in Gutter-lane, but I could not declare the mighty works of God there, as I did afterward at the Savoy in all simplicity. And the word did not return empty. Finding abundance of people greatly exasperated by gross misrepresentations of the words I had spoken, I went to as many of them in private as my time would permit. God gave me much love toward them all. Some were convinced that they had been mistaken. And who knoweth but God will soon return to the rest, and leave a blessing behind him?

Saturday, Sept. 23. I was enabled to speak strong words both at Newgate and at Mr. E.'s society; and the next day at St. Anne's, and twice at St. John's, Clerkenwell; so that I fear they will bear me there no longer.

Tuesday, Sept. 26. I declared the Gospel of peace to a small company at Windsor.

Additional Labors among Prisons and Paupers.

Sunday, Dec. 3. I began reading prayers at Bocardo, (the city prison,) which had been long discontinued.

Tuesday, Dec. 5. I began reading prayers, and preaching, in Gloucester Green work-house; and on *Thursday,* in that belonging to St. Thomas's parish. On both days I preached at the Castle.

A Glorious Love-Feast.

Monday, Jan. 1, 1739. Messrs. Hall, Kinchin, Ingham, Whitefield, Hotchins, and my brother Charles were present at our love-feast in Fetter-lane, with about sixty of our brethren. About three in the morning, as we were continuing instant in prayer, the power of God came mightily upon us, insomuch that many cried out for exceeding joy, and many fell to the ground. As soon as we were recovered a little from the awe and amazement at the presence of His Majesty, we broke out with one voice, "We praise thee, O God, we acknowledge thee to be the Lord."

Bleeding and Blistering no Cure for a Wounded Spirit.

Sunday, Jan. 21. We were surprised in the evening, while I was expounding in the Minories. A well-dressed, middle-aged woman, suddenly cried out as in the agonies of death. She continued so to do for some time, with all the signs of the sharpest anguish of spirit. When she was a little recovered, I desired her to call upon me the next day. She then told me, that about three years before she was under strong conviction of sin, and in such terror of mind that she had no comfort in any thing, nor any rest, day or night; that she sent for the minister of her parish, and told him the distress she was in: upon which he told her husband she was stark mad, and advised him to send for a physician immediately. A physician was sent for accordingly, who ordered her to be blooded, blistered, and so on. But this did not heal her wounded spirit, so that she continued much as she was before; till the last night, He whose word she at first found to be "sharper than any two-edged sword" gave her a faint hope that he would undertake her cause, and heal the soul which had sinned against him.

A Quick Conversion at Oxford.

Friday, March 2. It was the advice of all our brethren that I should spend a few days at Oxford, whither I accordingly went on *Saturday* 3d. A few names I found here, also, who had not denied the faith, neither been ashamed of their Lord, even in the midst of a perverse generation. And every day we were together we had convincing proof, such as it had not before entered into our hearts to conceive, that "He is able to save unto the uttermost all that come to God through him."

One of the most surprising instances of his power which I ever remember to have seen was on the Tuesday following, when I visited one who was above measure enraged at this *new way*, and zealous in opposing it. Finding argument to be of no other effect than to inflame her more and more, I broke off the dispute, and desired we might join in prayer, which she so far consented to as to kneel down. In a few minutes she fell into an extreme agony, both of body and soul; and soon after cried out with the utmost earnestness, "Now I know I am forgiven for Christ's sake." Many other words she uttered to the same effect, witnessing a hope full of immortality. And from that hour, God hath set her face as a flint to declare the faith which before she persecuted.

Mr. Wesley's first Field Preaching.

Thursday, March 29. I left London, and in the evening expounded to a small company at Basingstoke.

Saturday, 31. In the evening I reached Bristol, and met Mr. Whitefield there. I could scarce reconcile myself at first to this strange way of preaching in the fields, of which he set me an example on Sunday; having been all my life (till very lately) so tenacious of every point relating to decency and order, that I should have thought the saving of souls almost a sin if it had not been done in a church.

April 1. In the evening (Mr. Whitefield being gone)

I begun expounding our Lord's sermon on the mount, (one pretty remarkable precedent of field preaching, though I suppose there were churches at that time also) to a little society which was accustomed to meet once or twice a week in Nicholas-street.

Monday, 2. At four in the afternoon I submitted to be more vile, and proclaimed in the highways the glad tidings of salvation, speaking from a little eminence in the ground adjoining to the city to about three thousand people. The Scripture on which I spoke was this, (is it possible that any one should be ignorant that it is fulfilled in every true minister of Christ ?) "The Spirit of the Lord is upon me, because he hath anointed me to preach the Gospel to the poor ; he hath sent me to heal the broken-hearted, to preach deliverance to the captives, and recovering of sight to the blind, to set at liberty them that are bruised, to preach the acceptable year of the Lord." At seven I began expounding the Acts of the Apostles to a society meeting in Baldwin-street, and the next day the Gospel of St. John in the chapel at Newgate, where I also daily read the morning service of the Church.

A heavy Day's Work.

Sunday, April 15. I explained at seven o'clock, to five or six thousand persons, the story of the Pharisee and the Publican. About three thousand persons were present at Hannam Mount. I preached at Newgate after dinner to a crowded congregation. Between five and six o'clock we went to Rose Green. It rained hard at Bristol, but not a drop fell on us while I declared, to about five thousand, Christ our wisdom, and righteousness, and sanctification, and redemption. I concluded the day by showing at the society in Baldwin-street, "His blood cleanseth us from all sin."

A Rainy Day—Could Preach only Four Times.

Saturday, April 21. At Weaver's Hall a young man was suddenly seized with a violent trembling all over, and in a few minutes, the sorrows of his heart being enlarged, sunk down to the ground. But we ceased not calling upon God till he raised him up, full of "peace and joy in the Holy Ghost." On Easter Day, it being a thorough rain, I could only preach at Newgate at eight o'clock in the morning, and two in the afternoon; in a house near Hannam Mount at eleven; and in one near Rose Green at five. At the society in the evening many were cut to the heart, and many comforted.

Free Salvation joyfully received at Newgate.

Wednesday, April 24. To above two thousand, at Baptist Mills, I explained that glorious scripture, (describing the state of every true believer in Christ—every one who by faith is born of God,) "Ye have not received the spirit of bondage again to fear; but ye have received the spirit of adoption, whereby we cry, Abba, Father."

Thursday, April 25. While I was preaching at Newgate on these words, "He that believeth hath everlasting life," I was insensibly led, without any previous design, to declare strongly and explicitly that God willeth "all men to be" thus "saved;" and to pray that, "if this were not the truth of God, he would not suffer the blind to go out of the way; but, if it were, he would bear witness to his word." Immediately one, and another, and another sunk to the earth: they dropped on every side as if thunderstruck. One of them cried aloud. We besought God in her behalf, and he turned her heaviness into joy. A second being in the same agony, we called upon God for her also, and he spoke peace unto her soul. In the evening I was again pressed in spirit to declare that "Christ gave himself a ransom for all," and almost before we called upon him to set to his seal he answered. One was so wounded by the sword of the Spirit that you would have imagined she could not live a moment. But immediately his abundant kindness was showed, and she loudly sung of his righteousness.

Friday, April 26. All Newgate rang with the cries of those whom the word of God cut to the heart; two of whom were in a moment filled with joy, to the astonishment of those that beheld them.

Mr. Wesley Lays the Corner-stone of the First Methodist Chapel in the World.

Tuesday, May 8. I went to Bath, but was not suffered to be in the meadow where I was before, which occasioned the offer of a much more convenient place, where I preached Christ to about a thousand souls.

Wednesday, May 9. We took possession of a piece of ground near St. James's church-yard, in the Horse Fair, where it was designed to build a room large enough to contain both the societies of Nicholas and Baldwin-street, and such of their acquaintance as might desire to be present with them at such times as the Scripture was expounded. And on

Saturday, May 12. The first stone was laid with the voice of praise and thanksgiving.

Wesley preaches to the Rich at Clifton Church.

May. Seeing many of the rich at Clifton Church, my heart was much pained for them, and I was earnestly desirous that some of them might "enter into the kingdom of heaven." But full as I was, I knew not where to begin in warning them to flee from the wrath to come till my Testament opened on these words, "I came not to call the righteous but sinners to repentance;" in applying which my soul was so enlarged that methought I could have cried out, (in another sense than poor, vain Archimedes,) "Give me where to stand and I will shake the earth."

The "Lord answered for Himself."

Monday, May 21. Perhaps it might be because of the hardness of our hearts, unready to receive any thing unless we see it with our eyes and hear it with our ears, that God, in tender condescension to our weakness, suffered so many outward signs of the very time when he wrought this inward change to be continually seen and heard among us. But although they saw "signs and wonders," for so I must term them, yet many would not believe. They could not indeed *deny* the facts, but they could *explain* them away. Some said, "These were purely *natural* effects; the people fainted away only because of the heat and closeness of the rooms." And others were "sure it was all a cheat: they might help it if they would.

Else why were these things only in their private societies; why were they not done in the face of the sun." To-day our Lord answered for himself, for while I was enforcing these words, "Be still, and know that I am God," he began to make bare his arm, not in a close room, neither in private, but in the open air, and before more than two thousand witnesses. One, and another, and another was struck to the earth, exceedingly trembling at the presence of his power. Others cried, with a loud and bitter cry, "What must we do to be saved?" And in less than an hour seven persons, wholly unknown to me till that time, were rejoicing, and singing, and with all their might giving thanks to the God of their salvation.

Mr. Wesley guards against Intemperate Zeal.

Saturday, May 26. One came to us in deep despair, but after an hour spent in prayer, went away in peace. And the next day, having observed in many a zeal which did not suit with the sweetness and gentleness of love, I preached at Rose Green, to the largest congregation I ever had there, (I believe, upward of ten thousand souls,) on those words, "Ye know not what manner of spirit ye are of. For the Son of man is not come to destroy men's lives, but to save them."

A Noted Man Confounded.

Tuesday, June 5. There was great expectation at Bath of what a noted man was to do to me there, and I was much entreated not to preach, because no one knew what might happen. By this report I also gained a much larger audience, among whom were many of the rich and great. I told them plainly, the Scripture had concluded them all under sin; high and low, rich and poor, one with another. Many of them seemed to be a little surprised, and were sinking apace into seriousness, when their champion appeared, and coming close to me, asked by what authority I did these things. I replied, "By the authority of Jesus Christ, conveyed to me by the (now) Archbishop of Canterbury, when he laid hands upon me and said, 'Take thou authority to preach the Gospel.'" He said, "This is contrary to Act of Parliament: this is a conventicle." I answered, "Sir, the conventicles mentioned in that Act (as the preamble shows) are seditious meetings; but this is not such; here is no shadow of sedition; therefore it is not contrary to that Act." He replied, "I say it is; and, besides, your preaching frightens people out of their wits." "Sir, did you ever hear me preach?" "No." "How, then, can you judge of what you never heard?" "Sir, by common report." "Common report is not enough. Give me leave, sir, to ask, Is not your name Nash?" "My name is Nash." "Sir, I dare not judge of you by common report; I think it not enough to judge by." Here he paused awhile, and, having recovered himself, said, "I desire to know what this people comes here for?" on which one replied, "Sir, leave him to me: let an old woman answer him. You, Mr. Nash, take care of your body; we take care of our souls; and for the food of our souls we come here." He replied not a word, but walked away.

The Curiosity of Ladies Rebuked.

June 5. As I returned, the street was full of people, hurrying to and fro, and speaking great words. But when any of them asked, "Which is he?" and I replied, "I am he," they were immediately silent. Several ladies following me into Mr. Merchant's house, the servant told me there were some wanted to speak to me. I went to them and said, "I believe, ladies, the maid mistook; you only wanted to look at me." I added, "I do not expect that the rich and great should want either to speak with me, or to hear me, for I speak the plain truth—a thing you hear little of, and do not desire to hear."

Objections to Irregular Preaching Answered.

[One having made some objections to Mr. Wesley's irregularity in preaching wherever he found an open door, and having urged the acceptance of "a cure of souls," was answered by him thus :]

"But, in the meantime, you think I ought to sit still; because otherwise I should invade another's office if I interfered with other people's business, and intermeddled with souls that did not belong to me. You accordingly ask, 'How is it that I assemble Christians who are none of my charge, to sing psalms and pray, and hear the Scriptures expounded; and think it hard to justify doing this in other men's parishes, upon catholic principles.

"Permit me to speak plainly. If by catholic principles you mean any other than scriptural, they weigh nothing with me; I allow no other rule, whether of faith or practice, than the Holy Scriptures; but on scriptural principles, I do not think it hard to justify whatever I do. God in Scripture commands me, according to my power, to instruct the ignorant, reform the wicked, confirm the virtuous. Man forbids me to do this in another's parish; that is, in effect, to do it at all; seeing I have now no parish of my own, nor probably ever shall. Whom, then, shall I hear, God or man? 'If it be just to obey man rather than God, judge you.' A dispensation of the Gospel is committed to me, and woe is me if I preach not the Gospel.' But where shall I preach it upon the principles you mention? Why, not in Europe, Asia, Africa, or America; not in any of the Christian parts, at least, of the habitable earth: for all these are, after a sort, divided into parishes. If it be said, 'Go back, then, to the heathens from whence you came;' nay, but neither could I now (on your principles) preach to them, for all the heathens in Georgia belong to the parish either of Savannah or Frederica.

"Suffer me now to tell you my principles in this matter. I look upon all the world as my parish; thus far I mean, that, in whatever part of it I am, I judge it meet, right, and my bounden duty, to declare unto all that are willing to hear, the glad tidings of salvation. This is the work which I know God has called me to; and sure I am that his blessing attends it. Great encouragement have I, therefore, to be faithful. His servant I am, and, as such, am employed according to the plain direction of his word, as I have opportunity, doing 'good unto all men;' and his providence clearly concurs with his word; which has disengaged me from all things else, that I might singly attend to this very thing.

Wesley preaches for Mr. Whitefield Out of Doors.

Thursday, June 14. I went with Mr. Whitefield to Blackheath, where were, I believe, twelve or fourteen thousand people. He a little surprised me by desiring me to preach in his stead; which I did (though nature recoiled) on my favorite subject, "Jesus Christ, who of God is made unto us wisdom, righteousness, sanctification, and redemption." I was greatly moved with compassion for the rich that were there, to whom I made a particular application. Some of them seemed to attend, while others drove away their coaches from so uncouth a preacher.

Too Strict for the Quaker.

Friday, June 15. I had much talk with one who is called a Quaker, but he could not receive my saying. I was too strict for him, and talked of such a perfection as he could not think necessary; being persuaded there was no harm in costly apparel, provided it was plain and grave; or in putting scarlet or gold upon our houses, so it were not upon our clothes.

We did not Dispute, but Pray.

Sunday, June 17. I preached at seven, in Upper Moorfields, to, I believe, six or seven thousand people, on "Ho! every one that thirsteth, come ye to the waters." In the afternoon I saw poor R—d Y—n, who had left our society and the Church. We did not dispute, but pray, and in a short space the scales fell off from his eyes. He gladly returned to the Church, and was admitted into our society. In the evening I preached on Kennington Common to about fifteen thousand people on these words: "Look unto me, and be ye saved, all ye ends of the earth."

Whitefield's Preaching Produces "Outward Signs."

July 6. In the afternoon I was with Mr. Whitefield, just come from London, with whom I went to Baptist Mills, where he preached concerning the "Holy Ghost, which they that believe on him should receive;" not without a just, though severe, censure of those who preach as if there were no Holy Ghost. Next day I had an opportunity to talk with him of those outward signs which had so often accompanied the inward work of God. I found his objections were chiefly grounded on gross misrepresentations of matter of fact. But the next day he had an opportunity of informing himself better; for no sooner had he begun (in the application of his sermon) to invite all sinners to believe in Christ than four persons sunk down close to him, almost in the same moment. One of them lay without either sense or motion. A second trembled exceedingly. The third had strong convulsions all over his body, but made no noise, unless by groans. The fourth, equally convulsed, called upon God with strong cries and tears. From this time, I trust, we shall all suffer God to carry on his own work in the way which pleaseth him.

Wesley has an Interview with a Bigoted Churchman.

Monday, Aug. 27. For two hours I took up my cross in arguing with a zealous man, and laboring to convince him that I was not an enemy to the Church of England. He allowed I taught no other doctrines than those of the Church, but could not forgive my teaching them out of the church walls. He allowed, too, (which none indeed can deny, who has either any regard to truth or sense of shame,) that "by this teaching, many souls who, till that time, were 'perishing for lack of knowledge,' have been and are brought 'from darkness to light, and from the power of Satan unto God.'" But he added, "No one can tell what may be hereafter; and, therefore, I say these things ought not to be suffered."

Wesley charged with being a Papist.

Aug. 27. Indeed the report now current in Bristol was, that I was a Papist, if not a Jesuit. Some added that I was born and bred at Rome, which many cordially believed. O ye fools, when will ye understand that the preaching of justification by faith alone, the allowing no meritorious cause of justification but the death and righteousness of Christ, and no conditional or instrumental cause but faith, is overturning Popery from the foundation!

His Mother receives the Witness of the Spirit.

Monday, Sept. 3. I talked largely with my mother, who told me that till a short time since she had scarce heard such a thing mentioned as the having forgiveness of sins now, or God's Spirit bearing witness with our spirit; much less did she imagine that this was the common privilege of all true believers. "Therefore," said she, "I never durst ask for it myself. But two or three weeks ago, while my son Hall was pronouncing these words in delivering the cup to me, 'The blood of our Lord Jesus Christ, which was given for thee,' the words struck through my heart, and I knew God, for Christ's sake, had forgiven *me* all *my* sins."

I asked whether her father (Dr. Annesley) had not the same faith, and whether she had not heard him preach it to others. She answered, he had it himself; and declared, a little before his death, that for more than forty years he had no darkness, no fear, no doubt at all of his being "accepted in the Beloved." But that, nevertheless, she did not remember to have heard him preach, no not once, explicitly upon it; whence she supposed he also looked upon it as the peculiar blessing of a few, not as promised to all the people of God.

Wesley preaches to Twenty Thousand Persons.

Sunday, Sept. 9. I declared to ten thousand people in Moorfields, what they must do to be saved. My mother went with us about five to Kennington, where were supposed to be twenty thousand people. I again insisted on that foundation of all our hopes, "Believe on the Lord Jesus Christ, and thou shalt be saved."

A Churchman's Questions Promptly Answered.

Thursday, Sept. 13. A serious clergyman desired to know in what points we differed from the Church of England. I answered, "To the best of my knowledge, in none. The doctrines we preach are the doctrines of the Church of England; indeed, the fundamental doctrines of the Church, clearly laid down, both in her Prayers, Articles, and Homilies." He asked, "In what points, then, do you differ from the other clergy of the Church of England?" I answered, "In none from that part of the clergy who adhere to the doctrines of the Church; but from that part of the clergy who dissent from the Church (though they own it not) I differ in the points following:

"First. They speak of justification either as the same thing with sanctification, or as something consequent upon it. I believe justification to be wholly distinct from sanctification, and necessarily antecedent to it.

"Secondly. They speak of our own holiness, or good works, as the cause of our justification; or, that for the sake of which, on account of which, we are justified before God. I believe neither our own holiness nor good works are any part of the cause of our justification, but that the death and righteousness of Christ are the whole and sole cause of it; or, that for the sake of which, on account of which, we are justified before God.

"Thirdly. They speak of good works as a condition of justification, necessarily previous to it. I believe no good work can be previous to justification, nor, consequently, a condition of it; but that we are justified (being till that hour ungodly, and, therefore, incapable of doing any good work) by faith alone, faith without works, faith (though producing all, yet) including no good work.

"Fourthly. They speak of sanctification (or holiness) as if it were an outward thing, as if it consisted chiefly, if not wholly, in those two points: 1. The doing no harm; 2. The doing good, as it is called, that is, the using the means of grace and helping our neighbor.

"I believe it to be an inward thing, namely, the life of God in the soul of man, a participation of the divine nature, the mind that was in Christ, or the renewal of our heart after the image of him that created us.

"Lastly. They speak of the new birth as an outward thing, as if it were no more than baptism, or, at most, a change from outward wickedness to outward goodness ; from a vicious to (what is called) a virtuous life. I believe it to be an inward thing ; a change from inward wickedness to inward goodness ; an entire change of our inmost nature from the image of the devil (wherein we are born) to the image of God ; a change from the love of the creature to the love of the Creator ; from earthly and sensual to heavenly and holy affections ; in a word, a change from the tempers of the spirits of darkness to those of the angels of God in heaven.

"There is, therefore, a wide, essential, fundamental, irreconcilable difference between us ; so that if they speak the truth as it is in Jesus, I am found a false witness before God ; but if I teach the way of God in truth, they are blind leaders of the blind."

Satan Cast Out in Answer to Prayer.

Oct. 1739. Soon after I was sent for to one of those who was so strangely torn by the devil that I almost wondered her relations did not say, "Much religion hath made thee mad." We prayed God to bruise Satan under her feet. Immediately we had the petition we asked of him. She cried out vehemently, "He is gone! he is gone!" and was filled with the spirit of love and of a sound mind. I have seen her many times since, strong in the Lord. When I asked abruptly, "What do you desire now?" She answered, "Heaven." I asked, "What is in your heart?" She replied, "God." I asked, "But how is your heart when any thing provokes you?" She said, "By the grace of God, I am not provoked at any thing. All the things of this world pass by me as shadows." "Ye have seen the end of the Lord:" is he not "very pitiful and of tender mercy?"

A Sermon on the Beatitudes: Service three Hours Long.

Friday, Oct. 19. I preached in the morning at Newport on "What must I do to be saved?" to the most insensible, ill-behaved people I have ever seen in Wales. One ancient man, during a great part of the sermon, cursed and swore almost incessantly, and toward the conclusion took up a great stone, which he many times attempted to throw; but that he could not do. Such the champions, such the arms against field-preaching!

At four I preached at the Shire Hall of Cardiff again, where many gentry, I found, were present. Such freedom of speech I have seldom had as was given me in explaining those words, "The kingdom of God is not meat and drink; but righteousness, and peace, and joy in the Holy Ghost." At six almost the whole town, I was informed, came together, to whom I explained the six last beatitudes; but my heart was so enlarged I knew not how to give over, so that we continued three hours. O may the seed they have received have its fruit unto holiness, and in the end everlasting life!

A Wife Hopeful of Her Husband.

Wednesday, Oct. 24. I preached at Baptist Mills on those words of St. Paul, speaking in the person of one "under the law," (that is, still "carnal, and sold under sin," though groaning for deliverance,) "I know that in me dwelleth no good thing." A poor woman told me afterward, "I does hope as my husband wont hinder me any more, for I minded he did shiver every bone of him, and the tears ran down his cheeks like the rain."

An Objection with a Concession.

Sunday, Nov. 25. I preached at St. Mary's on "The kingdom of God is not meat and drink; but righteousness, and peace, and joy in the Holy Ghost." Dr. W. told me after sermon, "Sir, you must not preach in the afternoon. Not," said he, "that you preach any false doctrine. I allow all that you have said is true, and it is the doctrine of the Church of England; but it is not guarded. It is dangerous. It may lead people into enthusiasm or despair."

"Sick of this Sublime Divinity."

Sunday, Nov. 30. One came to me by whom I used to profit much; but her conversation was now too high for me: it was far above, out of my sight. My soul is sick of this sublime divinity! Let *me* think and speak as a little child! let *my* religion be plain, artless, simple! Meekness, temperance, patience, faith, and love, be these *my* highest gifts, and let the highest words wherein I teach them be those I learn from the book of God.

Who are Dissenters from the Church of England.

Feb. 1740. Our twentieth article defines a true Church, "a congregation of faithful people, wherein the true word of God is preached and the sacraments duly administered." According to this account the

Church of England is that body of faithful people, (or holy believers,) in England, among whom the pure word of God is preached, and the sacraments duly administered. Who, then, are the worst dissenters from this Church? 1. Unholy men of all kinds: swearers, Sabbath breakers, drunkards, fighters, whoremongers, liars, revilers, evil speakers; the passionate, the gay, the lovers of money, the lovers of dress or of praise, the lovers of pleasure more than the lovers of God; all these are dissenters of the highest sort, continually striking at the root of the Church, and themselves belonging, in truth, to no Church, but to the synagogue of Satan. 2. Men unsound in the faith, those who deny the Scriptures of truth, those who deny the Lord that bought them, those who deny justification by faith alone, or the present salvation which is by faith; these also are dissenters of a very high kind, for they likewise strike at the foundation; and were their principles universally to obtain there could be no true Church upon earth. Lastly, those who unduly administer the sacraments, who (to instance but in one point) administer the Lord's Supper to such as have neither the power nor the form of godliness. These, too, are gross dissenters from the Church of England, and should not cast the first stone at others.

First Mob at Bristol.

Tuesday, April 1. While I was expounding the former part of the twenty-third chapter of the Acts, (how wonderfully suited to the occasion, though not by my choice,) the floods began to lift up their voice. Some or other of the children of Belial had labored to disturb us several nights before, but now it seemed as if all the host of the aliens were come together with one consent. Not only the court and the alleys, but all the street, upward and downward, was filled with people, shouting, cursing, and swearing, and ready to swallow the ground with fierceness and rage. The mayor sent order that they should disperse, but they set him at naught. The chief constable came next in person, who was, till then, sufficiently prejudiced against us; but they insulted him, also, in so gross a manner as, I believe, fully opened his eyes. At length the Mayor sent several of his officers, who took the ringleaders into custody, and did not go till all the rest were dispersed. Surely he hath been to us "the minister of God for good."

Wednesday, April 2. The rioters were brought up to the court, the quarter sessions being held that day. They began to excuse themselves by saying many things of me. But the Mayor cut them all short, saying, "What Mr. Wesley is is nothing to you. I will keep the peace. I will have no rioting in this city."

Alderman Beecher—Citation.

April. Calling at Newgate in the afternoon, I was informed that the poor wretches under sentence of death were earnestly desirous to speak with me, but that it could not be, Alderman Beecher having just then sent an express order that they should not. I cite Alderman Beecher to answer for these souls at the judgment seat of Christ.

A Spirit of Controversy not Tolerated.

June. In the evening Mr. Acourt complained that Mr. Nowers had hindered his going into our society.

Mr. Nowers answered, "It was by Mr. C. Wesley's order." "What," said Mr. Acourt, "do you refuse admitting a person into your society only because he differs from you in opinion?" I answered, "No; but what opinion do you mean?" He said, "That of election. I hold a certain number is elected from eternity, and these must and shall be saved, and the rest of mankind must and shall be damned, and many of your society hold the same." I replied, "I never asked whether they hold it or no, only let them not trouble others by disputing about it." He said, "Nay, but I will dispute about it." "What, wherever you come?" "Yes, wherever I come." "Why, then, would you come among us, who, you know, are of another mind?" "Because you are all wrong, and I am resolved to set you all right." "I fear your coming with this view would neither profit you nor us." He concluded, "Then I will go and tell all the world that you and your brother are false prophets. And I tell you, in one fortnight, you will all be in confusion."

Decisive Disciplinary Action.

Sunday, July 20. At Mr. Seward's earnest request, I preached once more in Moorfields on "the work of faith," and "the patience of hope," and "the labor of love." A zealous man was so kind as to free us from most of the noisy, careless hearers, or spectators rather, by reading, meanwhile, at a small distance, a chapter in the "Whole Duty of Man." I wish neither he nor they may ever read a worse book; though I can tell them of a better—the Bible. In the evening I went with Mr. Seward to the love-feast in Fetter-lane; at the conclusion of which, having said nothing till then, I read a paper the substance whereof was as follows:

"About nine months ago certain of you began to speak contrary to the doctrine we had till then received. The sum of what you asserted is this: 1. That there is no such thing as *weak faith:* that there is no justifying faith where there is ever any doubt or fear, or where there is not, in the full sense, a new, a clean heart. 2. That a man ought not to use those ordinances of God, which our Church terms 'means of grace,' before he has such a faith as excludes all doubt and fear, and implies a new, a clean heart.

"You have often affirmed, that to search the Scriptures, to pray, or to communicate, before we have this faith, is to seek salvation by works; and that till these works are laid aside no man can receive faith. I believe these assertions to be flatly contrary to the word of God. I have warned you hereof again and again, and besought you to turn back to the law and the testimony. I have borne with you long, hoping you would turn. But as I find you more and more confirmed in the error of your ways, nothing now remains but that I give you up to God. You that are of the same judgment follow me."

I then, without saying any thing more, withdrew, as did eighteen or nineteen of the society.

First Meeting at the Foundry.

Wednesday, July 23. Our little company met at the Foundry instead of Fetter-lane. About twenty-five of our brethren God hath given us already, all of whom think and speak the same thing; seven or eight and forty likewise, of the fifty women that were in band, desired to cast in their lot with us.

Disturbers Confounded.

Aug. In the evening many were gathered together at Long-lane, on purpose to make a disturbance; having procured a woman to begin, well known in those parts as neither fearing God nor regarding man. The instant she broke out I turned full upon her, and declared the love our Lord had for *her* soul. We then prayed that he would confirm the word of his grace. She was struck to the heart, and shame covered her face. From her I turned to the rest, who melted away like water, and were as men that had no strength. But surely some of them shall find who is their "rock" and their "strong salvation."

Satan against Satan.

Tuesday, Sept. 16. Many more, who came in among us as lions, in a short space became as lambs; the tears trickling apace down their cheeks, who at first most loudly contradicted and blasphemed. I wonder the devil has not wisdom enough to discern that he is destroying his own kingdom. I believe he has never yet, any one time, caused this open opposition to the truth of God without losing one or more of his servants, who were found of God while they sought him not.

A Mob at Mr. Wesley's Door.

Sunday, Sept. 28. I began expounding the sermon on the mount at London. In the afternoon I described, to a numerous congregation at Kennington, the life of God in the soul. One person who stood on the mount made a little noise at first; but a gentleman, whom I knew not, walked up to him, and, without saying one word, mildly took him by the hand and led him down. From that time he was quiet till he went away. When I came home I found an innumerable mob round the door, who all opened their throats the moment they saw me. I desired my friends to go into the house; and then, walking into the midst of the people, proclaimed "the name of the Lord, gracious and merciful, and repenting him of the evil." They stood staring one at another. I told them they could not flee from the face of this great God, and therefore besought them, that we might all join together in crying to him for mercy. To this they readily agreed. I then commended them to his grace, and went undisturbed to the little company within.

A Churchman's Demonstration turned against Himself.

Friday, Nov. 28. A gentleman came to me full of good will, to exhort me not to leave the Church; or, which was the same thing in his account, to use extemporary prayer; which, said he, "I will prove to a demonstration to be no prayer at all. For you cannot do two things at once. But thinking how to pray, and praying, are two things. *Ergo*, you cannot both think and pray at once." Now, may it not be proved by the self-same demonstration, that praying by a form is no prayer at all? For example, "You cannot do two things at once. But reading and praying are two things. *Ergo*, you cannot both read and pray at once."

Labor Lost and Mischief Prevented.

Sunday, Feb. 1, 1741. A private letter, wrote to me by Mr. Whitefield, having being printed without either his leave or mine, great numbers of copies were given to our people, both at the door and in the Foundry itself. Having procured one of them, I re lated, after preaching, the naked fact to the congregation, and told them, "I will do just what I believe Mr. Whitefield would were he here himself." Upon which I tore it in pieces before them all. Every one who had received it did the same; so that in two minutes there was not a whole copy left. Ah! poor Ahithophel! *Ibi omnis effusus labor!* (So all the labor's lost!)

Three Petitions Immediately Granted.

Monday, Feb. 16. While I was preaching in Long-lane, the host of the aliens gathered together; and one large stone, many of which they threw, went just over my shoulder. But no one was hurt in any degree; for thy "kingdom ruleth over all." All things now being settled according to my wish, on *Tuesday*, 17, I left London. In the afternoon I reached Oxford, and leaving my horse there, set out on foot for Stanton Harcourt. The night overtook me in about an hour, accompanied with heavy rain. Being wet and weary, and not well knowing my way, I could not help saying in my heart, (though ashamed of my want of resignation to God's will,) O that thou wouldest "stay the bottles of heaven;" or, at least, give me light, or an honest guide, or some help in the manner thou knowest! Presently the rain ceased the moon broke out, and a friendly man overtook me, who set me upon his own horse, and walked by my side till we came to Mr. Gambold's door.

Wesley and Whitefield Diverge.

Saturday, March 28. Having heard much of Mr. Whitefield's unkind behavior since his return from Georgia, I went to him to hear him speak for himself, that I might know how to judge. I much approved of his plainness of speech. He told me he and I preached two different gospels, and therefore he not only would not join with, or give me the right hand of fellowship, but was resolved publicly to preach against me and my brother wheresoever he preached at all. Mr. Hall, who went with me, put him in mind of the promise he had made but a few days before, that, whatever his private opinion was, he would never publicly preach against us. He said that promise was only an effect of human weakness, and he was now of another mind.

Saturday, April 4. I believed both love and justice required that I should speak my sentiments freely to Mr. Wh—— concerning the letter he had published, said to be an answer to my sermon on free grace. The sum of what I observed to him was this, 1. That it was quite imprudent to publish it at all, as being only the putting of weapons into their hands, who loved neither the one nor the other. 2. That if he was constrained to bear his testimony, as he termed it, against the error I was in, he might have done it by publishing a treatise on this head, without ever calling my name in question. 3. That what he had published was a mere burlesque upon an answer, leaving four of my eight arguments untouched, and handling the other four in so gentle a manner, as if he was afraid they would burn his fingers; however, that, 4, he had said enough of what was wholly foreign to the question, to make an open and, probably, irreparable breach between him and me: seeing "for a treacherous wound, and for the bewraying of secrets, every friend will depart."

Mr. Wesley's Systematic Care of the Poor.

Thursday, May 7. I reminded the United Society that many of our brethren and sisters had not needful food; many were destitute of convenient clothing; many were out of business, and that without their own fault; and many sick and ready to perish; that I had done what in me lay to feed the hungry, to clothe the naked, to employ the poor, and to visit the sick; but was not, alone, sufficient for these things, and therefore desired all whose hearts were as my heart, 1. To bring what clothes each could spare, to be distributed among those that wanted most. 2. To give weekly a penny, or what they could afford, for the relief of the poor and sick. My design, I told them, is to employ, for the present, all the women who were out of business, and desire it, in knitting. To these we will first give the common price for that work they do, and then add, according as they need. Twelve persons are appointed to inspect these, and to visit and provide things needful for the sick. Each of these is to visit all the sick within their district every other day; and to meet on Tuesday evening to give an account of what they have done, and consult what can be done further.

An Experiment.

June. For these two days I had made an experiment which I had been so often and earnestly pressed to do: Speaking to none concerning the things of God, unless my heart was free to it. And what was the event? Why, 1. That I spoke to none at all for fourscore miles together: No, not even to him that traveled with me in the chaise, unless a few words at first setting out. 2. That I had no cross either to bear or to take up, and commonly in an hour or two fell fast asleep. 3. That I had much respect shown me wherever I came; every one behaving to me as to a civil, good-natured gentleman. O how pleasing is all this to flesh and blood! Need ye "compass sea and land" to make "proselytes" to this!

Wesley Preaches before the University at Oxford.

Friday, July 24. Several of our friends from London, and some from Kingswood and Bristol, came to Oxford. Alas! how long shall they "come from the east, and from the west, and sit down in the kingdom of God," while the children of the kingdom will not come in, but remain in utter darkness!

Saturday, July 25. It being my turn, (which comes about once in three years,) I preached at St. Mary's, before the University. The harvest truly is plenteous. So numerous a congregation (from whatever motives they came) I have seldom seen at Oxford. My text was the confession of poor Agrippa, "Almost thou persuadest me to be a Christian." I have cast my "bread upon the waters:" let me "find it again after many days!" In the afternoon I set out, (having no time to spare,) and on *Sunday,* 26, preached at the

Foundery, on the "liberty" we have "to enter into the holiest by the blood of Jesus."

Rumors of Treason.

Wednesday, August 26. I was informed of a remarkable conversation, at which one of our sisters was present a day or two before, wherein a gentleman was assuring his friends that he himself was in Charles' Square when a person told Mr. Wesley to his face that he, Mr. Wesley, had paid twenty pounds already, on being convicted for selling Geneva, and that he now kept two Popish priests in his house. This gave occasion to another to mention what he had himself heard at an eminent dissenting teacher's, namely, that it was beyond dispute Mr. Wesley had large remittances from Spain, in order to make a party among the poor; and that as soon as the Spaniards landed, he was to join them with twenty thousand men.

Wesley's Horse falls upon Him.

Sunday, Oct. 25. After the sacrament at All Saints, I took horse for Kingswood; but before I came to Lawrence Hill my horse fell, and attempting to rise again, fell down upon me. One or two women ran out of a neighboring house, and when I rose helped me in. I adore the wisdom of God. In this house were three persons who began to run well, but Satan had hindered them; but they resolved to set out again, and not one of them has looked back since.

A Severe Sickness and Joyous Experience.

Wednesday, Nov. 4. Many of our brethren agreed to seek God to-day by fasting and prayer. [Apparently for Mr. Wesley's restoration from serious illness.] About twelve my fever began to rage. At two I dozed a little, and suddenly awaked in such a disorder (only more violent) as that on Monday. The silver cord appeared to be just then loosing, and the wheel breaking at the cistern. The blood whirled to and fro, as if it would immediately force its way through all its vessels, especially in the breast; and excessive burning heat parched up my whole body, both within and without. About three, in a moment the commotion ceased, the heat was over, and the pain gone. Soon after it made another attack, but not near so violent as the former. This lasted till half past four, and then vanished away at once. I grew better and better till nine; then I fell asleep, and scarce awaked at all till morning.

Thursday, Nov. 5. The noisy joy of the people in the streets did not agree with me very well, though I am afraid it disordered their poor souls much more than it did my body. About five in the evening my cough returned, and soon after, the heat and other symptoms; but with this remarkable circumstance, that for fourteen or fifteen hours following I had more or less sleep in every hour. This was one cause why I was never light-headed at all, but had the use of my understanding from the first hour of my illness to the last, as fully as when in perfect health.

Friday, Nov. 6. Between ten and twelve the main shock began. I can give but a faint account of this, not for want of memory, but of words. I felt in my body nothing but storm and tempest, hail-stones, and coals of fire. But I do not remember that I felt any fear, (such was the mercy of God!) nor any murmuring. And yet I found but a dull, heavy kind of patience, which I knew was not what it ought to be. The fever came rushing upon me as a lion, ready to break all my bones in pieces. My body grew weaker every moment, but I did not feel my soul put on strength. Then it came into my mind, "Be still, and see the salvation of the Lord. I will not stir hand or foot, but let him do with me what is good in his own eyes." At once my heart was at ease. My "mouth was filled with laughter," and my "tongue with singing." My eyes overflowed with tears, and I began to sing aloud. One who stood by said, "Now he is light-headed." I told her, "O no; I am not light-headed, but I am praising God; God is come to my help, and pain is nothing; glory be to God on high!" I now found why it was not expedient for me to recover my health sooner; because then I should have lost this experimental proof, how little every thing is which can befall the body, so long as God carries the soul aloft, as it were, on the wings of an eagle.

No Sympathy for Mystic Writers.

Wednesday, Nov. I read over once again "Theologia Germanica." O, how was it that I could ever admire the affected obscurity of this unscriptural writer! Glory be to God, that I now prefer the plain Apostles and Prophets before him and all his mystic followers!

Faithful Discipline.

Wednesday, Dec. 9. God humbled us in the evening by the loss of more than thirty of our little company, who I was obliged to exclude as no longer adorning the Gospel of Christ. I believe it best openly to declare both their names and the reason why they were excluded. We then all cried unto God that this might be for their edification, and not for destruction.

Solitary Christians.

Friday, Dec. 11. I went to Bath. I had often reasoned with myself concerning this place, "Hath God left himself without witness?" Did he never raise up such as might be shining lights, even in the midst of this sinful generation? Doubtless he has; but they are either gone "to the desert," or hid under the bushel of prudence. Some of the most serious persons I have known at Bath are either *solitary Christians*, scarce known to each other, unless by name; or *prudent Christians*, as careful not to give offense as if that were the unpardonable sin: and as zealous to "keep their religion to themselves," as they should be, to "let it shine before men."

Preaches Christ on a Sick Bed.

Friday, Jan. 1, 1742. After a night of quiet sleep I waked in a strong fever, but without any sickness, or thirst, or pain. I consented, however, to keep my bed, but on condition that every one who desired it should have liberty to speak with me. I believe fifty or sixty persons did so this day; nor did I find any inconvenience from it. In the evening I sent for all the bands who were in the house, that we might magnify our Lord together. A near relation being with me when they came, I asked her afterward if she was not offended. "Offended!" said she: "I wish I could be always among you. I thought I was in heaven." This night also, by the blessing of God, I slept well, to the utter astonishment of those about me, the apothecary in particular, who said he had never seen such a fever in his life. I had a clear remission in the morning, but about two in the afternoon a stronger fit than any before; otherwise I had determined to have been at the meeting of the bands; but good is the will of the Lord.

Riotous Demonstrations, with Good Results.

Monday, Jan. 25. While I was explaining at Long-lane, "He that committeth sin is of the devil," his servants were above measure enraged. They not only made all possible noise, (although, as I had desired before, no man stirred from his place, or answered them a word,) but violently thrust many persons to and fro, struck others, and brake down part of the house. At length they began throwing large stones upon the house, which, forcing their way wherever they came, fell down, together with the tiles, among the people, so that they were in danger of their lives. I then told them, "You must not go on thus; I am ordered by the magistrate, who is, in this respect, to us the minister of God, to inform him of those who break the laws of God and the king: and I must do it, if you persist herein; otherwise I am a partaker of your sin." When I ceased speaking they were more outrageous than before. Upon this I said, "Let three or four calm men take hold of the foremost, and charge a constable with him, that the law may take its course." They did so, and brought him into the house, cursing and blaspheming in a dreadful manner. I desired five or six to go with him to justice Copeland, to whom they nakedly related the fact. The justice immediately bound him over to the next sessions at Guildford.

I observed when the man was brought into the house that many of his companions were loudly crying out, "Richard Smith, Richard Smith!" who, as it afterward appeared, was one of their stoutest champions. But Richard Smith answered not; he was fallen into the hands of one higher than they. God had struck him to the heart; as also a woman, who was speaking words not fit to be repeated, and throwing whatever came to hand, whom he overtook in the very act. She came into the house with Richard Smith, fell upon her knees before us all, and strongly exhorted him never to turn back, never to forget the mercy which God had shown to his soul. From this time we had never any considerable interruption or disturbance at Long-lane; although we withdrew our prosecution upon the offender's submission and promise of better behavior.

A Necessary Qualification.

Thursday, Feb. 4. A clergyman lately come from America, who was at the preaching last night, called upon me, appeared full of good desires, and seemed willing to cast in his lot with us. But I cannot suddenly answer in this matter. I must first know what spirit he is of; for none can labor with us, unless he "count all things dung and dross, that he may win Christ."

Origin of Classes in London.

Sunday, March 21. In the evening I rode to Marshfield; and on *Tuesday*, in the afternoon, came to London.

Wednesday, 24. I preached for the last time, in the French chapel at Wapping, on, "If ye continue in my word, then are ye my disciples indeed."

Thursday, 25. I appointed several earnest and sensible men to meet me, to whom I showed the great difficulty I had long found of knowing the people who desired to be under my care. After much discourse, they all agreed there could be no better way to come to a sure, thorough knowledge of each person than to divide them into classes, like those at Bristol, under the inspection of those in whom I could most confide. This was the origin of our classes at London, for which I can never sufficiently praise God; the unspeakable usefulness of the institution having ever since been more and more manifest.

First Watch-night in London.

Friday, April 9. We had the first watch-night in London. We commonly choose for this solemn service the Friday night nearest the full moon, either before or after, that those of the congregation who live at a distance may have light to their several homes. The service begins at half an hour past eight, and continues till a little after midnight. We have often found a peculiar blessing at these seasons. There is generally a deep awe upon the congregation, perhaps in some measure owing to the silence of the night, particularly in singing the hymn with which we commonly conclude:

Hearken to the solemn voice,
The awful midnight cry!
Waiting souls, rejoice, rejoice,
And feel the Bridegroom nigh.

A Running Debate.

On *Thursday, May* 20, I set out. The next afternoon I stopped a little at Newport Pagnell, and then rode on till I overtook a serious man, with whom I immediately fell into conversation. He presently gave me to know what his opinions were; therefore I said nothing to contradict them. But that did not content him; he was quite uneasy to know whether I held the doctrine of the decrees as he did; but I told him over and over, "We had better keep to practical things, lest we should be angry at one another." And so we did for two miles, till he caught me unawares, and dragged me into the dispute before I knew where I was. He then grew warmer and warmer; told me I was rotten at heart, and supposed I was one of John Wesley's followers. I told him, "No, I am John Wesley himself." Upon which,

> *Improvisum aspris veluti qui sentibus anguem*
> *Pressit*—(As one that has unawares trodden upon a snake,)

he would gladly have run away outright. But, being the better mounted of the two, I kept close to his side, and endeavored to show him his heart till we came into the street of Northampton.

How John Nelson was Led to Preach.

Tuesday, May 25. I set out early in the morning with John Taylor, (since settled in London;) and *Wednesday* 26, in the evening, reached Birstal, six miles beyond Wakefield. John Nelson had wrote to me some time before, but at that time I had little thought of seeing him. Hearing he was at home, I sent for him to our inn; whence he immediately carried me to his house, and gave me an account of the strange manner wherein he had been led on from the time of our parting at London.

He had full business there, and large wages. But from the time of his finding peace with God, it was continually upon his mind that he must return (though he knew not why) to his native place. He did so, about Christmas, in the year 1740. His relations and acquaintance soon began to inquire what he thought of this new faith, and whether he believed there was any such thing as a man's knowing that his sins were forgiven. John told them point blank that this new faith, as they called it, was the old faith of the Gospel; and that he himself was as sure his sins were forgiven, as he could be of the shining of the sun. This was soon noised abroad; more and more came to inquire concerning these strange things: some put him upon the proof of the great truths which such inquiries naturally led him to mention; and thus he was brought unawares to quote, explain, compare, and enforce several parts of Scripture. This he did at first, sitting in his house, till the company increased so that the house could not contain them. Then he stood at the door, which he was commonly obliged to do, in the evening, as soon as he came from work. God immediately set his seal to what was spoken; and several believed, and therefore declared, that God was merciful also to their unrighteousness, and had forgiven all their sins.

Mr. Wesley Preaches at Newcastle-upon-Tyne.

Sunday, May 30. At seven I walked down to Sandgate, the poorest and most contemptible part of the town, and, standing at the end of the street with John Taylor, began to sing the hundredth psalm. Three or four people came out to see what was the matter, who soon increased to four or five hundred. I suppose there might be twelve or fifteen hundred before I had done preaching, to whom I applied these solemn words: "He was wounded for our transgressions, he was bruised for our iniquities: the chastisement of our peace was upon him; and by his stripes we are healed." Observing the people, when I had done, to stand gaping and staring upon me with the most profound astonishment, I told them, "If you desire to know who I am, my name is John Wesley. At five in the evening, with God's help, I design to preach here again."

At five the hill on which I designed to preach was covered from the top to the bottom. I never saw so large a number of people together either in Moorfields or at Kennington Common. I knew it was not possible for the one half to hear, although my voice was then strong and clear, and I stood so as to have them all in view, as they were ranged on the side of the hill. The word of God which I set before them was, "I will heal their backsliding, I will love them freely." After preaching, the poor people were ready to tread me under foot out of pure love and kindness. It was some time before I could possibly get out of the press.

A Sharp Criticism.

Friday, June 4. At noon I preached at Bristol once more. All the hearers were deeply attentive, whom I now confidently and cheerfully committed to "the great Shepherd and Bishop of souls." Hence I rode to Beeston. Here I met once more with the works of a celebrated author, of whom many great men cannot speak without rapture and the strongest expressions of admiration—I mean Jacob Behmen. The book I now opened was his "Mysterium Magnum," or Exposition of Genesis. Being conscious of my ignorance, I earnestly besought God to enlighten my understanding. I seriously considered what I read, and endeavored to weigh it in the balance of the sanctuary. And what can I say concerning the part I read? I can and must say thus much, (and that with as full evidence as I can say that two and two make four,) it is most sublime nonsense, inimitable bombast, fustian not to be paralleled; all of a piece with his inspired interpretation of the word *Tetragrammaton,* on which (mistaking it for the unutterable name itself, whereas it means only a word consisting of four letters) he comments with such exquisite gravity and solemnity, telling you the meaning of every *syllable* of it.

Condemns Borrowed Phrases from Mystic Writers.

Saturday, June 5. I rode for Epworth. Before we came thither I made an end of Madam Guyon's "Short Method of Prayer," and "Les Torrents Spirituelles." Ah, my brethren, I can answer your riddle now I have plowed with your heifer. The very words I have so often heard some of you use are not your own no more than they are God's. They are only retailed from this poor Quietist, and that with the utmost faithfulness. O that ye knew how much God is wiser than man! Then would you drop

Quietists and Mystics together, and at all hazards keep to the plain, practical, written word of God.

Wesley Preaches on his Father's Tombstone.

June. It being many years since I had been in Epworth before, I went to an inn in the middle of the town, not knowing whether there were any left in it now who would not be ashamed of my acquaintance; but an old servant of my father's, with two or three poor women, presently found me out. I asked her, "Do you know any in Epworth who are in earnest to be saved?" She answered, "I am, by the grace of God, and I know I am saved through faith." I asked, "Have you, then, the peace of God? Do you know that he has forgiven your sins?" She replied, "I thank God, I know it well. And many here can say the same thing."

Sunday, June 6. A little before the service began I went to Mr. Romley, the curate, and offered to assist him either by preaching or reading prayers; but he did not care to accept of my assistance. The church was exceeding full in the afternoon, a rumor being spread that I was to preach. But the sermon, on "Quench not the Spirit," was not suitable to the expectation of many of the hearers. Mr. Romley told them one of the most dangerous ways of quenching the Spirit was by enthusiasm, and enlarged on the character of an enthusiast in a very florid and oratorical manner. After sermon John Taylor stood in the church-yard and gave notice, as the people were coming out, "Mr. Wesley, not being permitted to preach in the church, designs to preach here at six o'clock." Accordingly at six I came, and found such a congregation as I believe Epworth never saw before. I stood near the east end of the church, upon my father's tombstone, and cried, "The kingdom of heaven is not meat and drink; but righteousness, and peace, and joy in the Holy Ghost."

A Wagon Load of Heretics.

Wednesday, June 9. I rode over to a neighboring town to wait upon a justice of the peace, a man of candor and understanding, before whom, I was informed, their angry neighbors had carried a wagon load of these new heretics. But when he asked what they had done there was a deep silence, for that was a point their conductor had forgotten. At length one said, "Why, they pretend to be better than other people; and besides, they prayed from morning till night." Mr. S. asked, "But have they done nothing besides?" "Yes, sir," said an old man; "an't please your worship, they have *convarted* my wife. Till she went among them she had such a tongue, and now she is as quiet as a lamb." "Carry them back, carry them back," replied the justice, "and let them convert all the scolds in town."

A Shaking Among the Dry Bones at Epworth.

Friday, June 11. I visited the sick, and those who desired, but were not able, to come to me. At six I preached at Overthorp, near Haxey, (a little village about two miles from Epworth,) on that comfortable scripture, "When they had nothing to pay, he frankly forgave them both." I preached at Epworth, about eight, on Ezekiel's vision of the resurrection of the dry bones, and great indeed was the shaking among them ; lamentation and great mourning were heard, God bowing their hearts, so that on every side, as with one accord, they lift up their voice and wept aloud. Surely he who sent his Spirit to breathe upon them will hear their cry and will help them.

Saturday, June 12. I preached on the righteousness of the law and the righteousness of faith. While I was speaking several dropped down as dead ; and among the rest, such a cry was heard, of sinners groaning for the righteousness of faith, as almost drowned my voice ; but many of these soon lifted up their heads with joy and broke out into thanksgiving, being assured they now had the desire of their soul —the forgiveness of their sins. I observed a gentleman there who was remarkable for not pretending to be of any religion at all. I was informed he had not been at public worship of any kind for upward of thirty years. Seeing him stand as motionless as a statue, I asked him abruptly, "Sir, are you a sinner ?" He replied, with a deep and broken voice, "Sinner enough ;" and continued staring upward till his wife and a servant or two, who were all in tears, put him into his chaise and carried him home.

Fruit at Last.

Sunday, June 13. I preached for the last time in Epworth church-yard, (being to leave the town the next morning,) to a vast multitude, gathered together from all parts, on the beginning of our Lord's sermon on the mount. I continued among them for near three hours, and yet we scarce knew how to part. O let none think his labor of love is lost because the fruit does not immediately appear ! Near forty years did my father labor here, but he saw little fruit of his labor I took some pains among this people too, and my strength also seemed spent in vain, but now the fruit appeared. There were scarce any in the town on whom either my father or I had taken any pains formerly ; but the seed, sown so long since, now sprang up, bringing forth repentance and remission of sins.

Wesley present at the Death of his Mother.

Friday, July 23. About three in the afternoon I went to my mother, and found her change was near. I sat down on the bedside. She was in her last conflict, unable to speak, but I believe quite sensible. Her look was calm and serene, and her eyes fixed upward, while we commended her soul to God. From three to four the silver cord was loosing, and the wheel breaking at the cistern ; and then, without any struggle, or sigh, or groan, the soul was set at liberty. We stood round the bed and fulfilled her last request, uttered a little before she lost her speech : "Children, as soon as I am released sing a psalm of praise to God."

Her Burial and Epitaph.

Sunday, Aug. 1. Almost an innumerable company of people being gathered together about five in the afternoon, I committed to the earth the body of my mother, to sleep with her fathers. The portion of Scripture from which I afterward spoke was, "I saw a great white throne, and him that sat on it, from whose face the earth and the heaven fled away ; and there was found no place for them. And I saw the dead, small and great, stand before God ; and the books were opened: and the dead were judged out of those things which were written in the books, according to their works." It was one of the most solemn assemblies I ever saw, or expect to see on this side eternity. We set up a plain stone at the head of her grave inscribed with the following words:

HERE LIES THE BODY OF
MRS. SUSANNAH WESLEY,
THE YOUNGEST AND LAST SURVIVING DAUGHTER OF
DR. SAMUEL ANNESLEY.

In sure and steadfast hope to rise,
And claim her mansion in the skies,
A Christian here her flesh laid down,
The cross exchanging for a crown.

True daughter of affliction, she,
Inured to pain and misery,
Mourned a long night of griefs and fears,
A legal night of seventy years.

The Father then revealed his Son,
Him in the broken bread made known.
She knew and felt her sins forgiven,
And found the earnest of her heaven.

Meet for the fellowship above,
She heard the call, "Arise, my love!"
"I come," her dying looks replied,
And lamb-like, as her Lord, she died.

Wesley Visits Newgate Prisoners.

Saturday, Sept. 4. I was pressed to visit a poor murderer in Newgate, who was much afflicted both in body and soul. I objected; it could not be; for all the turnkeys, as well as the keeper, were so good Christians they abhorred the name of a Methodist, and had absolutely refused to admit me even to one who earnestly begged it the morning he was to die. However, I went, and found, by a surprising turn, that all the doors were now open to me. I exhorted the sick malefactor to cry unto God with all his might for grace to repent and believe the Gospel. It was not long before the rest of the felons flocked round, to whom I spoke strong words concerning the Friend of sinners, which they received with as great signs of amazement as if it had been a voice from heaven. When I came down into the Common Hall, (I think they called it,) one of the prisoners there asking me a question, gave me occasion to speak among them also; more and more still running together, while I declared, God was "not willing any of them should perish, but that all should come to repentance."

Blood Drawn in the Battle for Truth.

Sunday, Sept. 12. I was desired to preach in an open place, commonly called the Great Gardens, lying between Whitechapel and Coverlet Fields, where I found a vast multitude gathered together. Taking knowledge that a great part of them were little acquainted with the things of God, I called upon them in the words of our Lord, "Repent ye; and believe the Gospel." Many of the beasts of the people labored much to disturb those who were of a better mind. They endeavored to drive in a herd of cows among them; but the brutes were wiser than their masters. They then threw whole showers of stones, one of which struck me just between the eyes; but I felt no pain at all; and, when I had wiped away the blood, went on testifying with a loud voice that God hath given to them that believe, "not the spirit of fear, but of power, and of love, and of a sound mind." And by the spirit which now appeared through the whole congregation, I plainly saw what a blessing it is when it is given us, even in the lowest degree, to suffer for his name's sake.

Lamentation and Mourning give place to Thanksgiving and Praise.

Monday, Sept. 13. I preached, about nine, at Windsor, and the next evening came to Bristol. I spent the remainder of this, and the following week, in examining those of the society, speaking severally to each, that I might more perfectly know the state of their souls to Godward.

Thursday, Sept. 23. In the evening, almost as soon as I begun to pray in the society, a voice of lamentation and bitter mourning was heard from the whole congregation; but in a while loud thanksgivings were mixed therewith, which in a short space spread over all, so that nothing was to be heard on every side but "Praise to God and the Lamb for ever and ever!"

Notes of Thanks.

Friday, Sept. 24. I had notes from nineteen persons, desiring to return God thanks. Some of them follow:

"John Merriman, a blind man, desires to return thanks to Almighty God for the discovery of his love to him, an old sinner." "One desires to return God thanks for giving her a token of his love in removing all prejudices, and giving her love to all mankind." "Edith W—— desires to return thanks for great and unspeakable mercies which the Lord was pleased to reveal to her heart, even telling me, 'I am he that blotteth out thy transgressions, and thy sins I will remember no more.' And I desire that the praise of the Lord may be ever in my heart." "Ann Simmonds desires to return hearty thanks to God for the great mercies she received last night, for she has a full assurance of her redemption in the blood of Christ." "Mary K—— desires to return thanks to God for giving her a fresh sense of her forgiveness." "Mary F—— desires to return thanks for that the Lord hath made her triumph over sin, earth, and hell." "Mary W——n desires to return thanks to Almighty God for a fresh sense of forgiveness." "Sir,—I desire to return humble thanks to Almighty God for the comfortable assurance of his pardoning love. E. C——."

Prophets Waiting for a Predicted Event.

Wednesday, Nov. 3. Two of those who are called *prophets* desired to speak with me. They told me they were sent from God with a message to me, which was, that very shortly I should be *born'd* again. One of them added, they would stay in the house till it was done, unless I turned them out. I answered, gravely, "I will not turn you out," and showed them down into the society-room. It was tolerably cold, and they had neither meat nor drink; however, there they sat from morning to evening. They then went quietly away, and I have heard nothing from them since.

Wesley preaches in the midst of Storm and Tempest.

Monday, Dec. 27. I rode to Horsley. The house being too small, I was obliged again to preach in the open air; but so furious a storm have I seldom known. The wind drove upon us like a torrent, coming by turns from east, west, north, and south; the straw and thatch flew round our heads, so that one would have imagined it could not be long before the house must follow; but scarce any one stirred, much less went away, till I dismissed them with the peace of God.

Tuesday, Dec. 28. I preached in an open place at Swalwell, two or three miles from Newcastle. The wind was high, and extremely sharp; but I saw none go away till I went. Yet I observed none that seemed to be much convinced; only stunned, as if cut in the head.

Wednesday, Dec. 29. After preaching (as usual) in the Square, I took horse for Tanfield. More than once I was only not blown off my horse. However, at three I reached the Leigh, and explained to a multitude of people the salvation which is through faith. Afterward I met the society in a large upper room, which rocked to and fro with the violence of the storm. But all was calm within; and we rejoiced together in hope of a kingdom which cannot be moved.

Examination of Persons prostrated under Wesley's Preaching.

Thursday, Dec. 30. I carefully examined those who had lately cried out in the congregation. Some of these, I found, could give no account at all how or wherefore they had done so, only that of a sudden they dropped down, they knew not how, and what they afterward said or did they knew not. Others could just remember they were in fear, but could not tell what they were in fear of. Several said they were afraid of the devil, and this was all they knew. But a few gave a more intelligible account of the piercing sense they then had of their sins, both inward and outward, which were set in array against them round about; of the dread they were in of the wrath of God, and the punishment they had deserved, into which they seemed to be just falling, without any way to escape. One of them told me, "I was as if I was just falling down from the highest place I had ever seen. I thought the devil was pushing me off, and that God had forsaken me." Another said, "I felt the very fire of hell already kindled in my breast, and all my body was in as much pain as if I had been in a burning fiery furnace." What wisdom is that which rebuketh these, that they "should hold their peace!" Nay, let such a one cry after Jesus of Nazareth till he saith, "Thy faith hath made thee whole."

Sacrament denied Mr. Wesley at Epworth.

January, 1743. In the evening I rode to Epworth.

Sunday, *Jan.* 2. At five I preached on, "So is every one that is born of the Spirit." About eight, I preached from my father's tomb on Heb. viii, 11. Many from the neighboring towns asked if it would not be well, as it was sacrament Sunday, for them to receive it. I told them, "By all means; but it would be more respectful first to ask Mr. Romley, the curate's leave." One did so in the name of the rest, to whom he said, "Pray tell Mr. Wesley I shall not give *him* the sacrament, for he is not *fit*." How wise a God is our God! There could not have been so fit a place under heaven, where this should befall me first, as my father's house, the place of my nativity, and the very place where, "according to the straitest sect of our religion," I had so long "lived a Pharisee!" It was also fit, in the highest degree, that he who repelled me from that very table, where I had myself so often distributed the bread of life, should be one who owed his all in this world to the tender love which my father had shown to his, as well as personally to himself.

Two Noted Hearers differently affected.

Monday, Jan. 24. I preached at Bath. Some of the rich and great were present, to whom, as to the rest, I declared with all plainness of speech, 1. That, by nature, they were all children of wrath; 2. That all their natural tempers were corrupt and abominable; 3. Also all their words and works, which could never be any better but by faith; and that, 4. A natural man has no more faith than a devil, if so much. One of them, my Lord ——, stayed very patiently till I came to the middle of the fourth head; then, starting up, he said, "'Tis hot! 'tis very hot," and got down stairs as fast as he could. Several of the gentry desired to stay at the meeting of the society, to whom I explained the nature of inward religion, words flowing upon me faster than I could speak. One of them (a noted infidel) hung over the next seat in an attitude not to be described; and when he went, left half a guinea with Mary Naylor for the use of the poor.

Wesley preaches to the Colliers at Placey.

April 1. (Being *Good Friday*,) I had a great desire to visit a little village called Placey, about ten measured miles north of Newcastle. It is inhabited by colliers only, and such as had been always in the first rank for savage ignorance and wickedness of every kind. Their grand assembly used to be on the Lord's day, on which men, women, and children met together to dance, fight, curse, and swear, and play at chuck, ball, span-farthing, or whatever came next to hand. I felt great compassion for these poor creatures from the time I heard of them first; and the more, because all men seemed to despair of them. Between seven and eight I set out with John Heally, my guide. The north wind being unusually high, drove the sleet in our face, which froze as it fell, and cased us over presently. When we came to Placey we could very hardly stand. As soon as we were a little recovered, I went into the Square and declared Him who "was wounded for our transgressions" and "bruised for our iniquities." The poor sinners were quickly gathered together, and gave earnest heed to the things which were spoken. And so they did in the afternoon again, in spite of the wind and snow, when I besought them to receive Him for their King, to "repent and believe the Gospel." On *Easter Monday* and *Tuesday* I preached there again, the congregation continually increasing. And as most of these had never in their lives pretended to any religion of any kind, they were the more ready to cry to God as mere sinners, for the redemption which is in Jesus.

A Heavy Days' Work in London.

Sunday, May 29. (Being *Trinity Sunday*,) I began officiating at the chapel in West-street, near the Seven

Dials, of which (by a strange chain of providences) we have a lease for several years. I preached on the Gospel for the day, part of the third chapter of St. John and afterward administered the Lord's Supper to some hundreds of communicants. I was a little afraid at first that my strength would not suffice for the business of the day, when a service of five hours (for it lasted from ten to three) was added to my usual employment. But God looked to that; so I must think; and they that will call it enthusiasm may. I preached at the Great Gardens, at five, to an immense congregation, on "Ye must be born again." Then the leaders met, (who filled all the time that I was not speaking in public;) and after them, the bands. At ten at night I was less weary than at six in the morning. The following week I spent in visiting the Society.

Sunday, June 5. The service of the chapel lasted till near four in the afternoon; so that I found it needful, for the time to come, to divide the communicants into three parts, that we might not have above six hundred at once.

Wednesday, June 8. I ended my course of visiting, throughout which I found great cause to bless God, so very few having drawn back to perdition out of nineteen hundred and fifty souls!

Cause of the Riots in Staffordshire.

Saturday, June 18. I received a full account of the terrible riots which had been in Staffordshire. I was not surprised at all; neither should I have wondered if, after the advices they have so often received from the pulpit, as well as from the episcopal chair, the zealous high churchmen had rose and cut all that were Methodists in pieces.

Monday, June 20. Resolving to assist them as far as I could, I set out early in the morning; and after preaching at Wycomb about noon, in the evening came to Oxford.

Tuesday, June 21. We rode to Birmingham; and in the morning, *Wednesday, June* 22, to Francis Ward's, at Wednesbury.

Although I knew all that had been done here was as contrary to law as it was to justice and mercy, yet I knew not how to advise the poor sufferers, or to procure them any redress. I was then little acquainted with the English course of law, having long had scruples concerning it. But, as many of these were now removed, I thought it best to inquire whether there could be any help from the laws of the land. I therefore rode over to Counselor Littleton, at Tamworth, who assured us we might have an easy remedy if we resolutely prosecuted in the manner the law directed those rebels against God and the king.

Wesley defeated by "the Newcastle Wretches."

Monday, July 4, and the following days, I had time to finish the "Instructions for Children."

Sunday, July 10. I preached at eight on Chowden Fell on "Why will ye die, O house of Israel?" Ever since I came to Newcastle the first time, my spirit has been moved within me at the crowds of poor wretches who were every Sunday, in the afternoon, sauntering to and fro on the Sand-hill. I resolved, if possible, to find them a better employ; and as soon as the service at All Saints was over, walked straight from the church to the Sand-hill, and gave out a verse of a psalm. In a few minutes I had company enough, thousands upon thousands crowding together. But the prince of this world fought with all his might, lest his kingdom should be overthrown. Indeed, the very mob of Newcastle, in the height of their rudeness, have commonly some humanity left. I scarce observed that they threw any thing at all, neither did I receive the least personal hurt; but they continued thrusting one another to and fro, making such a noise that my voice could not be heard; so that, after spending near an hour in singing and prayer, I thought it best to adjourn to our own house.

Wesley Redeeming "Fragments of Time."

Monday, Aug. 22. After a few of us had joined in prayer, I set out and rode softly to Snowhill, where, the saddle slipping quite upon my mare's neck, I fell over her head, and she ran back into Smithfield. Some boys caught her and brought her to me again, cursing and swearing all the way. I spoke plainly to them, and they promised to amend. I was setting forward, when a man cried, "Sir, you have lost your saddle-cloth." Two or three more would needs help me to put it on; but these too swore at almost every word. I turned to one and another, and spoke in love. They all took it well, and thanked me much. I gave them two or three little books, which they promised to read over carefully. Before I reached Kensington I found my mare had lost a shoe. This gave me an opportunity of talking closely, for near half an hour, both to the smith and his servant. I mention these little circumstances to show how easy it is to redeem every fragment of time, (if I may so speak,) when we feel any love to those souls for which Christ died.

Wesley Quells a Mob.

Friday, Sept. 16. I preached to four or five hundred people on St. Hilary Downs, and many seemed amazed. But I could find none, as yet, who had any deep or lasting conviction. In the evening, as I was preaching at St. Ives Satan began to fight for his kingdom. The mob of the town burst into the room and created much disturbance, roaring and striking those that stood in their way, as though Legion himself possessed them. I would fain have persuaded our people to stand still; but the zeal of some, and the fear of others, had no ears; so that, finding the uproar increase, I went into the midst and brought the head of the mob up with me to the desk. I received but one blow on the side of the head, after which we reasoned the case, till he grew milder and milder, and at length undertook to quiet his companions.

An Open Heart for all who love God.

Thursday, Sept. 22. As we were riding through a village called Sticklepath one stopped me in the street and asked abruptly, "Is thy name John Wesley?" Immediately two or three more came up and told me I must stop there. I did so, and before we had spoken many words our souls took acquaintance with each other. I found they were called Quakers; but that hurt not me, seeing the love of God was in their hearts.

Personal Effort.

Monday, Sept. 26. I had a great desire to speak plain to a young man who went with us over the New Passage. To that end I rode with him three miles out of my way, but I could fix nothing upon him. Just as we parted, walking over Caerleon bridge, he stumbled, and was like to fall. I caught him, and began to speak of God's care over us. Immediately the tears stood in his eyes, and he appeared to feel every word which was said ; so I spoke, and spared not. The same I did to a poor man who had led my horse over the bridge, to our landlord and his wife, and to one who occasionally came in, and they all expressed a surprising thankfulness.

Watchful over his Societies.

Monday, Oct. 3. I returned to Bristol, and employed several days in examining and purging the Society, which still consisted (after many were put away) of more than seven hundred persons. The next week I examined the Society in Kingswood, in which I found but few things to reprove.

Saturday, Oct. 15. The leaders brought in what had been contributed in their several classes toward the public debt, and we found it was sufficient to discharge it.

Mob at Wednesbury—A Thrilling Account.

Thursday, Oct. 20. I rode to Wednesbury. At twelve I preached in a ground near the middle of the town, to a far larger congregation than was expected, on "Jesus Christ, the same yesterday, and to-day, and forever." I believe every one present felt the power of God, and no creature offered to molest us, either going or coming ; but the Lord fought for us, and we held our peace.

I was writing at Francis Ward's in the afternoon, when the cry arose that the mob had beset the house. We prayed that God would disperse them, and it was so! One went this way, and another that, so that in half an hour not a man was left. I told our brethren "now is the time for us to go," but they pressed me exceedingly to stay. So that I might not offend them I sat down, though I foresaw what would follow. Before five the mob surrounded the house again, in greater numbers than ever. The cry of one and all was, "bring out the minister; we will have the minister." I desired one to take their captain by the hand and bring him into the house. After a few sentences interchanged between us the lion was become a lamb. I desired him to go and bring one or two more of the most angry of his companions. He brought in two, who were ready to swallow the ground with rage ; but in two minutes they were as calm as he. I then bade them make way, that I might go out among the people. As soon as I was in the midst of them I called for a chair ; and, standing up, asked, "What do any of you want with me?" Some said, "We want you to go with us to the justice." I replied, "That I will with all my heart." I then spoke a few words, which God applied ; so that they cried out, with might and main, "The gentleman is an honest gentleman, and we will spill our blood in his defense." I asked, "Shall we go to the justice to-night, or in the morning?" Most of them cried, "To-night! to-night!" on which I went before, and two or three hundred followed, the rest returning whence they came.

The night came on before we had walked a mile, together with heavy rain. However, on we went to Bentley Hall, two miles from Wednesbury. One or two ran before to tell Mr. Lane they had brought Mr. Wesley before his worship. Mr. Lane replied, "What have I to do with Mr. Wesley? Go and carry him back again." By this time the main body came up, and began knocking at the door. A servant told them Mr. Lane was in bed. His son followed, and asked what was the matter. One replied, "Why, an't please you, they sing psalms all day; nay, and make folks rise at five in the morning. And what would your worship advise us to do?" "To go home," said Mr. Lane, "and be quiet."

Here they were at a full stop, till one advised to go to Justice Persehouse, at Walsal. All agreed to this; so we hastened on, and about seven came to his house. But Mr. P. likewise sent word that he was in bed. Now they were at a stand again, but at last they all thought it the wisest course to make the best of their way home. About fifty of them undertook to convoy me. But we had not gone a hundred yards when the mob of Walsal came, pouring in like a flood, and bore down all before them. The Darlaston mob made what defense they could; but they were weary, as well as outnumbered, so that in a short time, many being knocked down, the rest ran away, and left me in their hands.

To attempt speaking was vain, for the noise on every side was like the roaring of the sea. So they dragged me along till we came to the town, where, seeing the door of a large house open, I attempted to go in; but a man catching me by the hair pulled me back into the middle of the mob. They made no more stop till they had carried me through the main street, from one end of the town to the other. I continued speaking all the time to those within hearing, feeling no pain or weariness. At the west end of the town, seeing a door half open, I made toward it, and would have gone in; but a gentleman in the shop would not suffer me, saying they would pull the house down to the ground. However, I stood at the door and asked, "Are you willing to hear me speak?" Many cried out, "No, no! knock his brains out! down with him! kill him at once!" Others said, "Nay, but we will hear him first." I began asking, "What evil have I done? which of you all have I wronged in word or deed?" and continued speaking for above a quarter of an hour, till my voice suddenly failed: then the floods began to lift up their voice again, many crying out, "Bring him away! bring him away!"

In the meantime my strength and my voice returned, and I broke out aloud into prayer. And now the man who just before headed the mob turned and said, "Sir, I will spend my life for you: follow me, and not one soul here shall touch a hair of your head." Two or three of his fellows confirmed his words, and got close to me immediately. At the same time the gentleman in the shop cried out, "For shame! for shame! Let him go." An honest butcher, who was a little further off, said it was a shame they should do thus, and pulled back four or five, one after another, who were running on the most fiercely. The people then, as if it had been by common consent, fell back to the right and left, while those three or four men took me between them and carried me through them all. But on the bridge the mob rallied again: we therefore went on one side over the mill-dam, and thence through the meadows till, a little before ten, God brought me safe to Wednesbury, having lost only one flap of my waistcoat and a little skin from one of my hands. I never saw such a chain of providences before: so many convincing proofs that the hand of God is on every person and thing, overruling all as it seemeth him good.

The circumstances that follow, I thought, were particularly remarkable: 1. That many endeavored to throw me down while we were going down hill on a slippery path to the town; as well judging, that if I was once on the ground I should hardly rise any more. But I made no stumble at all, nor the least slip, till I was entirely out of their hands. 2. That although many strove to lay hold on my collar or clothes to pull me down, they could not fasten at all; only one got fast hold of the flap of my waistcoat, which was soon left in his hand; the other flap, in the pocket of which was a bank-note, was torn but half off. 3. That a lusty man just behind struck at me several times with a large oaken stick, with which if he had struck me once on the back part of my head it would have saved him all further trouble. But every time the blow was turned aside, I knew not how, for I could not move to the right hand or left. 4. That another came rushing through the press, and raising his arm to strike, on a sudden let it drop, and only stroked my head, saying, "What soft hair he has!" 5. That I stopped exactly at the mayor's door, as if I had known it, (which the mob thought I did,) and found him standing in the shop, which gave the first check to the madness of the people. 6. That the very first men whose hearts were turned were the heroes of the town, the captains of the rabble on all occasions, one of them having been a prize-fighter at the bear-garden. 7. That, from first to last, I heard none give a reviling word, or call me by any opprobrious name whatever; but the cry of one and all was, "The preacher! The preacher! The parson! The minister!" 8. That no creature, at least within my hearing, laid any thing to my charge, either true or false; having in the hurry quite forgot to provide themselves with an accusation of any kind. And, Lastly, That they were as utterly at a loss what they should do with me, none proposing any determinate thing; only, "Away with him! Kill him at once!"

By how gentle degrees does God prepare us for his will! Two years ago a piece of brick grazed my shoulders. It was a year after that the stone struck me between the eyes. Last month I received one blow, and this evening two—one before we came into the town, and one after we were gone out; but both were as nothing: for though one man struck me on the breast with all his might, and the other on the mouth with such a force that the blood gushed out immediately, I felt no more pain from either of the blows than if they had touched me with a straw.

Narrow Escape from Drowning.

Saturday, Oct. 22. I rode from Nottingham to Epworth, and on Monday set out for Grimsby; but at

Ferry we were at a full stop, the boatmen telling us we could not pass the Trent: it was as much as our lives were worth to put from shore before the storm abated. We waited an hour; but, being afraid it would do much hurt if I should disappoint the congregation at Gransby, I asked the men if they did not think it possible to get to the other shore. They said they could not tell; but if we would venture our lives, they would venture theirs. So we put off, having six men, two women, and three horses in the boat. Many stood looking after us on the river-side, in the middle of which we were, when, in an instant, the side of the boat was under water, and the horses and men rolling one over another. We expected the boat to sink every moment, but I did not doubt of being able to swim ashore. The boatmen were amazed as well as the rest; but they quickly recovered and rowed for life. Soon after, our horses leaping overboard lightened the boat, and we came unhurt to land.

They wondered what was the matter I did not rise, (for I lay along in the bottom of the boat,) and I wondered too, till, upon examination, I found that a large iron crow, which the boatmen sometimes used, was (none knew how) run through the string of my boot, which pinned me down that I could not stir; so that if the boat had sunk, I should have been safe enough from swimming any further. The same day, and, as near as we can judge, the same hour, the boat in which my brother was crossing the Severn, at the New Passage, was carried away by the wind, and in the utmost danger of splitting upon the rocks. But the same God, when all human hope was past, delivered them as well as us.

A High Debate and a Profound Decision.

Sunday, Oct. 30. Mr. Clayton read prayers, and I preached on "What must I do to be saved?" I showed, in the plainest words I could devise, that mere outside religion would not bring us to heaven; that none could go thither without inward holiness, which was only to be attained by faith. As I went back through the church-yard, many of the parish were in high debate what religion this preacher was of. Some said, "He must be a Quaker;" others, "an Anabaptist;" but, at length, one deeper learned than the rest brought them all clearly over to his opinion, that he was a *Presbyterian Papist.*

Methodism Caricatured on the Stage.

Monday, Oct. 31. We set out early in the morning, and in the evening came to Newcastle.

Wednesday, Nov. 2. The following advertisement was published:

FOR THE BENEFIT OF MR. ESTE.

By the Edinburgh Company of Comedians, on Friday, November 4, will be acted a Comedy called

THE CONSCIOUS LOVERS;

To which will be added a Farce called

TRICK UPON TRICK; OR, METHODISM DISPLAYED.

On *Friday* a vast multitude of spectators were assembled in the Moot Hall to see this. It was believed there could not be less than fifteen hundred people, some hundreds of whom sat on rows of seats built upon the stage. Soon after the comedians had begun the first act of the play, on a sudden all those seats fell down at once, the supporters of them breaking like a rotten stick. The people were thrown one upon another, about five foot forward, but not one of them hurt. After a short time the rest of the spectators were quiet, and the actors went on. In the middle of the second act, all the shilling seats gave a crack and sunk several inches down. A great noise and shrieking followed, and as many as could readily get to the door went out and returned no more. Notwithstanding this, when the noise was over the actors went on with the play. In the beginning of the third act the entire stage suddenly sunk about six inches: the players retired with great precipitation, yet in a while they began again. At the latter end of the third act all the sixpenny seats, without any kind of notice, fell to the ground. There was now a cry on every side, it being supposed that many were crushed in pieces; but, upon inquiry, not a single person (such was the mercy of God!) was either killed or dangerously hurt. Two or three hundred remaining still in the Hall, Mr. Este (who was to act the Methodist) came upon the stage and told them, for all this, he was resolved the farce should be acted. While he was speaking, the stage sunk six inches more; on which he ran back in the utmost confusion, and the people as fast as they could out of the door, none staying to look behind him. Which is most surprising, that those players acted this farce the next week, or that some hundreds of people came again to see it?

Care for the Poor.

Friday, Feb. 17, 1744, we observed as a day of solemn fasting and prayer. In the afternoon, many being met together, I exhorted them, now, while they had opportunity, to make to themselves "friends of the mammon of unrighteousness," to deal their bread to the hungry, to clothe the naked, and not to hide themselves from their own flesh. And God opened their hearts so that they contributed near fifty pounds, which I began laying out the very next hour in linen, woollen, and shoes for them whom I knew to be diligent and yet in want.

Mistakes Rectified.

Feb. 17. In the Whitehall and London Evening Post, Saturday, February 18, was a paragraph with some mistakes which it may not be amiss to rectify. "By a private letter from Staffordshire we have advice of an insurrection of the people called Methodists,"—the insurrection was not of the people called Methodists, but against them,—"who upon some pretended insults from the Church party,"—they pretended no insults from the Church party, being themselves no other than true members of the Church of England; but were more than insulted by a mixed multitude of church-goers, (who seldom, if ever, go near a church,) Dissenters, and Papists,—"have assembled themselves in a riotous manner." Here is another small *error personæ.* Many hundreds of the mob did assemble themselves in a riotous manner, having given public notice several days before (particularly by a paper set up in Walsal market-place) that on Shrove Tuesday they intended to come and destroy the Methodists, and inviting all the country to come and join them. "And having committed several outrages,"—without ever committing any, they have suffered all manner of outrages for several months past,—" they proceeded at last to burn the house of one of their adversaries." Without burning any house or making any resistance, some hundreds of them, on Shrove Tuesday last, had their own houses broken up, their windows, window-cases, beds, tools, goods of all sorts, broke all to pieces, or taken away by open violence; their live goods driven off, themselves forced to fly for their lives, and most of them stripped of all they had in the world.

John Nelson Impressed for a Soldier.

May 15. After comforting the little flock at Norton, I rode the shortest way to Birstal. Here I found our brethren partly mourning and partly rejoicing on account of John Nelson. On Friday, the 4th instant, (they informed me,) the constables took him just as he had ended his sermon at Adwalton, and the next day carried him before the Commissioners at Halifax, the most active of whom was Mr. Coleby, Vicar of Birstal. Many were ready to testify that he was in no respect such a person as the Act of Parliament specified. But they were not heard. He was a preacher: that was enough. So he was sent for a soldier at once.

A Chancery Bill!

Thursday, Dec. 27. I called on the solicitor whom I had employed in the suit lately commenced against me in chancery, and here I first saw that foul monster, *a chancery bill!* A scroll it was of forty-two pages, in large folio, to tell a story which needed not to have taken up forty lines! And stuffed with such stupid, senseless, improbable lies, many of them, too, quite foreign to the question, as, I believe, would have cost the compiler his life in any heathen court either of Greece or Rome. And this is *equity* in a Christian country! This is the English method of redressing other grievances!

Ten Thousand Cares of Little Weight.

Saturday, Jan., 1745. I had often wondered at myself, and sometimes mentioned it to others, that ten thousand cares of various kinds were no more weight or burden to my mind than ten thousand hairs were to my head. Perhaps I began to ascribe something of this to my own strength. And thence it might be that on *Sunday*, 13, that strength was withheld, and I felt what it was to be troubled about many things. One and another hurrying me continually, it seized upon my spirit more and more, till I found it absolutely necessary to fly for my life, and that without delay. So the next day, *Monday*, 14, I took horse and rode away for Bristol. Between Bath and Bristol, I was earnestly desired to turn aside and call at the house of a poor man, William Shalwood. I found him and his wife sick in one bed, and with small hope of the recovery of either. Yet, after prayer, I believed they would "not die but live, and declare the loving kindness of the Lord." The next time I called he was sitting below stairs, and his wife able to go abroad.

As soon as we came into the house at Bristol my soul was lightened of her load, of that insufferable weight, which had lain upon my mind more or less for several days.

A Rough Journey.

Friday, Feb. 22. There was so much snow about Boroughbridge that we could go on but very slowly;

insomuch that the night overtook us when we wanted six or seven miles to the place where we designed to lodge. But we pushed on at a venture across the moor, and about eight came safe to Sandhutton.

Saturday, Feb. 23. We found the roads abundantly worse than they had been the day before, not only because the snows were deeper, which made the causeways in many places unpassable, (and turnpike roads were not known in these parts of England till some years after,) but likewise because the hard frost succeeding the thaw had made all the ground like glass. We were often obliged to walk, it being impossible to ride, and our horses several times fell down while we were leading them, but not once while we were riding them, during the whole journey. It was past eight before we got to Gateshead Fell, which appeared a great pathless waste of white. The snow filling up and covering all the roads, we were at a loss how to proceed, when an honest man of Newcastle overtook and guided us safe into town. Many a rough journey have I had before, but one like this I never had; between wind, and hail, and rain, and ice, and snow, and driving sleet, and piercing cold! but it is past; these days will return no more, and are therefore as though they had never been.

Pain, disappointment, sickness, strife,
Whate'er molests or troubles life,
However grievous in its stay,
It shakes the tenement of clay,
When past, as nothing we esteem;
And pain, like pleasure, is a dream.

A Clear Statement of the Case between Wesley and the Clergy

Sunday, March 10. We had a useful sermon at All Saints, and another at our own church in the afternoon. I was much refreshed by both, and united in love to the two preachers and to the clergy in general. The next day I wrote to a friend as follows:

NEWCASTLE-UPON-TYNE, *March* 11, 1745.

I have been drawing up this morning a short state of the case between the clergy and us. I leave you to make any such use of it as you believe will be to the glory of God.

"1. About seven years since we began preaching inward, present salvation, as attainable by faith alone. 2. For preaching this doctrine we were forbidden to preach in the churches. 3. We then preached in private houses, as occasion offered; and when the houses could not contain the people, in the open air. 4. For this many of the clergy preached or printed against us, as both heretics and schismatics. 5. Persons who were convinced of sin begged us to advise them more particularlyh ow to flee from the wrath to come. We replied, if they would all come at one time (for they were numerous) we would endeavor it. 6. For this we were represented, both from the pulpit and the press, (we have heard it with our ears, and seen it with our eyes,) as introducing Popery, raising sedition, practicing both against Church and State; and all manner of evil was publicly said both of us, and those who were accustomed to meet with us. 7. Finding some truth herein, namely, that some of those who so met together walked disorderly, we immediately desired them not to come to us any more.

8. And the more steady were desired to overlook the rest, that we might know if they walked according to the Gospel. 9. But now several of the Bishops began to speak against us, either in conversation or in public. 10. On this encouragement, several of the clergy stirred up the people to treat us as outlaws or mad dogs. 11. The people did so, both in Staffordshire, Cornwall, and many other places. 12. And they do so still, wherever they are not restrained by their fear of the secular magistrate.

Thus the case stands at present. Now, what can we do, or what can you our brethren do, toward healing this breach? which is highly desirable, that we may withstand, with joint force, the still increasing flood of Popery, Deism, and immorality. Desire of us any thing we can do with a safe conscience, and we will do it immediately. Will you meet us here? Will you do what we desire of you, so far as you can, with a safe conscience?

"Let us come to particulars. Do you desire us, 1. To preach another, or to desist from preaching this, doctrine? We think you do not desire it, as knowing we cannot do this with a safe conscience. Do you desire us, 2. To desist from preaching in private houses or in the open air? As things are now circumstanced, this would be the same as desiring us not to preach at all. Do you desire us, 3. To desist from advising those who now meet together for that purpose? or, in other words, to dissolve our societies? We cannot do this with a safe conscience, for we apprehend many souls would be lost thereby, and that God would require their blood at our hands. Do you desire us, 4. To advise them only one by one? This is impossible because of their number. Do you desire us, 5. To suffer those who walk disorderly still to mix with the rest? Neither can we do this with a safe conscience, because 'evil communications corrupt good manners.' Do you desire us, 6. To discharge those leaders of bands or classes (as we term them) who overlook the rest? This is, in effect, to suffer the disorderly walkers still to mix with the rest, which we dare not do. Do you desire us, Lastly, To behave with reverence toward those who are overseers of the Church of God? And with tenderness, both to the character and persons of our brethren, the inferior clergy? By the grace of God we can and will do this. Yea, our conscience beareth us witness that we have already labored so to do, and that at all times and in all places.

"If you ask what we desire of you to do, we answer, 1. We do not desire any one of you to let us preach in your church, either if you believe us to preach false doctrine, or if you have, upon any other ground, the least scruple of conscience concerning it. But we desire any who believes us to preach true doctrine, and has no scruple at all in this matter, may not be either publicly or privately discouraged from inviting us to preach in his church.

"2. We do not desire that any one who thinks that we are heretics or schismatics, and that it is his duty to preach or print against us as such, should refrain therefrom so long as he thinks it his duty. (Although in this case the breach can never be healed.) But we desire that none will pass such a sentence till he has calmly considered both sides of the question; that he would not condemn us unheard; but first read what we have written, and pray earnestly that God may direct him in the right way.

"3. We do not desire any favor, if either Popery, sedition, or immorality be proved against us. But we desire you will not credit, without proof, any of those senseless tales that pass current with the vulgar. That if you do not credit them yourselves, you will not relate them to others, (which we have known done;) yea, that you will confute them so far as ye have opportunity, and discountenance those who still retail them abroad.

"4. We do not desire any preferment, favor, or recommendation from those that are in authority, either in Church or State; but we desire, (1.) That if any thing material be laid to our charge, we may be permitted to answer for ourselves. (2.) That you would hinder your dependents from stirring up the rabble against us, who are certainly not the proper judges of these matters. And, (3.) That you would effectually suppress, and thoroughly discountenance, all riots and popular insurrections, which evidently strike at the foundation of all government, whether of Church or State. Now these things you certainly can do, and that with a safe conscience. Therefore, till these things are done, the continuance of the breach is chargeable on you, and you only."

Water-Power and Voice-Power Antagonized.

Sunday, April 28. I preached at five, (as I had done overnight,) about a mile from Altringham, on "Watch and pray, that ye enter not into temptation." A plain man came to me afterward and said, "Sir, I find Mr. Hutchings and you do not preach the same way. You bid us read the Bible, and pray, and go to church; but he bids us let all this alone, and says, if we go to church and sacrament we shall never come to Christ." At nine I preached, near Stockport, to a large congregation; thence we rode to Bongs, in Derbyshire, a lone house on the side of a high, steep mountain, whither abundance of people were got before us. I preached on God's justifying the ungodly, and his word was as dew upon the tender herb. At five I preached at Mill Town, near Chapel-en-le-Frith. The poor miller, near whose pond we stood, endeavored to drown my voice by letting out the water, which fell with a great noise. But it was labor lost; for my strength was so increased that I was heard to the very skirts of the congregation.

Exhorted to Return to the Church.

Thursday, May 23. We had one more conversation with one that had often strengthened our hands, but now earnestly exhorted us (what is man!) to return to the Church, to renounce all our lay assistants, to dissolve our societies, to leave off field-preaching, and to accept of honorable preferment.

Insufferable Impudence.

Tuesday, June 25. We rode to St. Just. I preached at seven to the largest congregation I have seen since my coming. At the meeting of the earnest, loving society, all our hearts were in a flame; and again at five in the morning, while I explained, "There is no condemnation to them which are in Christ Jesus." When the preaching was ended the constable apprehended Edward Greenfield, (by a warrant from Dr.

Borlase,) a tinner, in the forty-sixth year of his age, having a wife and seven children. Three years ago he was eminent for cursing, swearing, drunkenness, and all manner of wickedness ; but those old things had been for some time passed away, and he was then remarkable for a quite contrary behavior. I asked a little gentleman at St. Just what objection there was to Edward Greenfield. He said, "Why, the man is well enough in other things, but his impudence the gentlemen cannot bear. Why, sir, he says he knows his sins are forgiven!" And for this cause he is adjudged to banishment or death!

Wesley Walks through the Mob.

Thursday, July 4, 1746. I rode to Falmouth. About three in the afternoon I went to see a gentlewoman who had been long indisposed. Almost as soon as I was set down, the house was beset on all sides by an innumerable multitude of people. A louder or more confused noise could hardly be at the taking of a city by storm. At first Mrs. B. and her daughter endeavored to quiet them. But it was labor lost. They might as well have attempted to still the raging of the sea. They were soon glad to shift for themselves, and leave K. E. and me to do as well as we could. The rabble roared with all their throats, "Bring out the Canorum! Where is the Canorum?" (an unmeaning word which the Cornish generally use instead of Methodist.) No anwer being given, they quickly forced open the door and filled the passage. Only a wainscot partition was between us, which was not likely to stand long. I immediately took down a large looking glass which hung against it, supposing the whole side would fall in at once. When they began their work with abundance of bitter imprecations poor Kitty was utterly astonished, and cried out, "O, sir, what must we do?" I said, "We must pray." Indeed, at that time, to all appearance, our lives were not worth an hour's purchase. She asked, "But, sir, is it not better for you to hide yourself? to get into the closet?" I answered, "No. It is best for me to stand just where I am." Among those without were the crews of some privateers, which were lately come into the harbor. Some of these being angry at the slowness of the rest, thrust them away, and, coming up all together, set their shoulders to the inner door and cried out, "Avast, lads, avast!" Away went all the hinges at once, and the door fell back into the room. I stepped forward at once into the midst of them, and said, "Here I am. Which of you has any thing to say to me? To which of you have I done any wrong? To you? Or you? Or you?" I continued speaking, till I came, bare-headed as I was, (for I purposely left my hat, that they all might see my face,) into the middle of the street, and then raising my voice, said, "Neighbors, countrymen! Do you desire to hear me speak?" They cried vehemently, "Yes, yes. He shall speak! He shall! Nobody shall hinder him." But having nothing to stand on, and no advantage of ground, I could be heard by few only. However, I spoke without intermission, and, as far as the sound reached, the people were still; till one or two of their captains turned about and swore not a man should touch him. Mr. Thomas, a clergyman, then came up and asked, "Are you not ashamed to use a stranger thus?" He was soon seconded by two or three gentlemen of the town, and one of the aldermen, with whom I walked down the town, speaking all the time, till I came to Mrs. Maddern's house. The gentlemen proposed sending for my horse to the door, and desired me to step in and rest the meantime. But on second thoughts, they judged it not advisable to let me go out among the people again; so they chose to send my horse before me to Penryn, and to send me thither by water, the sea running close by the backdoor of the house in which we were.

Count Zinzendorf's Prophecy.

Friday, Sept. 6. Many of our friends were grieved at the advertisement which James Hutton had just published, by order of Count Zinzendorf, declaring that he and his people had no connection with Mr. John and Charles Wesley. But I believed that declaration would do us no more harm than the prophecy which the Count subjoined to it—that we should soon run our heads against the wall. We will not if we can help it.

Wesley leaves his Horse in the Quagmire.

Saturday, Nov. 9. In the evening we came to Penkridge, and light on a poor drunken, cursing, swearing landlord, who seemed scarce to think there was either God or devil. But I had spoke very little when his countenance changed, and he was so full of his thanks and blessings that I could hardly make an end of my sentence. May salvation come to this house also! It was exceeding dark when we rode through Bilston. However, we did not stick fast till we came to Wednesbury town-end. Several coming with candles, I got out of the quagmire; and, leaving them to disengage my horse, walked to Francis Ward's, and preached on, "Fear not ye; for I know ye seek him that was crucified."

A Distributer of Tracts.

December. We had within a short time given away some thousands of little tracts among the common people, and it pleased God hereby to provoke others to jealousy, insomuch that the Lord Mayor had ordered a large quantity of papers, dissuading from cursing and swearing, to be printed and distributed to the train-bands. And this day "An Earnest Exhortation to Serious Repentance" was given at every church door in or near London to every person who came out, and one left at the house of every householder who was absent from church. I doubt not but God gave a blessing therewith. And perhaps then the sentence of desolation was recalled. It was on this very day that the Duke's army was so remarkably preserved in the midst of the ambuscades at Clifton Moor. The rebels fired many volleys upon the King's troops from the hedges and walls, behind which they lay. And yet, from first to last, only ten or twelve men fell, the shot flying over their heads.

Wesley Insists on the Right of Private Judgment.

June 7, 1746. In the afternoon an old friend (now with the Moravians) labored much to convince me that I could not continue in the Church of England, because I could not implicitly submit to her determinations; "for this," he said, "was essentially necessary to the continuing in any Church." Not to the continuing in any but that of the Brethren; if it were, I could be a member of no Church under heaven. For I must still insist on the right of private judgment. I dare call no man Rabbi. I cannot yield either implicit faith or obedience to any man or number of men under heaven.

Wesley's Plan for Relieving the Industrious Poor.

Thursday, July 17. I finished the little collection which I had made among my friends for a lending stock: it did not amount to thirty pounds, which a few persons afterward made up to fifty. And by this inconsiderable sum above two hundred and fifty persons were relieved in one year.

His rule always to look a Mob in the Face.

Weduesday, Aug. 6. I preached at Oak Hill. How is this? I have not known so many persons earnestly mourning after God, of any society of this size in England, and so unblamable in their behavior; and yet not one person has found a sense of the pardoning love of God from the first preaching here to this day! When I mentioned this to the society there was such a mourning as one would believe should pierce the clouds. My voice was quickly drowned. We continued crying to God with many loud and bitter cries, till I was constrained to break away, between four and five, and take horse for Shepton.

Here the good curate (I was informed) had hired a silly man, with a few other drunken champions, to make a disturbance. Almost as soon as I began, they began screaming out a psalm; but our singing quickly swallowed up theirs. Soon after, their orator named a text, and (as they termed it) preached a sermon; his attendants meantime being busy (not in hearing him, but) in throwing stones and dirt at our brethren—those of them, I mean, who were obliged to stand at the door. When I had done preaching I would have gone out to them, it being my rule, confirmed by long experience, always to look a mob in the face; but our people took me up, whether I would or no, and carried me into the house. The rabble melted away in a quarter of an hour, and we walked home in peace.

A Faithful Mayor.

Friday, Sept. 26. Mr. B. went to the Mayor and said, "Sir, I come to inform against a common swearer. I believe he swore a hundred oaths last night, but I marked down only twenty." "Sir," said the Mayor, "you do very right in bringing him to justice. What is his name?" He replied, "R. D." "R. D.?" answered the Mayor; "why, that is my son!"—"Yes, sir," said Mr. B., "so I understand."—"Nay sir," said he, "I have nothing to say in his defense. If he breaks the law he must take what follows."

Wesley Employs his Pen for Children.

Monday, Dec. 15. Most of this week I spent at Lewisham in writing "Lessons for Children," consisting of the most practical Scriptures, with a very few short explanatory notes.

A Remarkable Escape.

Wednesday, Jan. 14, 1747. I rode on to Bristol, and spent a week in great peace.

Thursday, Jan. 22. About half-hour after twelve I took horse for Wick, where I had appointed to preach at three. I was riding by the wall through St. Nicholas Gate (my horse having been brought to the house where I dined) just as a cart turned short from St. Nicholas-street, and came swiftly down the hill. There was just room to pass between the wheel of it and the wall, but that space was taken up by the cartman. I called him to go back, or I must ride over him; but the man, as if deaf, walked straight forward. This obliged me to hold back my horse. In the meantime the shaft of the cart came full against his shoulder with such a shock as beat him to the ground. He shot me forward over his head, as an arrow out of a bow, where I lay with my arms and legs, I know not how, stretched out in a line close to the wall. The wheel ran by close to my side, but only dirted my clothes. I found no flutter of spirit, but the same composure as if I had been sitting in my study. When the cart was gone I rose. Abundance of people gathered round, till a gentleman desired me to step into his shop. After cleaning myself a little I took horse again, and was at Wick by the time appointed. I returned to Bristol (where the report of my being killed had spread far and wide) time enough to praise God in the great congregation, and to preach on "Thou, Lord, shalt save both man and beast." My shoulders, and hands, and side, and both my legs, were a little bruised; my knees something more; my right thigh the most, which made it a little difficult to me to walk; but some warm treacle took away all the pain in an hour, and the lameness in a day or two.

Wesley's Endurance in Traveling.

Tuesday, Feb. 10. My brother returned from the north, and I prepared to supply his place there.

Sunday, 15. I was very weak and faint; but on *Monday*, 16, I rose soon after three, lively and strong, and found all my complaints were fled away like a dream. I was wondering, the day before, at the mildness of the weather; such as seldom attends me in my journeys. But my wonder now ceased: the wind was turned full north, and blew so exceeding hard and keen, that when we came to Hatfield neither my companions nor I had much use of our hands or feet. After resting an hour we bore up again through the wind and snow, which drove full in our faces. But this was only a squall. In Baldock-field the storm began in earnest. The large hail drove so vehemently in our faces that we could not see, nor hardly breathe. However, before two o'clock we reached Baldock, where one met and conducted us safe to Totten.

An Honest but Muddy Mind.

Friday, 27. Honest muddy M. B. conducted me to his house at Acomb. I now found out (which I could not comprehend before) what was the matter with him. He, and one or two more, since I saw them last, had been studying the profound Jacob Behmen. The event was, (as might easily have been foreseen,) he had utterly confounded their intellects, and filled them so full of sublime speculations that they had left Scripture and common sense far behind.

A Pulpit cordially Offered.

Sunday, *March* 1. I came to Osmotherly about ten o'clock, just as the minister (who lives some miles off) came into town. I sent my service to him, and told him, if he pleased, I would assist him, either by reading prayers or preaching. On receiving the message he came to me immediately, and said he would willingly accept of my assistance. As we walked to church he said, "Perhaps it would fatigue you too much to read prayers and preach too." I told him no; I would choose it if he pleased; which I did accordingly. After service was ended Mr. D. said, "Sir, I am sorry I have not a house here to entertain you. Pray let me know whenever you come this way." Several asking where I would preach in the afternoon, one went to Mr. D. again and asked if he was willing I should preach in the church. He said, "Yes, whenever Mr. Wesley pleases." We had a large congregation at three o'clock. Those who in time past had been the most bitter gainsayers seemed now to be melted into love. All were convinced we are no Papists. How wisely does God order all things in their season!

Wesley Instructs Young Men.

Wednesday, March 4. This week I read over with some young men a compendium of rhetoric, with a system of ethics. I see not why a man of tolerable understanding may not learn in six months' time more of solid philosophy than is commonly learned at Oxford in four (perhaps seven) years.

Wesley's Method of Examining Leaders.

March 8. On *Monday, Tuesday,* and *Thursday* I examined the classes. I had been often told it was impossible for me to distinguish the precious from the vile without the miraculous discernment of spirits. But I now saw more clearly than ever that this might be done, and without much difficulty, supposing only two things: First, Courage and steadiness in the examiner. Secondly, Common sense and common honesty in the leader of each class. I visit, for instance, the class in the close, of which Robert Peacock is leader. I ask, "Does this and this person in your class live in drunkenness, or any outward sin? Does he go to church, and use the other means of grace? Does he meet you as often as he has opportunity?" Now, if Robert Peacock has common sense he can answer these questions truly; and if he has common honesty he will. And if not, some other in the class has both, and can and will answer for him. Where is the difficulty, then, of finding out if there be any disorderly walker in this class, and, consequently, in any other? The question is not concerning the heart, but the life. And the general tenor of this I do not say cannot be known, but cannot be hid without a miracle.

What Mr. Wesley would do if he had but two days to live.

Thursday, March 19. I considered, "What would I do now if I was sure I had but two days to live?" All outward things are settled to my wish: the houses at Bristol, Kingswood, and Newcastle are safe; the deeds whereby they are conveyed to the trustees, took place on the 5th instant; my will is made; what have I more to do, but to commend my soul to my merciful and faithful Creator?

Christians may vindicate themselves.

Friday, April 10. Having settled all the Societies in the country, I began examining that at Newcastle again. It was my particular concern to remove, if possible, every hinderance of brotherly love, and one odd one I found creeping in upon us which had already occasioned much evil, namely, a fancy that we must not justify ourselves. (Some of the spawn of Mystic divinity.) Just contrary to the scriptural injunction, "Be ready to give a reason of the hope that is in you." For want of doing this in time some offenses were now grown incurable. I found it needful, therefore, to tear up this by the roots, to explain this duty from the foundation, and to require all who desired to remain with us to justify themselves whenever they were blamed unjustly, and not to swallow up both peace and love in their voluntary humility.

John Nelson Assaulted and left for Dead.

April 20. John Nelson met me at Osmotherly. On Thursday, Friday, and Saturday he had preached at Acomb and the neighboring places; on Good Friday in particular, on Heworth Moor, to a large and quiet congregation. On Easter Sunday, at eight, he preached there again to a large number of serious hearers. Toward the close of his discourse a mob came from York, hired and headed by some (miscalled) gentlemen. They stood still till an eminent Papist cried out, "Why do not you knock the dog's brains out?" On which they immediately began throwing all that came to hand, so that the congregation was quickly dispersed. John spoke a few words, and walked toward York. They followed with showers of bricks and stones, one of which struck him on the shoulder, one on the back, and, a little before he came to the city, part of a brick hit him on the back part of the head and felled him to the ground. When he came to himself, two of Acomb lifted him up and led him forward between them. The gentlemen followed, throwing as before, till he came to the city gate, near which lived an honest tradesmen, who took him by the arm and pulled him into his house. Some of the rioters swore they would break all his windows if he did not turn him out. But he told them resolutely, "I will not; and let any of you touch my house at your peril; I shall make you remember it as long as you live." On this they thought good to retire.

After a surgeon had dressed the wound in his head, John went softly on to Acomb. About five he went out in order to preach, and began singing a hymn. Before it was ended, the same gentlemen came in a coach from York with a numerous attendance. They threw clods and stones so fast on every side that the congregation soon dispersed. John walked down into a little ground not far from Thomas Slaton's house. Two men quickly followed, one of whom swore desperately he would have his life, and he seemed to be in good earnest. He struck him several times with all his force on the head and breast, and at length threw him down, and stamped upon him till he left him for dead. But, by the mercy of God, being carried into a house, he soon came to himself, and after a night's rest was so recovered that he was able to ride to Osmotherly.

A Far-reaching Argument.

Tuesday, April 21. I called at Thirsk; but, finding the town full of holiday folks, drinking, cursing, swearing, and cock-fighting, I did not stop at all, but rode on to Boroughbridge, and in the afternoon to Leeds.

Wednesday, April 22. I spent an hour with Mr. M., and pressed him to make good his assertion, that our preaching had done more harm than good. This he did not choose to pursue, but enlarged on the harm it might occasion in succeeding generations. I cannot see the force of this argument. I dare not neglect the doing certain, present good for fear of some probable ill in the succeeding century.

Mr. Wesley's first Street-Preaching in Manchester.

May. We came to Manchester between one and two. I had no thought of preaching here till I was informed John Nelson had given public notice that I would preach at one o'clock. I was now in a great strait. Their house would not contain a tenth part of the people; and how the unbroken spirits of so large a town would endure preaching in the street I knew not. Besides that, having rode a swift trot for several hours, and in so sultry a day, I was both faint and weary. But, after considering that I was not going a warfare at my own cost, I walked straight to Salford Cross. A numberless crowd of people partly ran before, partly followed after me. I thought it best not to sing, but, looking round, asked abruptly, "Why do you look as if you had never seen me before? Many of you have seen me in the neighboring church, both preaching and administering the sacrament." I then began, "Seek ye the Lord while he may be found; call upon him while he is near." None interrupted at all or made any disturbance till, as I was drawing to a conclusion, a big man thrust in, with three or four more, and bade them bring out the engine. Our friends desired me to remove into a yard just by, which I did, and concluded in peace. About six we reached Davy Hulme, five miles from Manchester, where I was much refreshed both in preaching and meeting the society. Their neighbors here used to disturb them much; but a Justice of Peace, who feared God, granting them a warrant for the chief of the rioters, from that time they were in peace,

A Brave Defender.

Saturday, June 27. I preached at four, and then spoke severally to part of the society. As yet I have found only one person among them who knew the love of God before my brother came. No wonder the devil was so stil, for his goods were in peace. About six in the evening I went to the place where I preached last year. A little before we had ended the hymn came the lieutenant, a famous man, with his retinue of soldiers, drummers, and mob. When the drums ceased a gentleman-barber began to speak; but his voice was quickly drowned in the shouts of the multitude, who grew fiercer and fiercer as their numbers increased. After waiting about a quarter of an hour, perceiving the violence of the rabble still increasing, I walked down into the thickest of them and took the captain of the mob by the hand. He immediately said, "Sir, I will see you safe home. Sir, no man shall touch you. Gentlemen, stand off! give back! I will knock the first man down that touches him." We walked on in great peace, my conductor every now and then stretching out his neck (he was a very tall man) and looking round, to see if any behaved rudely, till we came to Mr. Hide's door. We then parted in much love. I stayed in the street near half an hour after he was gone talking with the people, who had now forgot their anger, and went away in high good humor.

Paid Voters Return the Money.

Wednesday, July 1. I spoke severally to all those who had votes in the ensuing election. I found them such as I desired. Not one would even eat or drink at the expense of him for whom he voted. Five guineas had been given to W. C., but he returned them immediately. T. M. positively refused to accept any thing; and when he heard that his mother had received money privately he could not rest till she gave him the three guineas, which he instantly sent back.

Thursday, July 2, was the day of election for Parliament men. It was begun and ended without any hurry at all. I had a large congregation in the evening, among whom two or three roared for the disquietness of their heart; as did many at the meeting which followed, particularly those who had lost their first love.

"One may as well Blow against the Wind."

Monday, July 6. I preached, about twelve, at Bray; but neither the house nor the yard would contain the congregation, and all were serious. The scoffers are vanished away; I scarce saw one in the county. I preached in the evening at Camborne to an equally serious congregation. I looked about for John Rogers, the champion, who had so often sworn I should never more preach in that parish. But it seems he had given up the cause, saying, "One may as well blow against the wind."

Wesley Sifting the Exhorters.

Tuesday, July 7. I preached at St. Ives; *Wednesday* 8, at Sithney. On *Thursday* the stewards of all the societies met. I now diligently inquired what exhorters there were in each society; whether they had gifts meet for the work, whether their lives were eminently holy, and whether there appeared any fruit of their labor. I found, upon the whole, 1. That there were no less than eighteen exhorters in the county; 2. That three of these had no gifts at all for the work, neither natural nor supernatural; 3. That a fourth had neither gifts nor grace, but was a dull, empty, self-conceited man; 4. That a fifth had considerable gifts, but had evidently made shipwreck of the grace of God; these, therefore, I determined immediately to set aside, and advise our societies not to hear them; 5. That J. B., A. L., and J. W., had gifts and grace, and had been much blessed in the work. Lastly, that the rest might be helpful when there was no preacher in their own or the neighboring societies, provided they would take no step without the advice of those who had more experience than themselves.

A Romantic Ride.

Wednesday, Aug. 5. Taking horse early in the morning, we rode over the rough mountains of Radnorshire and Montgomeryshire into Merionethshire.

In the evening I was surprised with one of the finest prospects in its kind that ever I saw in my life. We rode in a green vale, shaded with rows of trees, which made an arbor for several miles. The river labored along on our left hand through broken rocks of every size, shape, and color. On the other side of the river the mountain rose to an immense height, almost perpendicular, and yet the tall, straight oaks stood, rank above rank, from the bottom to the very top, only here and there, where the mountain was not so steep, were interposed pastures or fields of corn. At a distance, as far as the eye could reach, as it were by way of contrast,

> A mountain huge upreared
> Its broad, bare back,

with vast, rugged rocks hanging over its brow, that seemed to nod portending ruin.

The Fault in his Head, not in the Heart.

Wednesday, Sept. 2. I spent some time with T. Prosser, who had filled the society with vain janglings. I found the fault lay in his head rather than his heart. He is an honest, well-meaning man; but no more qualified, either by nature or grace, to expound Scripture than to read lectures in logic or algebra. Yet even men of sense have taken this dull, mystical man to be far deeper than he is, and it is very natural so to do. If we look into a dark pit it seems deep, but the darkness only makes it seem so. Bring the light, and we shall see it is very shallow. In the evening I preached at Fonmon; but, the congregation being larger than the chapel would contain, I was obliged to preach in the court. I was myself much comforted in comforting the weary and heavy laden.

Alexander the Great and Judas.

Friday, Sept. 4. There was a very large congregation at Cardiff Castle yard in the evening. I afterward met the society, spoke plain to them, and left them once more in peace.

Saturday, Sept. 5. In my road to Bristol I read over Q. Curtius, a fine writer, both as to thought and language. But what a hero does he describe! whose murder of his old friend and companion, Clitus, (though not done of a sudden, as is commonly supposed, but deliberately, after some hours' consideration,) was a virtuous act in comparison of his butchering poor Philotas, and his good old father, Parmenio. Yet even this was a little thing compared to the thousands and ten thousands he slaughtered, both in battle and in and after taking cities, for no other crime than defending their wives and children. I doubt whether Judas claims so hot a place in hell as Alexander the Great.

A Captain of the Mob begins to Pray.

Friday, Feb. 12, 1748. After preaching at Oakhill about noon I rode to Shepton, and found them all under a strange consternation. A mob, they said, was hired, prepared, and made sufficiently drunk, in order to do all manner of mischief. I began preaching between four and five; none hindered or interrupted at all. We had a blessed opportunity, and the hearts of many were exceedingly comforted. I wondered what was become of the mob. But we were quickly informed they mistook the place, imagining I should alight (as I used to do) at William Stone's house, and had summoned, by drum, all their forces together to meet me at my coming; but Mr. Swindells innocently carrying me to the other end of the town, they did not find their mistake till I had done preaching, so that the hindering this, which was one of their designs, was utterly disappointed. However, they attended us from the preaching-house to William Stone's, throwing dirt, stones, and clods in abundance; but they could not hurt us; only Mr. Swindells had a little dirt on his coat, and I a few specks on my hat.

After we were gone into the house they began throwing great stones in order to break the door; but perceiving this would require some time, they dropped that design for the present. They first broke all the tiles on the penthouse over the door, and then poured in a shower of stones at the windows. One of their captains, in his great zeal, had followed us into the house, and was now shut in with us. He did not like this, and would fain have got out, but it was not possible, so he kept as close to me as he could, thinking himself safe when he was near me; but staying a little behind—when I went up two pair of stairs, and stood close on one side, where we were a little sheltered—a large stone struck him on the forehead, and the blood spouted out like a stream. He cried out, "O, sir, are we to die to-night? What must I do? What must I do?" I said, "Pray to God. He is able to deliver you from all danger." He took my advice, and began praying in such a manner as he had scarce done ever since he was born.

Wesley's Remarkable Preservation.

Feb. Mr. Swindells and I then went to prayer; after which I told him "we must not stay here; we must go down immediately." He said, "Sir, we cannot stir; you see how the stones fly about." I walked straight through the room, and down the stairs, and not a stone came in till we were at the bottom. The mob had just broke open the door when we came into the lower room, and exactly while they burst in at one door we walked out at the other; nor did one man take any notice of us, though we were within five yards of each other. They filled the house at once, and proposed setting it on fire; but one of them, happening to remember that his own house was next, with much ado persuaded them not to do it. Hearing one of them cry out, "They are gone over the grounds," I thought the advice was good; so we went over the grounds to the further end of the town, where Abraham Jenkins waited, and undertook to guide us to Oakhill. I was riding on in Shepton-lane, it being now quite dark, when he cried out, "Come down, come down from the bank!" I did as I was bid; but the bank being high, and the side very near perpendicular, I came down all at once, my horse and I tumbling one over another. But we both rose unhurt. In less than an hour we came to Oakhill, and the next morning to Bristol.

Sea Captains' Excuses for not Sailing.

Sunday, Feb. 28. In the evening I read prayers at our inn, and preached to a large and serious audience. I did the same on *Monday* and *Tuesday* evening.

Perhaps our stay here may not be in vain. I never knew men make such poor, lame excuses as these captains did for not sailing. It put me in mind of the epigram,

> There are, if rightly I methink,
> Five causes why a man should drink;

which, with a little alteration, would just suit them:

> There are, unless my memory fail,
> Five causes why we should not sail:
> The fog is thick, the wind is high,
> It rains, or may do by and by;
> Or—any other reason why.

Wesley Examines the Classes—Results.

Wednesday, March 23. I talked with a warm man, who was always very zealous for the Church when he was very drunk, and just able to stammer out the Irish proverb, "No gown, no crown." He was quickly convinced that, whatever we were, he was himself a child of the devil. We left him full of good resolutions, which held several days. I preached at Newgate at three, but found no stirring at all among the dry bones.

Friday, March 25. I preached in Marlborough-street at five to the largest congregation I have yet seen in a morning. At two I began in Ship-street, where were many of the rich and genteel. I was exceeding weak in body, having been examining classes all the day, but I felt it not after I had spoke two sentences. I was strengthened both in body and soul. I finished the classes the next day, and found them just as I expected. I left three hundred and ninety-four persons united together in August. I had now admitted between twenty and thirty, who had offered themselves since my return to Dublin, and the whole number was neither more nor less than three hundred and ninety-six.

Wesley holds his Congregation in a Hail-storm.

Tuesday, April 12. I rode to Clara, where I was quickly informed that there was to begin in an hour's time a famous cock-fight, to which almost all the country was coming from every side. Hoping to engage some part of them in a better employ, I began preaching in the street as soon as possible. One or two hundred stopped and listened awhile, and pulled off their hats, and forgot their diversion. The congregation at Tullamore in the evening was larger than ever before, and deep attention sat on every face. Toward the latter end of the sermon there began a violent storm of hail. I desired the people to cover their heads, but the greater part of them would not, nor did any one go away till I concluded my discourse.

Criticism on the History of St. Patrick.

Monday, April 25. Finding my fever greatly increased, I judged it would be best to keep my bed, and to live awhile on apples and apple-tea. On *Tuesday* I was quite well, and should have preached, but that Dr. Rutty (who had been with me twice) insisted on my resting for a time.

I read to-day what is accounted the most correct history of St. Patrick that is extant, and, on the maturest consideration, I was much inclined to believe that St. Patrick and St. George were of one family.

The whole story smells strong of romance. To touch only on a few particulars: I object to his first setting out. The Bishop of Rome had no such power in the beginning of the fifth century as this account supposes, nor would his uncle, the Bishop of Tours, have sent him in that age to Rome for a commission to convert Ireland, having himself as much authority over that land as any Italian bishop whatever. Again, if God had sent him thither, he would not so long have buried his talent in the earth. I never heard before of an apostle sleeping thirty-five years, and beginning to preach at three-score. But his success staggers me the most of all. No blood of the martyrs is here, no reproach, no scandal of the cross, no persecution to those that will live godly. Nothing is to be heard of, from the beginning to the end, but kings, nobles, warriors bowing down before him. Thousands are converted without any opposition at all: twelve thousand at one sermon. If these things were so, either there was then no devil in the world, or St. Patrick did not preach the Gospel of Christ.

Bareheaded Children the first to greet Wesley.

Friday, April 29. I rode to Temple Macqueteer, and thence toward Athlone. We came at least an hour before we were expected. Nevertheless, we were met by many of our brethren. The first I saw, about two miles from the town, were a dozen little boys running with all their might, some bareheaded, some barefooted and barelegged; so they had their desire of speaking to me first, the others being still behind.

Faithful Preaching and an Affectionate Parting.

Sunday, May 8. I preached at five, though I could not well stand. I then set out for Aghrim, in the county of Galway, thirteen Connaught (that is, Yorkshire) miles from Athlone. The morning prayers (so called) began about twelve, after which we had a warm sermon against enthusiasts. I could not have come at a better time, for I began immediately after; and all that were in the church, high and low, rich and poor, stopped to hear me. In explaining the inward kingdom of God, I had a fair occasion to consider what we had just heard; and God renewed my strength, and, I trust, applied his word to the hearts of most of the hearers. Mr. S., a neighboring Justice of Peace, as soon as I had done, desired me to dine with him. After dinner I hastened back to Athlone, and began preaching about six; five clergymen were of the audience, and abundance of Romanists. Such an opportunity I never had before in these parts.

Monday, May 9. Having not had an hour's sound sleep from the time I lay down till I rose, I was in doubt whether I could preach or not; however, I went to the market-place as usual, and found no want of strength till I had fully declared "the redemption that is in Jesus Christ." I had designed afterward to settle the society thoroughly; but I was not able to sit up so long. Many advised me not to go out at night, the wind being extremely cold and blustering. But I could in no wise consent to spare myself at such a time as this. I preached on, "Come unto me all ye that labor and are heavy laden," and

I found myself at least as well when I had done as I was before I begun.

Tuesday, May 10. With much difficulty I broke away from this immeasurably-loving people, and not so soon as I imagined neither; for when we drew near to the turnpike, about a mile from the town, a multitude waited for us at the top of the hill. They fell back on each side, to make us way, and then joined and closed us in. After singing two or three verses I put forward, when, on a sudden, I was a little surprised by such a cry of men, women, and children as I never heard before. Yet a little while, and we shall meet to part no more; and sorrow and sighing shall flee away for ever.

The Wish of a Popish Priest.

Sunday, May 15. Finding my strength greatly restored, I preached at five and at eight on Oxmantown Green. I expected to sail as soon as I had done, but the captain putting it off, (as their manner is,) gave me an opportunity of declaring the Gospel of peace to a larger congregation in the evening. One of them, after listening some time, cried out, shaking his head, "Aye, he is a Jesuit; that's plain." To which a Popish priest, who happened to be near, replied aloud, "No, he is not; I would to God he was."

Epworth greatly Reformed.

July. Mr. Hay, the Rector, reading prayers, I had once more the comfort of receiving the Lord's Supper at Epworth. After the evening service, I preached at the Cross again to almost the whole town. I see plainly we have often judged amiss when we have measured the increase of the work of God, in this and other places, by the increase of the society only. The society here is not large; but God has wrought upon the whole place. Sabbath-breaking and drunkenness are no more seen in these streets; cursing and swearing are rarely heard. Wickedness hides its head already. Who knows but, by and by, God may utterly take it away? I was peculiarly pleased with the deep seriousness of the congregation at church, both morning and evening; and all the way as we walked down the church lane, after the sermon was ended, I scarce saw one person look on either side, or speak one word to another.

Criticism on the Tenth Iliad of Homer.

Friday, Aug. 12. In riding to Newcastle I finished the tenth Iliad of Homer. What an amazing genius had this man! To write with such strength of thought, and beauty of expression, when he had none to go before him! And what a vein of piety runs through his whole work, in spite of his pagan prejudices! Yet one cannot but observe such improprieties intermixed as are shocking to the last degree. What excuse can any man of common sense make for "His scolding heroes, and his wounded gods?" Nay, does he not introduce even his "Father of gods and men," one while shaking heaven with his nod, and soon after using his sister and wife, the empress of heaven, with such language as a carman might be ashamed of? And what can be said for a king, full of days and wisdom, telling Achilles how often he had given him wine, when he was a child and sat in his lap, till he had vomited it up on his clothes? Are these some of those "divine boldnesses which naturally provoke short-sightedness and ignorance to show themselves?"

Wesley Preaches four times, and rides Fifty Miles in a Day.

Tuesday, Aug. 16. We left Newcastle. In riding to Leeds I read Dr. Hodge's "Account of the Plague in London." I was surprised, 1. That he did not learn, even from the symptoms related by himself, that the part first seized by the infection was the stomach; and, 2. That he so obstinately persevered in the hot regimen; though he continually saw the ill success of it, a majority of the patients dying under his hands. Soon after twelve I preached, near the market-place in Stockton, to a very large and very rude congregation. But they grew calmer and calmer, so that long before I had done they were quiet and serious. Some gentlemen of Yarm earnestly desired that I would preach there in the afternoon. I refused for some time, being weak and tired; so that I thought preaching thrice in the day, and riding upward of fifty miles, would be work enough. But they would take no denial; so I went with them about two o'clock, and preached at three, in the market-place there, to a great multitude of people, gathered together at a few minutes' warning. About seven I preached in the street at Osmotherly. It rained almost all the time, but none went away.

The Stones Hit the right Mark.

August. At one I went to the Cross at Bolton. There was a vast number of people, but many of them utterly wild. As soon as I began speaking, they began thrusting to and fro, endeavoring to throw me down from the steps on which I stood. They did so once or twice; but I went up again, and continued my discourse. They then began to throw stones; at the same time some got upon the Cross behind me to push me down; on which I could not but observe how God overrules even the minutest circumstances. One man was bawling just at my ear, when a stone struck him on the cheek, and he was still. A second was forcing his way down to me, till another stone hit him on the forehead; it bounded back, the blood ran down, and he came no further. The third, being got close to me, stretched out his hand, and in the instant a sharp stone came upon the joints of his fingers. He shook his hand, and was very quiet till I concluded my discourse and went away.

Silver-tongued Antichrist.

August. We came to Shackerley, six miles further, before five in the evening. Abundance of people were gathered before six—many of whom were disciples of Dr. Taylor—laughing at Original Sin, and, consequently, at the whole frame of scriptural Christianity. O what a providence is it, which has brought us here also among these silver-tongued Antichrists! Surely a few, at least, will recover out of the snare, and know Jesus Christ as their wisdom and righteousness!

Satan's Device exposed.

Sunday, Oct. 9. I began examining the classes in Kingswood, and was never before so fully convinced of the device of Satan, which has often made our hands hang down, and our minds evil affected to our brethren. Now, as ten times before, a cry was gone forth, "What a scandal do these people bring upon the Gospel! What a society is this, with all these drunkards, and tale-bearers, and evil-speakers in it!" I expected, therefore, that I should find a heavy task upon my hands; and that none of these scandalous people might be concealed, I first met all the leaders, and inquired particularly of each person in every class. I repeated this inquiry when the classes themselves met. And what was the ground of all this outcry? Why, two persons had relapsed into drunkenness within three months' time; and one woman was proved to have made, or at least related, an idle story concerning another. I should rather have expected two and twenty instances of the former, and one hundred of the latter kind.

Mr. Wesley Instructs his Preachers in Logic and Elocution.

Tuesday, Feb. 21, 1749. I rode to Ragland, and the next day to Kingswood.

Thursday, Feb. 23. My design was to have as many of our preachers here, during the Lent, as could possibly be spared, and to read lectures to them every day, as I did to my pupils in Oxford. I had seventeen of them in all. These I divided into two classes, and read to one Bishop Pearson on the Creed, to the other Aldrich's Logic; and to both, "Rules for Action and Utterance."

Meets the Children Weekly.

Tuesday, March 14. Having set apart an hour weekly for that purpose, I met the children of our four schools together: namely, the boys boarded in the new house, the girls boarded in the old; the day scholars (boys) taught by James Harding, and the girls taught by Sarah Dimmock. We soon found the effect of it in the children, some of whom were deeply affected.

A false Report—Dr. B. the Sinner.

Friday, June 2. I was sent for by a clergyman, who had come twelve miles on purpose to talk with me. We had no dispute, but simply endeavored to strengthen each other's hands in God. In the evening a gentlewoman informed me that Dr. B. had averred to her and many others, 1. That both John and Charles Wesley had been expelled the University of Oxford long ago. 2. That there was not a Methodist left in Dublin, or any where in Ireland, but Cork and Bandon, all the rest having been rooted out by order of the government. 3. That neither were there any Methodists left in England. And, 4. That it was all Jesuitism at the bottom. Alas for poor Dr. B.! God be merciful unto thee, a sinner!

Quick Response to an Important Question.

Saturday, June 17. The wind blowing very tempestuous in the evening, I preached in our new built house. Toward the close of the sermon I asked, "Which of you will give yourself, soul and body, to God?" "O, I will! I will!" one cried out, with a cry that almost shook the house; and, as soon as she could stand, she came forth in the midst to witness it before all the congregation. It was Mrs. Glass. Her words pierced like lightning. Presently another witnessed the same resolution. And not long after, one who had been sorrowing as without hope, Mrs. Meecham, lifted up her head with joy, and continued singing and praising God to the dawn of the next day.

Perceiving this was an acceptable time, I laid aside my design of meeting the society, and continued in prayer with the whole congregation, all our hearts being as the heart of one man. When I had at length pronounced the blessing no man stirred, but each stayed in his place till I walked through them. I was soon called back by one crying out, "My God! my God! thou hast forgotten me." Having spoken this, she sank to the earth. We called upon God in her behalf. The cries both of her and of several others, mourning after God, redoubled. But we continued wrestling with God in prayer till he gave us an answer of peace.

Presentment of a Grand Jury in Cork.

Tuesday, Aug. 1. I spent a solemn hour with our children at Kingswood. After having settled all things there and at Bristol I returned to London, where I received a remarkable account from Cork. On *August* 19 twenty-eight depositions were laid before the Grand Jury there, but they threw them all out, and at the same time made that memorable presentment, which is worthy to be preserved in the annals of Ireland to all succeeding generations:

"We find and present Charles Wesley to be a person of ill fame, a vagabond, and a common disturber of his Majesty's peace; and we pray he may be transported.

"We find and present James Williams, etc. We find and present Robert Swindle, etc. We find and present Jonathan Reeves, etc. We find and present John Larwood, etc. We find and present Joseph M'Auliff, etc. We find and present Charles Skaron, etc. We find and present William Tooker, etc.

"We find and present Daniel Sullivan to be a person of ill fame, a vagabond, and a common disturber of his Majesty's peace; and we pray he may be transported."

Daniel Sullivan was an honest baker, who had lived in Cork many years, I suppose in as good fame as any of his trade in the city; but he had entertained my brother, and several other Methodists; nay, and suffered them to preach in his house. The other names (only most of them miserably mangled and murdered) were designed for the names of eight preachers who had been there.

How Mr. Wesley took Rest.

Wednesday, *Sept.* 6. I reached Newcastle; and after resting a day, and preaching two evenings and two mornings, with such a blessing as we have not often found, on *Friday* set out to visit the northern societies. I began with that of Morpeth, where I preached at twelve, on one side of the market-place. It was feared the market would draw the people from the sermon; but it was just the contrary: they quitted their stalls, and there was no buying or selling till the sermon was concluded. At Alnwick likewise I stood in the market-place in the evening, and exhorted a numerous congregation to be always ready for death, for judgment, for heaven. I felt what I spoke; as I believe did most that were present, both then and in the morning, while I besought them to "present" themselves "a living sacrifice, holy, acceptable to God."

Saturday, Sept. 9. I rode slowly forward to Berwick. I was myself much out of order; but I would not lose the opportunity of calling, in the evening, all that were "weary and heavy laden" to Him who hath said, "I will give you rest."

Sunday, Sept. 10. I preached at eight, and at four in the afternoon; and in the hours between, spoke with the members of the society. I met them all at seven, and a glorious meeting it was. I forgot all my pain while we were praising God together; but after they were gone I yielded to my friends, and determined to give myself a day's rest. So I spent *Monday*, the 11th, in writing; only I could not refrain from meeting the society in the evening. The next evening God enabled me to speak searching words to an earnestly attentive congregation.

Could not Send them Away Empty.

Sunday, Sept. 24. At eight I preached at the Gins, another village full of colliers about half a mile from the town. The congregation was very large and deeply attentive. Between one and two I preached again at Hensingham, to as many as my voice could command, on "Repent ye and believe the Gospel." Thence I hastened to church, and in the midst of the service I felt a sudden stroke. Immediately a shivering ran through me, and in a few minutes I was in a fever. I thought of taking a vomit immediately and going to bed. But when I came from church, hearing there was a vast congregation in the market-place, I could not send them away empty.

And while I was speaking to them God remembered me and strengthened me both in soul and body.

Lions at Rochdale and Bolton.

Wednesday, Oct. 18. I rode, at the desire of John Bennet, to Rochdale, in Lancashire. As soon as ever we entered the town, we found the streets lined on both sides with multitudes of people, shouting, cursing, blaspheming, and gnashing upon us with their teeth. Perceiving it would not be practicable to preach abroad, I went into a large room open to the street, and called aloud, "Let the wicked forsake his way, and the unrighteous man his thoughts." The word of God prevailed over the fierceness of man. None opposed or interrupted, and there was a very remarkable change in the behavior of the people as we afterward went through the town.

We came to Bolton about five in the evening. We had no sooner entered the main street than we perceived the lions at Rochdale were lambs in comparison of those at Bolton. Such rage and bitterness I scarce ever saw before in any creatures that bore the form of men. They followed us in full cry to the house where we went; and as soon as we were gone in, took possession of all the avenues to it, and filled the street from one end to the other. After some time the waves did not roar quite so loud. Mr. P. thought he might then venture out. They immediately closed in, threw him down, and rolled him in the mire; so that when he scrambled from them, and got into the house again, one could scarce tell who or what he was. When the first stone came among us through the window I expected a shower to follow, and the rather because they had now procured a bell to call their whole forces together. But they did not design to carry on the attack at a distance; presently one ran up and told us the mob had burst into the house; he added, that they had got J. B. in the midst of them. They had; and he laid hold on the opportunity to tell them of "the terrors of the Lord." Meantime D. T. engaged another part of them with smoother and softer words. Believing the time was now come, I walked down into the thickest of them. They had now filled all the rooms below. I called for a chair. The winds were hushed, and all was calm and still. My heart was filled with love, my eyes with tears, and my mouth with arguments. They were amazed, they were ashamed, they were melted down, they devoured every word. What a turn was this! O how did God change the counsel of the old Ahithophel into foolishness, and bring all the drunkards, swearers, Sabbath-breakers, and mere sinners in the place to hear of his plenteous redemption!

"Who Maketh me to Differ."

Saturday, Oct. 21. By conversing with several here, I found we were not now among publicans and sinners, but among those who, awhile ago, supposed they needed no repentance. Many of them had been long "exercising themselves unto godliness," in much the same manner as we did at Oxford; but they were now thoroughly willing to renounce their own, and accept "the righteousness which is of God by faith." A gentleman who had several years before heard me preach at Bath, sending to invite me to dinner, I had three or four hours' serious conversation with him. O, who maketh me to differ! Every objection he made to the Christian system has passed through my mind also; but God did not suffer them to rest there, or to remove me from the hope of the Gospel. I was not surprised when word was brought that the Vicar of Acton had not the courage to stand to his word; neither was I troubled. I love indeed to preach in a church; but God can work wherever it pleaseth him.

A Remarkable Event Brought to Mind.

Friday, Feb. 9, 1750. We had a comfortable watch-night at the chapel. About eleven o'clock it came into my mind that this was the very day and hour in which, forty years ago, I was taken out of the flames. I stopped, and gave a short account of that wonderful providence. The voice of praise and thanksgiving went up on high, and great was our rejoicing before the Lord.

Wesley Shut Out of Newgate and Bedlam.

Wednesday, Feb. 21. I preached in the old French church in Grey-eagle-street, Spitalfields. It was extremely full, and many of the hearers were greatly moved; but who will endure to the end?

Thursday, Feb. 22. Having been sent for several times, I went to see a young woman in Bedlam. But I had not talked with her long, before one gave me to know that none of these preachers were to come there. So we are forbid to go to Newgate for fear of making them wicked; and to Bedlam, for fear of driving them mad!

Always at Work.

Saturday, March 24. We set out at five, and at six came to the sands. But the tide was in, so that we could not pass; so I sat down in a little cottage for three or four hours and translated Aldrich's "Logic."

A Congregation Daubed with Gold and Silver.

Thursday, March 29. In the evening I was surprised to see, instead of some poor, plain people, a room full of men daubed with gold and silver. That I might not go out of their depth, I began expounding the story of Dives and Lazarus. It was more applicable than I was aware, several of them (as I afterward learned) being eminently wicked men. I delivered my own soul; but they could in no wise bear it. One and another walked away murmuring sorely. Four stayed till I drew to a close; they then put on their hats, and began talking to one another. I mildly reproved them; on which they rose up and went away, railing and blaspheming. I had then a comfortable hour with a company of plain, honest Welshmen.

The Mayor of Cork in Concert with the Mob.

Saturday, May 19. I preached about eleven, and in the afternoon rode on to Cork. About nine in the evening I came to Alderman Pembrock's.

Sunday, May 20. Understanding the usual place of preaching would by no means contain those who desired to hear, about eight I went to Hammond's Marsh. The congregation was large and deeply attentive. A few of the rabble gathered at a distance; but by little and little they drew near, and mixed with the congregation; so that I have seldom seen a more quiet and orderly assembly at any church in England or Ireland.

In the afternoon, a report being spread abroad that the Mayor designed to hinder my preaching on the Marsh in the evening, I desired Mr. Skelton and Mr. Jones to wait upon him and inquire concerning it. Mr. Skelton asked if my preaching there would be disagreeable to him; adding, "Sir, if it would, Mr. Wesley will not do it." He replied warmly, "Sir, I will have no mobbing." Mr. Skelton replied, "Sir, there was none this morning." He answered, "There was. Are there not churches and meeting-houses enough? I will have no more mobs and riots." Mr. Skelton replied, "Sir, neither Mr. Wesley nor they that heard him made either mobs or riots." He answered plain, "I will have no more preaching; and if Mr. Wesley attempts to preach I am prepared for him."

I began preaching in our own house soon after five. Mr. Mayor meantime was walking in the 'Change, and giving orders to the town drummers and to his sergeants—doubtless to go down and *keep the peace!* They accordingly came down to the house with an innumerable mob attending them. They continued drumming, and I continued preaching till I had finished my discourse. When I came out the mob immediately closed me in. Observing one of the sergeants standing by, I desired him to keep the King's peace; but he replied, "Sir, I have no orders to do that." As soon as I came into the street the rabble threw whatever came to hand, but all went by me or flew over my head, nor do I remember that one thing touched me. I walked on straight through the midst of the rabble, looking every man before me in the face, and they opened on the right and left till I came near Dant's bridge. A large party had taken possession of this, one of whom was bawling out, "Now, hey for the Romans!" When I came up they likewise shrunk back, and I walked through them to Mr. Jenkins's house; but a Papist stood just within the door and endeavored to hinder my going in, till one of the mob (I suppose aiming at me, but missing) knocked her down flat. I then went in, and God restrained the wild beasts, so that not one attempted to follow me.

But many of the congregation were more roughly handled, particularly Mr. Jones, who was covered with dirt, and escaped with his life almost by miracle. The main body of the mob then went to the house, brought out all the seats and benches, tore up the floor, the door, the frames, of the windows, and whatever of wood-work remained; part of which they carried off for their own use, and the rest they burned in the open street. Finding there was no probability of their dispersing I sent to Alderman Pembrock, who immediately desired Mr. Alderman Winthrop, his nephew, to go down to Mr. Jenkins's, with whom I walked up the street, none giving me an unkind or disrespectful word.

Monday, May 21. I rode on to Bandon. From three in the afternoon till past seven the mob of Cork marched in grand procession, and then burned me in effigy near Dant's bridge. While they were so busily employed, Mr. Haughton took the opportunity of going down to Hammond's Marsh. He called at a friend's house there, where the good woman, in great care, locked him in; but observing many people were met, he threw up the sash and preached to them out of the window. Many seemed deeply affected, even of those who had been persecutors before; and they all quietly retired to their several homes before the mob was at leisure to attend them.

Tuesday, May 22. The mob and drummers were moving again between three and four in the morning. The same evening they came down to the Marsh, but stood at a distance from Mr. Stockdale's house till the drums beat, and the Mayor's sergeant beckoned to them, on which they drew up and began the attack. The Mayor being sent for, came with a party of soldiers and said to the mob, "Lads, once, twice, thrice, I bid you go home; now I have done." He then went back, taking the soldiers with him; on which the mob, pursuant to instructions, went on and broke all the glass and most of the window-frames in pieces.

The Three Champions.

Friday, May 25. All this time God gave us great peace at Bandon, notwithstanding the unwearied labors, both public and private, of good Dr. B—— to stir up the people. But, *Saturday, May* 26, many were under great apprehensions of what was to be done in the evening. I began preaching in the main street at the usual hour, but to more than twice the usual congregation. After I had spoken about a quarter of an hour a clergyman, who had planted himself near me, with a very large stick in his hand, according to agreement, opened the scene. (Indeed, his friends assured me he was drunk or he would not have done it,) but before he had uttered many words, two or three resolute women, by main strength pulled him into a house, and after expostulating a little sent him away through the garden.

The next champion that appeared was one Mr. M——, a young gentleman of the town. He was attended by two others with pistols in their hands. But his triumph, too, was short. Some of the people quickly bore him away, though with much gentleness and civility.

The third came on with greater fury; but he was encountered by a butcher of the town, (not one of the Methodists,) who used him as he would an ox, bestowing one or two hearty blows upon his head. This cooled his courage, especially as none took his part. So I quietly finished my discourse.

An Irish Howl at the Burial of the Dead.

Thursday, May 31. I rode to Rathcormuck. There being a great burying in the afternoon, to which people came from all parts, Mr. Lloyd read part of the burial service in the church, after which I preached on, "The end of all things is at hand." I was exceedingly shocked at (what I had only heard of before) the Irish howl which followed. It was not a song, as I supposed, but a dismal, inarticulate yell, set up at the grave by four shrill-voiced women, who (we understood) were hired for that purpose. But I saw not one that shed a tear; for that, it seems, was not in their bargain.

Wesley's Longest Day's Ride.

June 15. My horse tired in the afternoon, so I left him behind, and borrowed that of my companion. I came to Aymo about eleven, and would very willingly have passed the rest of the night there, but the good woman of the inn was not minded that I should. For some time she would not answer; at last she opened the door just wide enough to let out four dogs upon me. So I rode on to Ballybrittas, expecting a rough salute here too from a large dog which used to be in the yard. But he never stirred till the hostler waked and came out. About twelve I laid me down. I think this was the longest day's journey I ever rode; being fifty old Irish, that is, about ninety English miles.

Wesley Sighs for Retirement.

Thursday, June 21. I returned to Closeland, and preached in the evening to a little, earnest company. O, who should drag me into a great city if I did not know that there is another world! How gladly could I spend the remainder of a busy life in solitude and retirement.

A Remedy for Anger successfully applied.

Friday, June 22. We had a watch-night at Portarlington. I began before the usual time, but it was not easy to leave off, so great was our rejoicing in the Lord.

Saturday, June 23. I heard, face to face, two that were deeply prejudiced against each other, Mrs. E—— and Mrs. M——. But the longer they talked the warmer they grew; till, in about three hours, they were almost distracted. One who came in as a witness was as hot as either. I perceived there was no remedy but prayer, so a few of us wrestled with God for above two hours. When we arose, Mrs. M—— ran and fell on the other's neck. Anger and revenge were vanished away, and melted down into love. One only, M——t B——, continued still in bitter agony of soul. We besought God in her behalf, and did not let him go till she also was set at liberty.

Discharged from Preaching by the Mayor of Shaftesbury.

Monday, Sept. 3. About noon I preached at Hill-farrance, three miles from Taunton. Three or four boors would have been rude if they durst, but the odds against them was too great. At five I preached in Bridgewater to a well-behaved company, and then rode on to Middlesey. We rode from hence to Shaftesbury, where I preached between six and seven to a serious and quiet congregation. We had another happy opportunity at five in the morning, when abundance of people were present. I preached at noon in the most riotous part of the town, just where four ways met; but none made any noise, or spoke one word, while I called "the wicked to forsake his way." As we walked back one or two foul-mouthed women spoke unseemly; but none regarded, or answered them a word. Soon after I was sat down, a constable came and said, "Sir, the Mayor discharges you from preaching in this borough any more." I replied, "While King George gives me leave to preach I shall not ask leave of the Mayor of Shaftesbury."

Some Days of Literary Work for the Children.

Monday, Sept. 24. I reached Kingswood in the evening, and the next day selected passages of Milton for the eldest children to transcribe and repeat weekly.

Thursday, Sept. 27. I went into the school and

heard half the children their lessons, and then selected passages of the "Moral and Sacred Poems."

Friday, Sept. 28. I heard the other half of the children.

Saturday, Sept. 29. I was with them from four to five in the morning. I spent most of the day in revising Kennet's "Antiquities," and marking what was worth reading in the school.

Wednesday, Oct. 3. I revised for the use of the children Archbishop Potter's "Grecian Antiquities;" a dry, dull, heavy book.

Thursday, Oct. 4. I revised Mr. Lewis's "Hebrew Antiquities;" something more entertaining than the other, and abundantly more instructive.

Saturday, Oct. 6. I nearly finished the abridgment of Dr. Cave's "Primitive Christianity," a book wrote with as much learning and as little judgment as any I remember to have read in my whole life; serving the ancient Christians just as Xenophon did Socrates; relating every weak thing they ever said or did.

Wednesday, Oct. 10. I dined at P—— S——'s who, with his wife and daughter, are wonderful monuments of God's mercy. They were convinced of the truth when I first preached at Bristol, and Mrs. Sk—— was a living witness of it; yet Satan was afterward suffered to sift her as wheat, it seems, to take possession of her body. He tormented her many years in an unheard-of manner, but God has now set her at full liberty.

Thursday, Oct. 11. I prepared a short "History of England" for the use of the children; and on *Friday* and *Saturday* a short "Roman History," as an introduction to the Latin historians.

Mr. Wesley takes a Journey in Order to Vote.

Wednesday, January 30, 1751. Having received a pressing letter from Dr. Isham, then the Rector of our college, to give my vote at the election for member of Parliament, which was to be the next day, I set out early in a severe frost, with the northwest wind full in my face. The roads were so slippery that it was scarce possible for our horses to keep their feet; indeed, one of them could not, but fell upon his head and cut it terribly. Nevertheless, about seven in the evening God brought us safe to Oxford. A congregation was waiting for me at Mr. Evans's, whom I immediately addressed in those awful words, "What is a man profited, if he shall gain the whole world and lose his own soul?"

Thursday, Jan. 31. I went to the schools where the convocation was met, but I did not find the decency and order which I expected. The gentleman for whom I came to vote was not elected; yet I did not repent of my coming. I owe much more than this to that generous, friendly man, who now rests from his labors. I was much surprised, wherever I went, at the civility of the people, gentlemen as well as others. There was no pointing, no calling of names, as once; no, nor even laughter. What can this mean? Am I become a servant of men? Or is the scandal of the cross ceased?

His Marriage, and Reasons for it, with Advice to Single Men.

Saturday, Feb. 2. Having received a full answer from Mr. P——, I was clearly convinced that I ought to marry. For many years I remained single, because

I believed I could be more useful in a single than in a married state; and I praise God who enabled me so to do. I now as fully believed that in my present circumstances I might be more useful in a married state; into which, upon this clear conviction, and by the advice of my friends, I entered a few days after.

Wednesday, Feb. 6. I met the single men, and showed them on how many accounts it was good for those who had received that gift from God to remain "single for the kingdom of heaven's sake," unless where a particular case might be an exception to the general rule.

Wesley Meets with an Accident.

Sunday, Feb. 10. After preaching at five, I was hastening to take my leave of the congregation at Snowfields, proposing to set out in the morning for the north, when on the middle of London Bridge both my feet slipped on the ice, and I fell with great force, the bone of my ankle lighting on the top of a stone. However, I got on with some help to the chapel, being resolved not to disappoint the people. After preaching I had my leg bound up by a surgeon, and made a shift to walk to the Seven Dials. It was with much difficulty that I got up into the pulpit, but God then comforted many of our hearts. I went back in a coach to Mr. B——'s, and from thence in a chair to the Foundry; but I was not able to preach, my sprain growing worse. I removed to Threadneedle-street, where I spent the remainder of the week, partly in prayer, reading, and conversation, partly in writing a "Hebrew Grammar" and "Lessons for Children."

Preaching in a Kneeling Posture.

Sunday, Feb. 17. I was carried to the Foundry, and preached, kneeling, (as I could not stand,) on part of the Twenty-third Psalm, my heart being enlarged and my mouth opened to declare the wonders of God's love.

Monday, Feb. 18, was the second day I had appointed for my journey; but I was disappointed again, not being yet able to set my foot to the ground. However, I preached (kneeling) on *Tuesday* evening and *Wednesday* morning.

Sunday, Feb. 24, I preached morning and evening at Spitalfields, where many who had been wandering from God for several years seemed at length to have fresh desires of returning to him. How is it that we are so ready to despair of one another? For want of the "love" that "hopeth all things."

Bristol Conference of one Heart and Mind.

Monday, March 11. Our Conference began, and the more we conversed the more brotherly love increased. The same spirit we found on *Tuesday* and *Wednesday*. I expected to have heard many objections to our first doctrines, but none appeared to have any. We seemed to be all of one mind, as well as one heart.

Friday, March 15. I mentioned whatever I thought was amiss or wanting in any of our brethren. It was received in a right spirit, with much love, and serious, earnest attention; and, I trust, not one went from the Conference discontented, but rather blessing God for the consolation.

The Marriage State no Excuse for Less Work.

Tuesday, March 19. Having finished the business for which I came to Bristol I set out again for London, being desired by many to spend a few days there before I entered upon our northern journey. I came to London on *Thursday*, and having settled all affairs, left it again on *Wednesday, March* 27. I cannot understand how a Methodist preacher can answer it to God to preach one sermon or travel one day less in a married than in a single state. In this respect surely, "it remaineth that they who have wives be as though they had none."

Disastrous Results from Doubtful Disputations.

Wednesday, April 1. I had desired John Haine to preach at Wednesbury, but when I came he had but just began the hymn, so I had an opportunity, which I did not expect, of speaking again to that willing people. What a work would have been in all these parts if it had not been for doubtful dispensations! If the predestinarians had not thrown back those who had began to run well, partly into the world, partly to the Baptists, and partly into endless disputes, concerning the secret counsels of God! While we carried our lives in our hands none of these came near—the waves ran too high for them; but when all was calm they poured in on every side, and bereaved us of our children. Out of these they formed one society here, one at Dudley, and another at Birmingham. Many indeed, though torn from us, would not stay with them, but broke out into the wildest enthusiasm. But still they were called

Methodists, and so all their drunkenness and blasphemies (not imputed to a believer) were imputed to us.

Mr. Wesley in Scotland.

Wednesday, April 24. Mr. Hopper and I took horse between three and four, and about seven came to Old Carmus. Whether the country was good or bad we could not see, having a thick mist all the way. The Scotch towns are like none which I ever saw, either in England, Wales, or Ireland; there is such an air of antiquity in them all, and such a peculiar oddness in their manner of building. But we were most surprised at the entertainment we met with in every place, so far different from common report. We had all things good, cheap, in great abundance, and remarkably well-dressed. In the afternoon we rode by Preston Field, and saw the place of battle, and Colonel Gardiner's house. The Scotch here affirm that he fought on foot after he was dismounted, and refused to take quarter. Be it as it may, he is now "where the wicked cease from troubling, and where the weary are at rest." We reached Musselburgh between four and five. I had no intention to preach in Scotland, nor did I imagine there were any that desired I should. But I was mistaken. Curiosity (if nothing else) brought abundance of people together in the evening. And whereas in the kirk (Mrs. G—— informed me) there used to be laughing and talking, and all the marks of the grossest inattention, it was [now] far otherwise here. They remained as statues from the beginning of the sermon to the end.

Thursday, April 25. We rode to Edinburgh, one of

the dirtiest cities I had ever seen, not excepting Cōlen in Germany. We returned to Musselburgh to dinner, whither we were followed in the afternoon by a little party of gentlemen from Edinburgh. I know not why any should complain of the shyness of the Scots toward strangers. All I spoke with were as free and open with me as the people of Newcastle or Bristol; nor did any person move any dispute of any kind, or ask me any question concerning my opinion.

I preached again at six on "Seek ye the Lord while he may be found." I used great plainness of speech toward them, and they received it in love; so that the prejudice which the devil had been several years planting was torn up by the roots in one hour. After preaching, one of the bailies of the town, with one of the elders of the kirk, came to me and begged I would stay with them awhile, if it were but two or three days, and they would fit up a far larger place than the school, and prepare seats for the congregation. Had not my time been fixed I should gladly have complied. All I could now do was to give them a promise that Mr. Hopper would come back the next week and spend a few days with them.

The Times changed at Wakefield.

Sunday, April 12, 1752. I came to Wakefield as the bells were ringing in, and went directly to Mr. W——, in the vestry. The behavior of the congregation surprised me. I saw none light, none careless or unaffected, while I enforced, "What is a man profited, if he shall gain the whole world and lose his own soul?" Hath not God the hearts of all men in his hand? Who would have expected to see me preaching in Wakefield church to so attentive a congregation, a few years ago, when all the people were as roaring lions ; and the honest man did not dare to let me preach in his yard lest the mob should pull down his houses!

Monday, April 13. In the evening I preached at Sheffield, in the shell of the new house. All is peace here now since the trial at York, at which the magistrates were sentenced to rebuild the house which the mob had pulled down. Surely the magistrate has been the minister of God to us for good!

A Strange Desire.

Friday, April 24. We rode by a fine seat, the owner of which (not much above fourscore years old) says he desires only to live thirty years longer: ten to hunt, ten to get money, (having at present but twenty thousand pounds a year,) and ten years to repent. O that God may not say unto him, "Thou fool, this night shall thy soul be required of thee!" When I landed at the quay in Hull it was covered with people, inquiring, "Which is he? Which is he?" But they only stared and laughed, and we walked unmolested to Mr. A——'s house. I was quite surprised at the miserable condition of the fortifications, far more ruinous and decayed than those at Newcastle even before the rebellion. It is well there is no enemy near.

Nine Years' Labor without Success.

Friday, May 15. In the afternoon I preached at Alemouth. How plain an evidence have we here that even our outward work, even the societies, are not of man's building. With all our labor and skill we cannot in nine years' time form a society in this place, even though there is none that opposes, poor or rich; nay, though the two richest men in the town, and the only gentlemen there, have done all which was in their power to further it.

Wesley's Strength remarkably restored.

Tuesday, May 26. We rode to Weardale. I had been out of order all night, and found myself now much weaker. However, I trusted in the Strong for strength, and began preaching to a numerous congregation, and I did not want strength till I had finished my discourse, nor did the people want a blessing. In the evening we came to Allandale, and found the poor society well-nigh shattered in pieces. Slackness and offense had eaten them up. When I came into the room I was just like one of them, having neither life nor strength, and being scarce able either to speak or to stand. But immediately we had a token for good. In a moment I was well. My voice and strength were entirely restored, and I cried aloud, "How shall I give thee up, Ephraim?" The mountains again flowed down at his presence, and the rocks were once more broken in pieces.

The Colliers build Mr. Wesley a Pulpit.

Thursday, June 2. I rode to Seaton, a town of colliers, ten measured miles from Whitehaven. The poor people had prepared a kind of pulpit for me, covered at the top and on both sides, and had placed a cushion to kneel upon of the greenest turf in the country.

Wesley Sleeps Under-ground.

Tuesday, June 9. I preached at six to abundance of people near Ewood, and with an uncommon blessing. Hence we rode to Todmorden. The minister was slowly recovering from a violent fit of a palsy, with which he was struck immediately after he had been preaching a virulent sermon against the Methodists. I preached on the side of a mountain to a large and earnest congregation, and then went on to Mellarbarn. I preached at six in the town, and I suppose all the inhabitants, young and old, were present. Nor have I often seen so large a congregation so universally and deeply affected. My lodging was not such as I should have chosen, but what Providence chooses is always good. My bed was considerably under-ground, the room serving both for a bed-chamber and a cellar. The closeness was more troublesome at first than the coolness ; but I let in a little fresh air by breaking a pane of paper (put by way of glass) in the window, and then slept sound till the morning.

"A Comfortable Pain."

Monday, July 27. I preached in Edinderry at one, and at Closeland in the evening.

Tuesday, July 28. I preached at Portarlington, though I was extremely ill, and it was a pain to me to speak ; but it was a comfortable pain. I could from my heart praise God for his fatherly visitation.

Wednesday, July 29. I rode to Mount Mellick, but was so hoarse and weak that I could only preach in the house.

Friday, July 31. Being not well able to ride, I

borrowed Mr. P——'s chair to Tullamore, and on *Saturday* reached Cooly Lough, and met many of my friends from all parts. I now found my strength increasing daily; it must be as my day is.

The Sword usefully employed.

Tuesday, Aug. 25. I preached in the market-place at Kinsale. The next morning at eight I walked to the Fort. On the hill above it we found a large, deep hollow, capable of containing two or three thousand people. On one side of this the soldiers soon cut a place with their swords for me to stand, where I was screened both from the wind and sun, while the congregation sat on the grass before me. Many eminent sinners were present, particularly of the army, and I believe God gave them a loud call to repentance. In the evening I called sinners to repentance in the main street of Bandon. On *Thursday* and *Friday* the rain drove us into the market-house. Indeed, I hardly remember two dry days together since I landed in Ireland.

Wesley completes his Christian Library.

November 3. In the remaining part of this and the following month I prepared the rest of the books for the "Christian Library," a work by which I have lost above two hundred pounds. Perhaps the next generation may know the value of it.

Visits the Neglected Sick.

Thursday, Feb. 8, 1753. In the afternoon I visited many of the sick, but such scenes who could see unmoved? There are none such to be found in a Pagan country. If any of the Indians in Georgia were sick, (which indeed exceedingly rarely happened, till they learned gluttony and drunkenness from the Christians,) those that were near him gave him whatever he wanted. O who will convert the English into honest heathens!

On *Friday* and *Saturday* I visited as many more as I could. I found some in their cells under-ground; others in their garrets, half starved both with cold and hunger, added to weakness and pain. But I found not one of them unemployed who was able to crawl about the room. So wickedly, devilishly false is that common objection, "They are poor only because they are idle." If you saw these things with your own eyes, could you lay out money in ornaments or superfluities?

Synopsis of Dr. Franklin's Letters.

Saturday, Feb. 17. From Dr. Franklin's Letters I learned, 1. That electrical fire (or ether) is a species of fire infinitely finer than any other yet known. 2. That it is diffused, and in nearly equal proportions, through almost all substances. 3. That as long as it is thus diffused it has no discernible effect. 4. That if any quantity of it be collected together, whether by art or nature, it then becomes visible in the form of fire, and inexpressibly powerful. 5. That it is essentially different from the light of the sun, for it pervades a thousand bodies which light cannot penetrate, and yet cannot penetrate glass, which light pervades so freely. 6. That lightning is no other than electrical fire collected by one or more clouds. 7. That all the effects of lightning may be performed by the artificial electric fire. 8. That any thing pointed, as a spire or tree, attracts the lightning, just as a needle does the electric fire. 9. That the electrical fire discharged on a rat or a fowl will kill it instantly; but discharged on one dipped in water will slide off, and do it no hurt at all. In like manner the lightning, which will kill a man in a moment, will not hurt him if he be thoroughly wet. What an amazing scene is here opened for after ages to improve upon!

How God carries on his Work in England and America.

Wednesday, Feb. 28. We rode to Bristol. I now looked over Mr. Prince's "Christian History." What an amazing difference is there in the manner wherein God has carried on his work in England and in America! There, above a hundred of the established clergy, men of age and experience, and of the greatest note for sense and learning in those parts, are zealously engaged in the work. Here, almost the whole body of the aged, experienced, learned clergy are zealously engaged against it; and few, but a handful of raw young men engaged in it, without name, learning, or eminent sense. And yet by that large number of honorable men the work seldom flourished above six months at a time, and then followed a lamentable and general decay before the next revival of it; whereas that which God hath wrought by these despised instruments has continually increased for fifteen years together, and at whatever time it has declined in any one place has more eminently flourished in others.

Contention not Tolerated.

Thursday, April 26. I spoke severally to those of the society, and found that they had been harassed above measure by a few violent predestinarians, who had at length separated themselves from us. It was well they saved me the trouble, for I have no connection with those who will be contentious. These I reject, not for their opinion, but for their sins; for their unchristian temper and unchristian practice; for being haters of reproof, haters of peace, haters of their brethren, and, consequently, of God.

A Time of Power at York.

Sunday, May 13. I began preaching at seven, and God applied it to the hearts of the hearers. Tears and groans were on every side, among high and low. God, as it were, bowed the heavens and came down. The flame of love went before him, the rocks were broken in pieces, and the mountains flowed down at his presence. I had designed to set out for Lincolnshire this morning. But, finding that a day of God's power was come, I sent one thither in my place; and, after preaching (as I had appointed) at Stamford Bridge and at Pocklington, returned to York in the evening. Let us work together with him when, and where, and as he pleases! Every night while I stayed many of the rich and honorable crowded in among us. And is not "God able, even of these stones, to raise up children to Abraham?"

Wesley Preaches in the Isle of Wight.

Tuesday, July 10. I went on board a hoy, and in three hours landed at Cowes, in the Isle of Wight; as far exceeding the Isle of Anglesey, both in pleasantness and fruitfulness, as that exceeds the rocks of Scilly. We rode straight to Newport, the chief town in the Isle, and found a little society in tolerable order. Several of them had found peace with God. One informed me it was about eight years ago since she first knew her interest in Christ, by means of one who called there in his way to Pennsylvania; but having none to speak to or advise with, she was long tormented with doubts and fears. After some years she received a fresh manifestation of his love, and could not doubt or fear any more. She is now (and has been long) confined to her bed, and consuming away with pining sickness; but all is good to her, for she has learned in every thing to give thanks.

At half an hour after six I preached in the market-place to a numerous congregation, but they were not so serious as those of Portsmouth. Many children made much noise, and many grown persons were talking aloud almost all the time I was preaching. It was quite otherwise at five in the morning. There was a large congregation again, and every person therein seemed to know this was the word whereby God would judge them in the last day.

In the afternoon I walked to Carisbrook Castle, or rather the poor remains of it. It stands upon a solid rock on the top of a hill, and commands a beautiful prospect. There is a well in it, cut quite through the rock, said to be seventy-two yards deep; and another in the citadel, near a hundred. They drew up the water by an ass, which they assured us was sixty years old. But all the stately apartments lie in ruins. Only just enough of them is left to show the chamber where poor King Charles was confined, and the window through which he attempted to escape. In the evening the congregation at Newport was more numerous and more serious than the night before. Only one drunken man made a little disturbance. But the Mayor ordered him to be taken away.

An Accursed Thing at St. Ives.

On *Wednesday, July* 25, the Stewards met at St. Ives from the western part of Cornwall. The next day I began examining the society. I found an accursed thing among them; well-nigh one and all bought and sold uncustomed goods. I therefore delayed speaking to any more till I had met them all together. This I did in the evening, and told them plain, either they must put this abomination away, or they would see my face no more.

Friday, July 27. They severally promised to do so. So I trust this plague is stayed.

A Wise Providence.

Monday, Sept. 10. I preached to the condemned malefactors in Newgate, but I could make little impression upon them. I then took horse for Paulton, where I called on Stephen Plummer, once of our society, but now a zealous Quaker. He was much pleased with my calling, and came to hear me preach. Being straitened for time I concluded sooner than usual; but as soon as I had done Stephen began. After I had listened half an hour, finding he was no nearer the end, I rose up to go away. His sister then begged him to leave off, on which he flew into a violent rage, and roared louder and louder, till an honest man took him in his arms and gently carried him away. What a wise providence was it that this young man turned Quaker some years before he ran mad! So the honor of turning his brain now rests upon them, which otherwise must have fallen upon the Methodists.

Wesley Sick, but Preaching.

Monday, Nov. 12. I set out in a chaise for Leigh, having delayed my journey as long as I could. I preached at seven, but was extremely cold: my feet felt just as if I had stood in cold water.

Tuesday, Nov. 13. The chamber wherein I sat, though with a large fire, was much colder than the garden, so that I could not keep myself tolerably warm even when I was close to the chimney. As we rode home on *Wednesday, Nov.* 14, the wind was high and piercing cold and blew just in our face, so that the open chaise was no defense, but my feet were quite chilled. When I came home I had a settled pain in my left breast, a violent cough, and a slow fever; but in a day or two, by following Dr. Fothergill's prescriptions, I found much alteration for the better; and on *Sunday, Nov.* 18, I preached at Spitalfields, and administered the sacrament to a large congregation.

Monday, Nov. 19. I retired to Shoreham and gained strength continually, till about eleven at night on *Wednesday, Nov.* 21, I was obliged by the cramp to leap out of bed, and continue for some time walking up and down the room, though it was a sharp frost. My cough now returned with greater violence, and that by day as well as by night.

Saturday, Nov. 24. I rode home and was pretty well till night, but my cough was then worse than ever. My fever returned at the same time, together with the pain in my left breast; so that I should probably have stayed at home on *Sunday, Nov.* 25, had it not been advertised in the public papers that I would preach a charity sermon at the chapel both morning and afternoon. My cough did not interrupt me while I preached in the morning, but it was extremely troublesome while I administered the sacrament. In the afternoon I consulted my friends whether I should attempt to preach again or no. They thought I should, as it had been advertised. I did so, but very few could hear. My fever increased much while I was preaching; however, I ventured to meet the society, and for near an hour my voice and strength were restored, so that I felt neither pain nor weakness

Wesley Writes his Epitaph.

Monday, Nov. 26. Dr. F—— told me plain I must not stay in town a day longer, adding, "If any thing does thee good it must be the country air, with rest, asses' milk, and riding daily." So (not being able to sit a horse) about noon I took a coach for Lewisham. In the evening, (not knowing how it might please God to dispose of me,) to prevent vile panegyric I wrote as follows:

HERE LIETH THE BODY
OF
JOHN WESLEY,
A BRAND PLUCKED OUT OF THE BURNING:
WHO DIED OF A CONSUMPTION IN THE FIFTY-FIRST YEAR OF HIS AGE, NOT LEAVING, AFTER HIS DEBTS ARE PAID,
TEN POUNDS BEHIND HIM:
PRAYING,
GOD BE MERCIFUL TO ME, AN UNPROFITABLE SERVANT!

He ordered that this, if any, inscription should be placed on his tombstone.

Wesley's Notes on the New Testament the Result of Sickness.

Tuesday, Jan. 1, 1754. I returned once more to London. On *Wednesday, Jan.* 2, I set out in the machine, and the next afternoon came to Chippenham. Here I took a post-chaise, in which I reached Bristol about eight in the evening.

Friday, Jan. 4. I began drinking the water at the Hot Well, having a lodging at a small distance from it; and on *Sunday, Jan.* 6, I began writing Notes on the New Testament—a work which I should scarce ever have attempted had I not been so ill as not to be able to travel or preach, and yet so well as to be able to read and write.

Monday, Jan. 7. I went on now in a regular method, rising at my hour, and writing from five to nine at night, except the time of riding, half an hour for each meal, and the hour between five and six in the evening.

Preaches again after an intermission of Four Months.

Sunday, March 10. I took my leave of the Hot Well, and removed to Bristol.

Tuesday, March 19. Having finished the rough draft, I began transcribing the Notes on the Gospels.

Tuesday, March 26. I preached for the first time after an intermission of four months. What reason have I to praise God that he does not take the word of his truth utterly out of my mouth!

Baxter's "History of the Councils."

Monday, Aug. 5. I set out for Canterbury. On the way I read Mr. Baxter's "History of the Councils." It is utterly astonishing, and would be wholly incredible, but that his vouchers are beyond all exception. What a company of execrable wretches have they been, (one cannot justly give them a milder title,) who have almost in every age since St. Cyprian taken upon them to govern the Church! How has one Council been perpetually cursing another, and delivering all over to Satan, whether predecessors or contemporaries, who did not implicitly receive their determinations, though generally trifling, sometimes false, and frequently unintelligible or self-contradictory? Surely Mohammedanism was let loose to reform the Christians! I know not but Constantinople has gained by the change.

Strong Words to a Rich Man.

October. Upon the whole, I must once more earnestly entreat you to consider yourself, and God, and eternity. As to yourself, you are not the proprietor of any thing; no, not of one shilling in the world. You are only a steward of what another intrusts you with, to be laid out not according to your will but his. And what would you think of your steward if he laid out what is called your money according to his own will and pleasure? 2. Is not God the sole proprietor of all things? And are not you to give an account to him for every part of his goods? And O how dreadful an account if you have expended any part of them not according to his will, but your own! 3. Is not death at hand? And are not you and I just stepping into eternity? Are we not just going to appear in the presence of God, and that naked of all worldly goods? Will you then rejoice in the money you have left behind you? Or in that you have given to support a family, as it is called; that is, in truth to support the pride, and vanity, and luxury which you have yourself despised all your life long? O, sir, I beseech you, for the sake of God, for the sake of your own immortal soul, examine yourself whether you do not love money? If so, you cannot love God. And if we die without the fear of God, what remains? Only to be banished from him for ever and ever.

An Answer to Prayer.

Thursday, April 24, 1755. We rode in less than four hours the eight miles (so called) to Newell Hay. Just as I began to preach the sun broke out, and shone exceeding hot on the side of my head. I found if it continued I should not be able to speak long, and lifted up my heart to God. In a minute or two it was covered with clouds, which continued till the service was over. Let any who please call this *chance;* I call it an answer to prayer.

"A Pen dipped in Tears."

Wednesday, May 1. I finished the "Gentleman's Reasons," (who is a Dissenting Minister at Exeter.) In how different a spirit does this man write from honest Richard Baxter! The one dipping his pen as it were in tears, the other in vinegar and gall. Surely one page of that loving, serious Christian weighs more than volumes of this bitter, sarcastic jester.

Decision of the Leeds Conference.

Tuesday, May 6. Our Conference began at Leeds. The point on which we desired all the preachers to speak their minds at large was, "Whether we ought to separate from the Church?" Whatever was advanced on one side or the other was seriously and calmly considered; and on the third day we were all fully agreed in that conclusion—that (whether it was *lawful* or not) it was no ways *expedient.*

Monday, May 12. We rode (my wife and I) to Northallerton.

Tuesday, May 13. I rode to Newcastle. I did not find things here in the order I expected. Many were on the point of leaving the Church, which some had done already; and, as they supposed, on my authority! O how much discord is caused by one jarring string! How much trouble by one man who does not walk by the same rule, and agree in the same judgment with his brethren!

Retiring from the World.

Wednesday, Oct. 15. I preached at Bath. Even here a few joined together, and hope they shall be scattered no more. I dined with some serious persons in a large, stately house, standing on the brow of a delightful hill. In this paradise they live in ease, in honor, and in elegant abundance. And this they call retiring from the world! What would Gregory Lopez have called it? In the evening the society met at Bristol. I had desired again and again that no person would come who had not calmly and deliberately resolved to give himself up to God. But I believe not ten of them were wanting; and we now solemnly and of set purpose, by our own free act and deed, jointly agreed to take the Lord for our God. I think it will not soon be forgotten; I hope, not to all eternity.

A Heavy Day's Work in London.

Monday, Oct. 20. I left Bristol, and, taking several societies on the way, on *Thursday, Oct.* 23, preached at Reading. Several soldiers were there, and many more the next night, when I set before them "the terrors of the Lord." And I scarce ever saw so much impression made on this dull, senseless people.

Saturday, Oct. 25. I reached London, notwithstanding all the foreboding of my friends, in at least as good health as I left it.

Sunday, Oct. 26. I entered upon my London duty, reading prayers, preaching, and giving the sacrament, at Snowsfields in the morning; preaching and giving the sacrament at noon in West-street chapel, meeting the leaders at three, burying a corpse at four, and preaching at five in the afternoon. Afterward I met the society, and concluded the day with a general love-feast.

A Visit from Mr. Whitefield.

Thursday, Nov. 5. Mr. Whitefield called upon me; disputings are now no more. We love one another, and join hand in hand to promote the cause of our common Master.

Wesley Suits his Subject to the Occasion.

Monday, Nov. 17. As we were walking toward Wapping the rain poured down with such violence that we were obliged to take shelter till it abated. We then held on to Gravel-lane, in many parts of which the waters were like a river. However, we got on pretty well till the rain put out the candle in our lantern. We then were obliged to wade through all till we came to the chapel-yard. Just as we entered it a little streak of lightning appeared in the south-west. There was likewise a small clap of thunder and a vehement burst of rain, which rushed so plentifully through our shattered tiles that the vestry was all in a float. Soon after I began reading prayers the lightning flamed all round it, and the thunder rolled just over our heads. When it grew louder and louder, perceiving many of the strangers to be much affrighted I broke off the prayers after the collect, "Lighten our darkness, we beseech thee, O Lord," and began applying, "The Lord sitteth above the water-flood; the Lord remaineth a king forever." Presently the lightning, thunder, and rain ceased, and we had a remarkably calm evening. It was observed, that exactly at this hour they were acting "Macbeth" in Drury-lane, and just as the mock thunder began the Lord began to thunder out of heaven. For a while it put them to a stand, but they soon took courage and went on. Otherwise it might have been suspected that the fear of God had crept into the very theater!

Without the Hurry and Pomp of Dying.

Friday, Dec. 12. As I was returning from Zoar I came as well as usual to Moorfields, but there my strength entirely failed, and such a faintness and weariness seized me that it was with difficulty I got home. I could not but think how happy it would be (suppose we were ready for the Bridegroom) to sink down and steal away at once without any of the hurry and pomp of dying!

Wesley in the King's Robe-chamber.

Tuesday, Dec. 23. I was in the robe-chamber adjoining the House of Lords when the King put on his robes. His brow was much furrowed with age, and quite clouded with care. And is this all the world can give even to a king? All the grandeur it can afford? A blanket of ermine round his shoulders so heavy and cumbersome he can scarce move under it! A huge heap of borrowed hair, with a few plates of gold and glittering stones upon his head? Alas, what a bauble is human greatness!

Peter the Great no Christian.

Friday, Jan. 30, 1756. In returning to London I read the life of the late Czar, Peter the Great. Undoubtedly he was a soldier, a general, and a statesman scarce inferior to any. But why was he called a Christian? What has Christianity to do either with deep dissimulation or savage cruelty?

Conference at Bristol.

Wednesday, Aug. 25. We rode on to Bristol.

Thursday, Aug. 26. About fifty of us being met, the rules of the society were read over and carefully considered one by one, but we did not find any that could be spared. So we all agreed to abide by them all, and to recommend them with our might. We then largely considered the necessity of keeping in the Church and using the clergy with tenderness, and there was no dissenting voice. God gave us all to be of one mind and of one judgment.

Friday, Aug. 27. The rules of the bands were

read over and considered one by one; which, after some verbal alterations, we all agreed to observe and enforce.

Wesley's Gain by Printing and Preaching.

Monday, Sept. 6. I set out in the machine, and on *Tuesday* evening came to London. *Wednesday* and *Thursday* I settled my temporal business. It is now about eighteen years since I began writing and printing books, and how much in that time have I gained by printing? Why, on summing up my accounts I found on March 1, 1756, (the day I left London last,) I had gained by printing and preaching together a debt of twelve hundred and thirty-six pounds.

Criticism on the French Language.

Monday, Oct. 11. I went to Leigh. Where we dined, a poor woman came to the door with two little children. They seemed to be half-starved as well as their mother, who was also shivering with an ague. She was extremely thankful for a little food, and still more so for a few pills, which seldom fail to cure that disorder. In this little journey I read over a curiosity indeed—a French heroic poem, "Voltaire's Henriade." He is a very lively writer, of a fine imagination; and allowed, I suppose, by all competent judges, to be a perfect master of the French language; and by him I was more than ever convinced that the French is the poorest, meanest language in Europe; that it is no more comparable to the German or Spanish than a bagpipe is to an organ; and that, with regard to poetry in particular, considering the incorrigible uncouthness of their measure, and their always writing in rhyme, (to say nothing of their vile double rhymes, nay, and frequent false rhymes,) it is as impossible to write a fine poem in French as to make fine music upon a Jew's-harp.

Strength and Help from God.

Sunday, Feb. 27, 1757. After the service at Snowsfields I found myself much weaker than usual, and feared I should not be able to go through the work of the day, which is equal to preaching eight times. I therefore prayed that God would send me help; and as soon as I had done preaching at West-street, a clergyman, who was come to town for a few days, came and offered me his service. So when I asked for strength, God gave me strength; when for help, he gave this also.

Sunday, March 6. I had no help, and I wanted none, for God renewed my strength; but on *Sunday, Mar.* 13, finding myself weak at Snowsfields, I prayed (if he saw good) that God would send me help at the chapel, and I had it. A clergyman, whom I never saw before, came and offered me his assistance, and as soon as I had done preaching Mr. Fletcher came, who had just then been ordained priest, and hastened to the chapel on purpose to assist, as he supposed me to be alone.

Sunday, March 20. Mr. Fletcher helped me again. How wonderful are the ways of God! When my bodily health failed, and none in England were able and willing to assist me, he sent me help from the mountains of Switzerland, and a helpmeet for me in every respect. Where could I have found such another?

A Society Meeting of Twelve Hundred.

Monday, April 11. At five in the evening about twelve hundred of the society met at Spitalfields. I expected two to help me, but none came. I held out till between seven and eight. I was then scarce able to walk or speak; but I looked up and received strength. At half-hour after nine God broke in mightily upon the congregation. "Great" indeed "was our glorying" in him; we were "filled with consolation." And when I returned home between ten and eleven, I was no more tired than at ten in the morning.

The People of Huddersfield.

Monday, May 9. I rode over the mountains to Huddersfield. A wilder people I never saw in England. The men, women, and children filled the street as we rode along, and appeared just ready to devour us. They were, however, tolerably quiet while I preached; only a few pieces of dirt were thrown, and the bellman came in the middle of the sermon, but was stopped by a gentleman of the town. I had almost done, when they began to ring the bells, so that it did us small disservice. How intolerable a thing is the Gospel of Christ to them who are resolved to serve the devil!

Wesley Preaches on the Mountain-Top.

Wednesday, May 18. I rode in the afternoon from Halifax over the huge, but extremely pleasant and fruitful, mountains to Heptonstal. A large congregation was waiting for us, not only on the ground, but on the side and tops of the neighboring houses. But no scoffer or trifler was seen among them. It rained

12

in the adjoining valley all or most of the time that I was preaching; but it was fair with us on the top of the mountain. What an emblem of God's taking up his people into a place of safety while the storm falls on all below!

An Audience of Lunatics and Paupers.

Wednesday, June 1. We rode on to Glasgow, a mile short of which we met Mr. Gillies riding out to meet us. In the evening the tent (so they call a covered pulpit) was placed in the yard of the poor-house, a very large and commodious place. Fronting the pulpit was the Infirmary, with most of the patients at or near the windows. Adjoining to this was the hospital for lunatics; several of them gave deep attention. And cannot God give them also the spirit of a sound mind? After sermon they brought four children to baptize. I was at the kirk in the morning while the minister baptized several immediately after sermon, so I was not at a loss as to their manner of baptizing. I believe this removed much prejudice.

Singing a Scotch Psalm.

Friday, June 10. I found myself much out of order till the flux stopped at once without any medicine; but being still weak, and the sun shining extremely hot, I was afraid I should not be able to go round by Kelso. Vain fear! God took care for this also. The wind, which had been full east for several days, turned this morning full west, and blew just in our face; and about ten the clouds rose and kept us cool till we came to Kelso. At six William Coward and I went to the market-house; we stayed some time, and neither man, woman, nor child came near us. At length I began singing a Scotch psalm, and fifteen or twenty people came within hearing, but with great circumspection keeping their distance, as though they knew not what might follow. But while I prayed their numbers increased, so that in a few minutes there was a pretty large congregation. I suppose the chief men of the town were there, and I spared neither rich nor poor. I almost wondered at myself, it not being usual with me to use so keen and cutting expressions; and I believe many felt that, for all their form, they were but heathens still.

Robbing the King.

Thursday, June 16. In the evening I preached at Sunderland. I then met the society and told them plain none could stay with us unless he would part with all sin; particularly, robbing the King, selling or buying run goods, which I could no more suffer than robbing on the highway; this I enforced on every member the next day. A few would not promise to refrain, so these I was forced to cut off. About two hundred and fifty were of a better mind.

Wesley Rides Ninety Miles in a Day.

March, 1758. Rest was now the more sweet, because both our horses were lame. However, resolving to reach Epworth at the time appointed, I set out in a post-chaise between four and five in the morning; but the frost made it so bad driving that my companion came with the lame horses into Stamford as soon as me. The next stage I went on horseback; but I was then obliged to leave my mare and take another post-chaise. I came to Bawtry about six. Some from Epworth had come to meet me, but were gone half an hour before I came. I knew no chaise could go the rest of the road, so it remained only to hire horses and a guide. We set out about seven, but I soon found my guide knew no more of the way than myself. However, we got pretty well to Idlestop, about four miles from Bawtry, where we had just light to discern the river at our side, and the country covered with water. I had heard that one Richard Wright lived thereabouts, who knew the road over the moor perfectly well. Hearing one speak, (for we could not see him,) I called, "Who is there?" He answered, "Richard Wright." I soon agreed with him, and he quickly mounted his horse and rode boldly forward. The north-east wind blew full in our face, and I heard them say, "It is very cold!" But neither my face, nor hands, nor feet were cold till, between nine and ten, we came to Epworth; after traveling more than ninety miles, I was little more tired than when I rose in the morning.

A timely Supply of Money.

Monday, March 13. I preached in the shell of the new house, and then set out for York. The banks over which we crept along were ready to swallow up man and beast; however, we came safe to York in the afternoon. After settling the little affairs, on *Wednesday,* 15, I rode to Leeds, where, in the evening, a multitude of people were present. I never before saw things in so good order here, and took knowledge the assistant had not been idle. I was apprehensive, having been at an uncommon expense, of being a little straitened for money; but after preaching, one with whom I had never exchanged a word put a letter into my hand in which was a bill for ten pounds. Is not "the earth the Lord's, and the fullness thereof?"

Two Lost Hours.

Friday, April 21. I dined at Lady ——'s. We need great grace to converse with great people! From which, therefore, (unless in some rare instances,) I am glad to be excused. *Horæ fugiunt et imputantur!* [The moments fly away, and must be accounted for!] Of these two hours I can give no account.

A Church built of Mud and Straw.

Friday, May 5. In the evening I preached at Drumcree, in the new room built in the taste of the country. The roof is thatch, the walls mud; on which a ladder was suspended by ropes of straw.

The Preachers' Room at Terryhugan.

Tuesday, May 9. We rode by the side of the Canal, through a pleasant vale, to Terryhugan. The room built on purpose for us here is three yards long, two and a quarter broad, and six feet high. The walls, floor, and ceiling are mud; and we had a clean chaff bed. At seven I preached in a neighboring ground, having a rock behind me and a large congregation sitting on the grass before me. Thence we retired to our hut, and found it true:

Licet, sub paupere tecto,
Reges et regum vitâ præcurrere amicos.

[It is possible, under a humble roof, to live more happily than kings and their courtiers.]

Wesley Visits the dying Thomas Walsh.

Saturday, June 17. I met Thomas Walsh once more in Limerick alive, and but just alive. Three of the best physicians in these parts have attended him, and all agree that it is a lost case; that, by violent straining of his voice, added to frequent colds, he has contracted a pulmonary consumption, which is now in the last stage, and consequently beyond the reach of any human help. O what a man to be snatched away in the strength of his years! Surely thy judgments are a great deep!

Holds Conference at Limerick.

Wednesday, June 21. Our little Conference began, at which fourteen preachers were present. We settled all things here which we judged would be of use to the preachers or the societies, and consulted how to remove whatever might be a hinderance to the work of God.

Preaches to a Colony of Germans.

Friday, June 23. I rode over to Court Mattress, a colony of Germans, whose parents came out of the Palatinate about fifty years ago. Twenty families of them settled here; twenty more at Killiheen, a mile off; fifty at Balligarane, about two miles eastward, and twenty at Pallas, four miles further. Each family had a few acres of ground, on which they built as many little houses. They are since considerably increased in number of souls, though decreased in number of families. Having no minister, they were become eminent for drunkenness, cursing, swearing, and an utter neglect of religion. But they are washed since they heard and received the truth which is able to save their souls. An oath is now rarely heard among them, or a drunkard seen in their borders. Court Mattress is built in the form of a square, in the middle of which they have placed a pretty large preaching-house; but it would not contain one half of the congregation, so I stood in a large yard. The wind kept off the rain while I was preaching. As soon as I ended it began.

Oliver Cromwell's Camp.

Sunday, June 25. About six I preached in the island in a square green inclosure, which was formerly Oliver Cromwell's camp. I have not seen such a congregation since we left London. To how much better purpose is this ground employed than it was in the last century!

Symptoms of Consumption return.

Sunday, July 2. I preached in the island near Limerick both morning and evening, standing on the side of a large hollow adjoining to the old camp. The ground on the sides of it sloped upward, so that the people sat on the grass row above row. Such an amphitheater I never saw before, in which thousands of hearers were so commodiously placed; and they seemed earnestly to attend to our Lord's invitation, "Come, for all things are now ready." I did not then observe that I strained myself, but in the morning I was extremely hoarse. This increased all day, together with a load and stoppage in my breast. On Tuesday morning I began spitting blood, found a pain in my left side, a sensible decay of strength, and a deep wheezing cough, just the symptoms which I had some years since.

Blessed Work among Children.

Sunday, July 30. I began meeting the children in the afternoon, though with little hopes of doing them good. But I had not spoke long on our natural state before many of them were in tears, and five or six so affected that they could not refrain from crying aloud to God. When I began to pray their cries increased, so that my voice was soon lost. I have seen no such work among children for eighteen or nineteen years.

Wesley always Preaching!

Monday, August 7. Being detained at Cork, in the afternoon I went to the middle of the town. Abundance of people ran together, but they were far too wild and noisy to admit of my giving out a psalm, or naming a text, in the usual way; so I fell abruptly upon as many as could hear in a free and familiar manner. In a few minutes the whole body were quiet and tolerably attentive. They were more and more serious till I concluded with a hymn and a short prayer. Immediately after preaching I was sent for to a gentleman who was struck with the palsy. I found the house full of his friends and relations, to whom I spoke freely and largely. They seemed to be more than ordinarily affected. Perhaps for this also we were detained at Cove.

Prejudice overcome.

Wednesday, Dec. 20. I rode to Norwich. James Wheatley now repeated his offer of the Tabernacle. But I was in no haste. I wanted to consult my friends, and consider the thing thoroughly. One glaring objection to it was, "The congregation there will not hear me." He replied, "Sir, you cannot tell that, unless you make the trial." I consented so to do on *Thursday*, 21. But many declared, "No, he shall never come into that pulpit," and planted themselves in the way to prevent it. Hitherto only could they go. I went up and preached to a large congregation without any let or hinderance. I preached there again on *Saturday* evening, and again God stopped the mouths of the lions.

Sunday, Dec. 24. I preached in the Tabernacle at eight to a very serious congregation, and at the Foundery between four and five. About six the Tabernacle was thoroughly filled, and mostly with quiet hearers. I saw none who behaved amiss but two soldiers, who struck some that desired them to be silent. But they were seized and carried to the commanding officer, who ordered them to be soundly whipped.

Monday, Dec. 25. Our service began in the Foundery at four; in the Tabernacle at eight. God was now especially pleased to make bare his arm. There was a great cry among the people. Stony hearts were broke, many mourners comforted, many believers strengthened. Prejudice vanished away; a few only kept their fierceness till the afternoon. One of these, still vehemently angry, planted himself just over against me. But before I concluded he cried out, "I am overcome! I am overcome!" Having now weighed the matter thoroughly, I yielded to the importunity of our brethren. So in the evening the copy of the lease was perfected, which was executed the next morning. A whole train of providences so plainly concurred thereto, that all might clearly see the hand of God.

Famous Castle at Colchester.

Friday, Dec. 29. To-day I walked all over the famous Castle, perhaps the most ancient in England. A considerable part of it is, without question, fourteen or fifteen hundred years old. It was mostly built with Roman bricks, each of which is about two inches thick, seven broad, and thirteen or fourteen long. Seat of ancient kings, British and Roman, once dreaded far and near! But what are they now? Is not "a living dog better than a dead lion?" And what is it wherein they pride themselves, as do the present great ones of the earth?

> A little pomp, a little sway,
> A sunbeam in a winter's day,
> Is all the great and mighty have
> Between the cradle and the grave!

Wesley Resting.

Saturday, Dec. 30. I returned to London, and received a pressing letter from Bristol; in consequence of which I took horse on *Monday* morning, *Jan.* 1, 1759, and came hither the next evening. After resting two days, (only preaching morning and evening,) I examined severally the members of the society. This was one great end of my coming down. Another was to provide for the poor. Accordingly on *Sunday, Jan.* 7, I preached a sermon for them, to which God was pleased to give his blessing; so that the collection was a great deal more than double what it used to be.

Let them have their Own Way.

Sunday, March 18, 1759. I administered the Lord's Supper to near two hundred communicants; so solemn a season I never remember to have known in the city of Norwich. As a considerable part of them were dissenters, I desired every one to use what posture he judged best. Had I required them to kneel, probably half would have sat. Now all but one kneeled down. Finding it was needful to see them once more at Colchester, I took horse between four and five in the morning. The frost was extremely sharp for some hours; it was then a fair, mild day. About two in the afternoon it began to rain, but we reached Colchester before we were wet through. The room was more than filled in the evening, so that many were obliged to go away.

Wednesday, March 21. I baptized seven adults, two of them by immersion; and in the evening (their own ministers having cast them out for going to hear the Methodists) I administered the Lord's Supper to them, and many others, whom their several teachers had repelled for the same reason.

New regulations.

Sunday, April 1. I met them all at six, requiring every one to show his ticket when he came in, a thing they had never heard of before. I likewise insisted on another strange regulation: that the men and women should sit apart. A third was made the same day. It had been the custom, ever since the Tabernacle was built, to have the galleries full of spectators while the Lord's Supper was administered. This I judged highly improper, and therefore ordered none to be admitted but those who desired to communicate. And I found far less difficulty than I expected in bringing them to submit to this also. The society now contained above five hundred and seventy members, a hundred and three of whom were in no society before, although many of them had found peace with God. I believe they would have increased to a thousand if I could have stayed a fortnight longer. Which of these will hold fast their profession? The fowls of the air will devour some, the sun will scorch more, and others will be choked by the thorns springing up. I wonder we should ever expect that half of those who "hear the word with joy" will bring forth fruit unto perfection.

Smugglers not tolerated.

Friday, June 22. I rode to S——k, and preached to my old congregation of colliers on "Why will ye die, O house of Israel?" After preaching, a servant of Mr. —— came and said, "Sir, my master discharges you from preaching any more on his ground; not out of any disrespect to you, but he will stand by the Church." "Simple master Shallow!" as Shakspeare has it; wise master Rector, his counselor!

Saturday, June 23. I spoke to each of the society in Sunderland. Most of the robbers, commonly called smugglers, have left us; but more than twice the number of honest people are already come in their place; and if none had come, yet should I not dare to keep those who steal either from the King or subject.

The Devil does not love Field-Preaching.

Sunday, June 24. I preached in the street at eight; about one at South Shields, and at five in North Shields. The greatest part of them seemed to hear as for their lives. So are these lions also become lambs. O for zealous, active, faithful laborers! How white are the fields unto the harvest! On *Monday* and *Tuesday* evening I preached abroad, near the Keelmen's Hospital, to twice the people we should have had at the house. What marvel the devil does not love field-preaching? Neither do I. I love a commodious room, a soft cushion, a handsome pulpit. But where is my zeal if I do not trample all these under foot in order to save one more soul!

Wesley's Letter to Dr. Taylor.

Tuesday, July 3. I wrote to Dr. Taylor as follows:

"REV. SIR: I esteem you as a person of uncommon sense and learning; but your doctrine I cannot esteem. And some time since I believed it my duty to speak my sentiments at large concerning your doctrine of Original Sin. When Mr. Newton, of Liverpool, mentioned this, and asked whether you designed to answer, you said you thought not, for it would only be a personal controversy between Jo. W——y and Jo. T——r. How gladly, if I durst, would I accept of this discharge from so unequal a contest! For I am thoroughly sensible, humanly speaking, it is *formica contra leonem*, [an ant against a lion.] How gladly, were it indeed no other than a personal controversy! But certainly it is not; it is a controversy *de re*, [concerning a thing,] if ever there was one in the world. Indeed, concerning a thing of the highest importance; nay, all the things that concern our eternal peace. It is Christianity or Heathenism! For take away the scriptural doctrine of redemption or justification, and that of the new birth, the beginning of sanctification; or, which amounts to the same, explain them as you do, suitably to your doctrine of Original Sin, and what is Christianity better than Heathenism? Wherein (save in rectifying some of our notions) has the religion of St. Paul any pre-eminence over that of Socrates or Epictetus?

"This is, therefore, to my apprehension, the least personal controversy of any in the world. Your person and mine are out of the question. The point is, 'Are those things that have been believed for many ages throughout the Christian world real solid truths, or monkish dreams and vain imaginations?'

"But further, it is certain between you and me there need be no personal controversy at all. For we may agree to leave each other's person and character absolutely untouched, while we sum up and answer the several arguments advanced as plainly and closely as we can. Either I or you mistake the whole of Christianity from the beginning to the end. Either my scheme or yours is as contrary to the scriptural as the Koran is. Is it mine or yours? Yours has gone through all England and made numerous converts. I attack it from end to end; let all England judge whether it can be defended or not.

"Earnestly praying that God may give you and me a right understanding in all things, I am, reverend sir,

"Your servant for Christ's sake, J. W."

Plain Talk.

Wednesday, Aug. 29. I rode to Lakenheath, and spoke exceeding plain to an honest, drowsy people.

Thursday, Aug. 30. I preached at the Tabernacle in Norwich to a large, rude, noisy congregation. I took knowledge what manner of teachers they had been accustomed to, and determined to mend them or end them. Accordingly, the next evening, after sermon, I reminded them of two things: the one, that it was not decent to begin talking aloud as soon as service was ended, and hurrying to and fro as in a bear-garden; the other, that it was a bad custom to gather into knots just after sermon and turn a place of worship into a coffee-house. I, therefore, desired that none would talk under that roof, but go quietly and silently away. And on *Sunday, Sept.* 2, I had the pleasure to observe that all went as quietly away as if they had been accustomed to it for many years.

Monday, Sept. 3. I met the society at five, and explained the nature and use of meeting in a class. Upon inquiry, I found we have now about five hundred members. But a hundred and fifty of these do not *pretend* to meet at all. Of those, therefore, I make no account. They hang on but a single thread.

Tuesday, Sept. 4. I walked to Kemnal, nine miles from Norwich, and preached at one o'clock. The ringleader of the mob came with his horn, as usual, before I began. But one quickly catched and threw away his horn, and in a few minutes he was deserted by all his companions, who were seriously and deeply attentive to the great truth, "By grace ye are saved, through faith."

Sunday, Sept. 9. I met the society at seven, and told them in plain terms that they were the most ignorant, self-conceited, self-willed, fickle, untractable, disorderly, disjointed society that I knew in the three kingdoms. And God applied it to their hearts, so that many were profited; but I do not find that one was offended. At ten we had another happy opportunity, and many stubborn hearts were melted down. Just at two the great congregation met, and the power of God was again present to heal; though not so eminently as at five, while I was describing "the peace that passeth all understanding."

Wesley's Loss of a Night's Sleep.

Monday, Sept. 10. We took horse at half-hour after four. Before eight it was as warm as it is usually at midsummer. And from ten we had the sun in our face all the way to Colchester. But we had the wind in our face too, or the heat would have been insupportable. I was in a fever from the moment I came into the house. But it did not hinder me from preaching on the Green, and afterward meeting the society. I then lay down as soon as possible, but could not sleep a quarter of an hour till between two and three in the morning. I do not know that I have lost a night's sleep before, sick or well, since I was six years old. But it is all one: God is able to give strength, either with sleep or without it. I rose at my usual time, and preached at five, without any faintness or drowsiness.

Expediency of Field-Preaching.

Sunday, Sept. 23. A vast majority of the immense congregation in Moorfields were deeply serious. One such hour might convince any impartial man of the expediency of field-preaching. What building, except St. Paul's Church, would contain such a congregation? And if it would, what human voice could have reached them there? By repeated observations I find I can command thrice the number in the open air that I can under a roof. And who can say the time for field-preaching is over, while, 1. Greater numbers than ever attend. 2. The converting, as well as the convincing, power of *God is eminently with them!*

His Care for French Prisoners.

Monday, Oct. 15. I walked up to Knowle, a mile from Bristol, to see the French prisoners. Above eleven hundred of them, we were informed, were confined in that little place without any thing to lie upon but a little dirty straw, or any thing to cover them but a few foul thin rags, either by day or night, so that they died like rotten sheep. I was much affected, and preached in the evening on, (Exodus xxiii, 9,) "Thou shalt not oppress a stranger; for ye know the heart of a stranger, seeing ye were strangers in the land of Egypt." Eighteen pounds were contributed immediately, which were made up four-and-twenty the next day. With this we bought linen and woolen cloth, which were made up into shirts, waistcoats, and breeches. Some dozen of stockings were added, all of which were carefully distributed where there was the greatest want. Presently after, the Corporation of Bristol sent a large quantity of mattresses and blankets. And it was not long before contributions were set on foot in London, and in various parts of the kingdom; so that I believe from this time they were pretty well provided with all the necessaries of life.

Wesley prefers to Preach to the Poor.

Saturday, Nov. 17. I spent an hour agreeably and profitably with Lady G—— H—— and Sir C—— H——. It is well a few of the rich and noble are called. O that God would increase their number! But I should rejoice (were it the will of God) if it were done by the ministry of others. If I might choose I should say, (as I have done hitherto,) preach the Gospel to the poor.

A Strange Preaching-Place.

Friday, Nov. 23. The roads were so extremely slippery it was with much difficulty we reached Bedford. We had a pretty large congregation; but the stench from the swine under the room was scarce supportable. Was ever a preaching-place over a hogsty before! Surely they love the Gospel who come to hear it in such a place.

Wesley's Views of Visions and Trances.

Saturday, Nov. 24. We rode to Everton, Mr. Berridge being gone to preach before the University at Cambridge. Many people came to his house in the evening, and it was a season of great refreshment.

Sunday, Nov. 25. I was a little afraid my strength would not suffice for reading prayers, and preaching, and administering the Lord's Supper alone to a large number of communicants; but all was well. Mr. Hicks began his own service early, and came before

I had ended my sermon. So we finished the whole before two, and I had time to breathe before the evening service. In the afternoon God was eminently present with us, though rather to comfort than convince. But I observed a remarkable difference since I was here before as to the manner of the work. None now were in trances, none cried out, none fell down or were convulsed; only some trembled exceedingly, a low murmur was heard, and many were refreshed with the multitude of peace.

The danger *was*, to guard extraordinary circumstances too much, such as outcries, convulsions, visions, trances, as if these were essential to the inward work, so that it could not go on without them. Perhaps the danger *is*, to regard them too little, to condemn them all together, to imagine they had nothing of God in them, and were a hinderance to his work. Whereas the truth is, 1. God suddenly and strongly convinced many that they were lost sinners; the natural consequence whereof were sudden outcries and strong bodily convulsions. 2. To strengthen and encourage them that believed, and to make his work more apparent, he favored several of them with divine dreams, others with trances and visions. 3. In some of these instances, after a time, nature mixed with grace. 4. Satan likewise mimicked this work of God, in order to discourage the whole work; and yet it is not wise to give up this part any more than to give up the whole. At first it was, doubtless, wholly from God. It is partly so at this day; and he will enable us to discern how far in every case the work is pure, and where it mixes or degenerates.

Let us even suppose that in some few cases there was a mixture of dissimulation, that persons pretended to see or feel what they did not, and imitated the cries or convulsive motions of those who were really overpowered by the Spirit of God; yet even this should not make us either deny or undervalue the real work of the Spirit. The shadow is no disparagement of the substance, nor the counterfeit of the real diamond. We may further suppose, that Satan will make these visions an occasion of pride; but what can be inferred from hence? Nothing, but that we should guard against it; that we should diligently exhort all to be little in their own eyes, knowing that nothing avails with God but humble love. But still, to slight or censure visions in general would be both irrational and unchristian.

Pretended Message from God.

Wednesday, Jan. 16, 1760. One came to me, as she said, with a message from the Lord, to tell me I was laying up treasures on earth, taking my ease, and minding only my eating and drinking. I told her God knew me better; and if he had sent her, he would have sent her with a more proper message.

As clear a Witness of Sanctification as of Justification.

Wednesday, March 12. Having desired that as many as could of the neighboring towns, who believed they were saved from sin, would meet me, I spent the greatest part of this day in examining them one by one. The testimony of some I could not receive; but, concerning the far greatest part, it is plain, (unless they could be supposed to tell willful and deliberate lies,) 1. That they feel no inward sin; and, to the best of their knowledge, commit no outward sin. 2. That they see and love God every moment, and pray, rejoice, give thanks evermore. 3. That they have constantly as clear a witness from God of sanctification as they have of justification. Now in this I do rejoice, and will rejoice, call it what you please; and I would to God thousands had experienced thus much: let them afterward experience as much more as God pleases.

Causes of Ireland's Troubles.

Monday, April 21. In riding to Rosmead I read Sir John Davis's "Historical Relations concerning Ireland." None who reads these can wonder that, fruitful as it is, it was always so thinly inhabited; for he makes it plain, 1. That murder was never capital among the native Irish; the murderer only paid a small fine to the Chief of his Sept. 2. When the English settled here, still the Irish had no benefit of the English laws. They could not so much as sue an Englishman. So the English beat, plundered, yea, murdered them at pleasure. Hence, 3, arose continual wars between them for three hundred and fifty years together; and hereby both the English and Irish natives were kept few, as well as poor. 4. When they were multiplied during a peace of forty years, from 1600 to 1641, the general massacre, with the ensuing war, again thinned their numbers; not so few as a million of men, women, and children being destroyed in four years' time. 5. Great numbers have ever since, year by year, left the land merely for want of employment. 6. The gentry are continually driving away hundreds, yea, thousands, of them that remain, by throwing such quantities of arable land into pasture, which leaves them neither business nor food. This it is that now dispeoples many parts of Ireland, of Connaught in particular, which, it is supposed, has scarce half the inhabitants at this day which it had fourscore years ago.

The Prophet's Chamber built of Marble.

Monday, April 28. I rode to Rathfriland, seven Irish miles from Newry, a small town built on the top of a mountain, surrounded first by a deep valley, and at a small distance by higher mountains. The Presbyterian minister had wrote to the Popish priest to keep his people from hearing. But they would not be kept; Protestants and Papists flocked together to the meadow where I preached, and sat on the grass still as night, while I exhorted them to "repent and believe the Gospel." The same attention appeared in the whole congregation at Terryhugan in the evening, where I spent a comfortable night in the Prophet's Chamber, nine feet long, seven broad, and six high. The ceiling, floor, and walls were all of the same marble, vulgarly called clay.

A Justice of the Peace heads the Mob.

June 10. At noon William Ley, James Glasbrook, and I rode to Carrick-upon-Shannon. In less than an hour an Esquire and Justice of the Peace came down with a drum, and what mob he could gather. I went into the garden with the congregation while he was making a speech to his followers in the street. He then attacked William Ley, (who stood at the door,) being armed with a halbert and long sword, and ran at him with the halbert, but missing his thrust he then struck at him, and broke it short upon his wrist. Having made his way through the house to the other door he was at a full stop. James Glasbrook held it fast on the other side. While he was endeavoring to force it open one told him I was preaching in the garden. On this he quitted the door in haste, ran round the house, and, with part of his retinue, climbed over the wall into the garden, and with a whole volley of oaths and curses declared, "You shall not preach here to-day." I told him, "Sir, I do not intend it, for I have preached already." This made him ready to tear the ground. Finding he was not to be reasoned with I went into the house. Soon after he revenged himself on James Glasbrook (by breaking the truncheon of his halbert on his arm) and on my hat, which he beat and kicked most valiantly; but a gentleman rescued it out of his hands, and we rode quietly out of the town.

German Settlements in Ireland.

Wednesday, July 9. I rode over to Killiheen, a German settlement near twenty miles south of Limerick. It rained all the way, but the earnestness of the poor people made us quite forget it. In the evening I preached to another colony of Germans at Ballygarane. The third is at Court Mattress, a mile from Killiheen. I suppose three such towns are scarce to be found again in England or Ireland. There is no cursing or swearing, no Sabbath breaking, no drunkenness, no ale-house, in any of them. How will these poor foreigners rise up in the judgment against those that are round about them?

Character of Wesley's Hearers at St. Ives.

Wednesday, Sept. 10. When I came to St. Ives I was determined to preach abroad, but the wind was so high I could not stand where I had intended. But we found a little inclosure near it, one end of which was native rock, rising ten or twelve feet perpendicular, from which the ground fell with an easy descent. A jutting out of the rock, about four feet from the ground, gave me a very convenient pulpit. Here well-nigh the whole town, high and low, rich and poor, assembled together. Nor was there a word to be heard, or a smile seen, from one end of the congregation to the other. It was just the same the three following evenings. Indeed, I was afraid on *Saturday* that the roaring of the sea raised by the north wind would have prevented their hearing. But God gave me so clear and strong a voice that I believe scarce one word was lost.

Sunday, Sept. 14. At eight I chose a large ground, the sloping side of a meadow, where the congregation stood, row above row, so that all might see as well as hear. It was a beautiful sight. Every one seemed to take to himself what was spoken. I believe every backslider in the town was there. And surely God was there to "heal their backslidings." I began at Zennor, as soon as the Church-service was ended. I suppose scarce six persons went away. Seeing many there who did once run well, I addressed myself to them in particular. The spirit of mourning was soon poured out, and some of them wept bitterly. O that the Lord may yet return unto them, and "leave a blessing behind him!" At five I went once more into the ground of St. Ives and found such a congregation as I think was never seen in a place before (Gwennap excepted) in this country. Some of the chief of the town were now not in the skirts, but in the thickest of the people. The clear sky, the setting sun, the smooth, still water, all agreed with the state of the audience. Is any thing too hard for God? May we not say in every sense,

> Thou dost the raging sea control,
>   And smooth the prospect of the deep;
> Thou mak'st the sleeping billows roll,
>   Thou mak'st the rolling billows sleep!

Wesley Preaches Thirty Times in Eleven Days.

Monday, Sept. 22. I preached at Penryn in the evening. It rained before and after, but not while I was preaching. While we were at prayer a sheet of light seemed to fill the yard, and "the voice of the Lord" was heard over our heads. This fixed the impression they had received upon the minds of many, as if it had said in express terms, "Prepare to meet thy God!" On *Wednesday* evening, having (over and above meeting the societies) preached thirty times in eleven days, I found myself a little exhausted; but a day's rest set me up; so on *Friday, Sept.* 26, I preached at noon again near Liskeard. In the afternoon we had rain and wind enough, and when we came to Saltash no boat would venture out, so we were obliged to take up our lodgings there.

Meets the Children at Bristol.

Sunday, Oct. 12. I visited the classes at Kingswood. Here only there is no increase; and yet, where was there such a prospect till that weak man,

John Cennick, confounded the poor people with strange doctrines? O what mischief may be done by one that means well! We see no end of it to this day. In the afternoon I had appointed the children to meet at Bristol, whose parents were of the society. Thirty of came to-day, and above fifty more on the Sunday and Thursday following. About half of these I divided into four classes, two of boys and two of girls, and appointed proper leaders to meet them separate. I met them all together twice a week, and it was not long before God began to touch some of their hearts. On *Tuesday* and *Wednesday* I visited some of the societies in the country. On *Thursday* I returned to Bristol, and in the afternoon preached a charity sermon in Newgate for the use of the poor prisoners. On the three following days I spoke severally to the members of the society. As many of them increase in worldly goods, the great danger I apprehended now is their relapsing into the spirit-world, and then their religion is but a dream.

King George gathered to his Fathers.

Saturday, Oct. 25. King George was gathered to his fathers. When will England have a better prince? Many of us agreed to observe *Friday, Oct.* 31, as a day of fasting and prayer for the blessing of God upon our nation, and in particular on his present majesty. We met at five, at nine, at one, and at half hour past eight. I expected to be a little tired, but was more lively after twelve at night than I was at six in the morning.

Comforted by the Law.

Thursday, Jan. 22, 1761. We had our first watch-night at the Tabernacle, at which I could not but observe, though I preached the law from the beginning of my sermon to the end, yet many were exceedingly comforted. So plain is it that God can send either terror or comfort to the heart by whatever means it pleaseth him.

Chapels Filled on Fast-Day.

Monday, Feb. 9, and the following days, I visited the classes.

Friday, Feb. 13, being the general fast-day, the chapel in West-street, as well as the rest, was thoroughly filled with serious hearers. Surely God is well pleased with even these outward humiliations, as an acknowledgment that he is the Disposer of all events; and they give some check, if it be but for a time, to the floods of ungodliness. Besides, we cannot doubt but there are some good men in most of the congregations then assembled, and we know "the effectual fervent prayer," even of one "righteous man, availeth much."

The True Catholic Church.

The Catholic Church is, the whole body of men, endued with faith working by love, dispersed over the whole earth, in Europe, Asia, Africa, and America. And this Church is "ever one;" in all ages and nations it is the one body of Christ. It is "ever holy," for no unholy man can possibly be a member of it. It is "ever orthodox;" so is every holy man, in all things necessary to salvation, "secured against error" in things essential "by the perpetual presence of Christ, and ever directed by the Spirit of truth" in the truth that is after godliness. This Church has a "perpetual succession of Pastors and Teachers, divinely appointed and divinely assisted." And there has never been wanting in the Reformed Churches such a succession of Pastors and Teachers, men both divinely appointed and divinely assisted, for they convert sinners to God, a work none can do unless God himself doth appoint them thereto, and assist them therein; therefore, every part of this character is applicable to them. Their Teachers are the proper successors of those who have delivered down through all generations the faith once delivered to the saints, and their members have true spiritual communion with the "one holy" society of true believers; consequently, although they are not the whole "people of God," yet are they an undeniable part of his people.

On the contrary, the Church of Rome, in its present form, was not "founded by Christ himself." All the doctrines and practices wherein she differs from us were not instituted by Christ—they were unknown to the ancient Church of Christ—they are unscriptural, novel corruptions: neither is that Church "propagated throughout the world." Therefore, if either antiquity or universality be essential thereto, the Church of Rome cannot be "the true Church of Christ."

Nor is the Church of Rome one; it is not in unity with itself; it is to this day torn with numberless divisions. And it is impossible it should be "the one Church," unless a part can be the whole; seeing the Asiatic, the African, and the Muscovite Churches (to name no more) never were contained in it. Neither is it holy; the generality of its members are no holier than Turks or Heathens. You need not go far for proof of this; look at the Romanists in London or Dublin. Are these the holy, the only holy Church? Just such holiness is in the bottomless pit. Nor is it "secured against error" either "by Christ" or "his Spirit;" witness Pope against Pope, Council against Council, contradicting, anathematizing each other. The instances are too numerous to be recited.

Neither are the generality of her "Pastors and Teachers" either "divinely appointed" or "divinely assisted." If God had sent them he would confirm the word of his messengers; but he does not. They convert no sinners to God. They convert many to their own opinion, but not to the knowledge or love of God. He that was a drunkard is a drunkard still; he that was filthy is filthy still; therefore, neither are they "assisted by him; so they and their flocks wallow in sin together; consequently (whatever may be the case of some particular souls) it must be said, the Roman Catholics in general are not "the people of God."

Ready at a Moment's Notice.

May 4. About noon I took a walk to the King's College, in Old Aberdeen. It has three sides of a square, handsomely built, not unlike Queen's College in Oxford. Going up to see the hall, we found a large company of ladies, with several gentlemen. They looked and spoke to one another, after which one of the gentlemen took courage and came to me. He said, "We came last night to the college close, but could not hear, and should be extremely obliged if you would give us a short discourse here." I knew not what God might have to do, and so began without delay on, "God was in Christ reconciling the world unto himself." I believe the word was not lost; it fell as dew on the tender grass.

An Ancient Chapel.

May 16. About noon I preached at Warksworth to a congregation as quiet and attentive as that at Alnwick. How long shall we forget that God can raise the dead? Were not we dead till he quickened us? A little above the town, on one side of the river, stands the remains of a magnificent castle. On the other side, toward the bottom of a steep hill, covered with wood, is an ancient chapel, with several apartments adjoining to it, hewn in the solid rock. The windows, the pillars, the communion table, and several other parts, are entire. But where are the inhabitants? Gathered to their fathers, some of them, I hope, in Abraham's bosom, till rocks, and rivers, and mountains flee away, and the dead, small and great, stand before God!

Unfaithful Pastors.

Monday, May 25. I rode to Shields, and preached in an open place to a listening multitude. Many of them followed me to South Shields, where I preached in the evening to almost double the congregation. How ripe for the Gospel are these also! What is wanting but more laborers? More! Why is there not here (as in every parish in England) a particular minister, who takes care of all their souls? There is one here who takes *charge* of all their souls; what *care* of them he takes is another question. It may be he neither knows nor cares whether they are going to heaven or hell. Does he ask man, woman, or child any questions about it from one Christmas to the next? O what account will such a pastor give to the Great Shepherd in that day!

Wesley finds a Limit to his Physical Powers.

Monday, June 15. I rode to Durham, having appointed to preach there at noon. The meadow near the river side was quite convenient, and the small rain neither disturbed me nor the congregation. In the afternoon I rode to Hartlepool, but I had much ado to preach; my strength was gone as well as my voice, and, indeed, they generally go together. Three days in a week I can preach thrice a day without hurting myself; but I had now far exceeded this, besides meeting classes and exhorting the societies. I was obliged to lie down a good part of *Tuesday;* however, in the afternoon I preached at Cherington, and in the evening at Hartlepool again, though not without difficulty.

Wednesday, June 17. I rode to Stockton, where, a little before the time of preaching, my voice and strength were restored at once. The next evening it began to rain just as I began to preach; but it was suspended till the service was over. It then rained again till eight in the morning.

Two Bands of Children.

Monday, June 22. I spoke, one by one, to the society at Hutton Rugby. They were about eighty in number, of whom near seventy were believers, and sixteen (probably) renewed in love. Here were two bands of children, one of boys and one of girls, most of whom were walking in the light. Four of those who seemed to be saved from sin were of one family, and all of them walked holy and unblamable, adorning the doctrine of God their Saviour.

Conversion of a Condemned Criminal.

Wednesday, Oct. 21. I was desired by the condemned prisoners to give them one sermon more. And on *Thursday*, Patrick Ward, who was to die on that day, sent to request I would administer the sacrament to him. He was one-and-twenty years of age, and had scarce ever had a serious thought till he shot the man who went to take away his gun. From that instant he felt a turn within, and never swore an oath more. His whole behavior in prison was serious and composed; he read, prayed, and wept much, especially after one of his fellow-prisoners had found peace with God. His hope gradually increased till this day, and was much strengthened at the Lord's Supper; but still he complained, " I am not afraid, but I am not desirous to die. I do not find that warmth in my heart; I am not sure my sins are forgiven." He went into the cart about twelve, in calmness, but mixed with sadness. But in a quarter of an hour, while he was wrestling with God in prayer, (not seeming to know that any one was near him,) "The Holy Ghost," said he, "came upon me, and I knew that Christ was mine." From that moment his whole deportment breathed a peace and joy beyond all utterance till, after having spent about ten minutes in private prayer, he gave the sign.

"A Fool of a Saint."

December. Preaching at Deptford, Welling, and Sevenoaks, in my way, on *Thursday, December* 3, I came to Shoreham. There I read the celebrated "Life of St. Katharine, of Genoa." Mr. Lesley calls one a devil of a saint; I am sure this was a fool of a saint; that is, if it was not the folly of the historian, who has aggrandized her into a mere idiot. Indeed, we seldom find a saint of God's making sainted by the Bishop of Rome.

Perseverance Rewarded.

Wednesday, March 30, 1762. Having been invited to preach at Wem, Mrs. Glynne desired she might take me thither in a post-chaise; but in little more than an hour we were fast enough; however, the horses pulled till the traces broke. I should then have walked on had I been alone, though the mud was deep, and the snow drove impetuously; but I could not leave my friend, so I waited patiently till the man had made shift to mend the traces, and the horses pulled amain; so that with much ado, not long after the time appointed, I came to Wem.

I came, but the person who invited me was gone; gone out of town at four in the morning, and I could find no one who seemed either to expect or desire my company. I inquired after the place where Mr.

Mather preached, but it was filled with hemp. It remained only to go into the market-house, but neither any man, woman, nor child cared to follow us, the north wind roared so loud on every side, and poured in from every quarter. However, before I had done singing two or three crept in, and after them two or three hundred; and the power of God was so present among them that I believe many forgot the storm. The wind grew still higher in the afternoon, so that it was difficult to sit our horses; and it blew full in our face, but could not prevent our reaching Chester in the evening. Though the warning was short, the room was full; and full of serious, earnest hearers, many of whom expressed a longing desire of the whole salvation of God.

Absolution no Antidote to the Fear of Death.

July 6. In the evening I preached at Waterford, in a court adjoining to the main street.

Wednesday, July 7. Four of the Whiteboys, lately condemned for breaking open houses, were executed. They were all, notwithstanding the absolution of their priest, ready to die for fear of death. Two or three of them laid fast hold on the ladder, and could not be persuaded to let it go. One in particular gave such violent shrieks as might be heard near a mile off. O what but love can cast out the fear of death! And how inexpressibly miserable is that bondage! On this and the two following days God remembered poor Waterford also. Several backsliders were healed, and many awoke out of sleep; and some mightily rejoiced in God their Saviour.

"Be silent, or begone."

July 11. At six in the evening I began preaching in the old Bowling Green near the castle. Abundance of people, Protestants and Papists, gathered from all parts. They were very still during the former part of the sermon; then the Papists ran together, set up a shout, and would have gone further, but they were restrained, they knew not how. I turned to them and said, "Be silent, or begone!" Their noise ceased, and we heard them no more; so I resumed and went on with my discourse, and concluded without interruption. When I came out of the Green they gathered again, and gnashed upon me with their teeth; one cried out, "O what is Kilkenny come to!" But they could go no further. Only two or three large stones were thrown, but none was hurt, save he that threw them; for as he was going to throw again, one seized him by the neck and gave him a kick and a cuff, which spoiled his diversion.

Poor dead Portarlington.

Saturday, July 17. I went on to poor dead Portarlington. And no wonder it should be so, while the preachers coop themselves up in a room with twenty or thirty hearers. I went straight to the market-place and cried aloud, "Hearken! Behold a sower went forth to sow." God made his word quick and powerful, and sharp as a two-edged sword. Abundantly more than the room could contain were present at five in the morning. At eight I began in the market-place again on, "How shall I give thee up, Ephraim?" Solemn attention sat on every face, and

God repeated his call to many hearts. In the evening I preached in the market-place at Tullamore.

Monday, July 19. Between two and three in the morning was such thunder and lightning as I never knew in Europe. The crack and the flash were in the same instant. Most of the houses shook, and yet no hurt was done in the whole town; but some good was done, for at five o'clock the preaching-house was quite filled, and the inward voice of the Lord was mighty in operation. This also was "a glorious voice."

The Work of Holiness in Dublin and London.

July. On examination I found three or four-and-forty in Dublin who seemed to enjoy the pure love of God; at least forty of these had been set at liberty within four months. Some others, who had received the same blessing, were removed out of the city. The same, if not a larger number, had found remission of sins. Nor was the hand of the Lord shortened yet: he still wrought as swiftly as ever.

In some respects the work of God in this place was more remarkable than even that in London. 1. It is far greater in proportion to the time and to the number of people. That society had above seven-and-twenty hundred members; this not a fifth part of the number. Six months after the flame broke out there we had about thirty witnesses of the great salvation. In Dublin there were above forty in less than four months. 2. The work was more pure. In all this time, while they were mildly and tenderly treated, there were none of them headstrong or unadvisable; none that were wiser than their teachers; none who dreamed of being immortal or infallible, or incapable of temptation ; in short, no whimsical or enthusiastic persons; all were calm and sober-minded. I know several of these were, in process of time, moved from their steadfastness. I am nothing surprised at this ; it was no more than might be expected ; I rather wonder that more were not moved. Nor does this, in any degree, alter my judgment concerning the great work which God then wrought.

Wesley's old opponent, the Bishop of Lavington.

Sunday, Aug. 29. I preached at eight on Southernay Green to an extremely quiet congregation. At the cathedral we had a useful sermon, and the whole service was performed with great seriousness and decency. Such an organ I never saw or heard before, so large, beautiful, and so finely toned ; and the music of "Glory be to God in the highest," I think, exceeded the Messiah itself. I was well pleased to partake of the Lord's Supper with my old opponent, Bishop Lavington. O may we sit down together in the kingdom of our Father! At five I went to Southernay Green again, and found a multitude of people ; but a lewd, profane, drunken vagabond had so stirred up many of the baser sort that there was much noise, hurry, and confusion. While I was preaching several things were thrown, and much pains taken to overturn the table ; and, after I concluded, many endeavored to throw me down, but I walked through the midst and left them.

Pretty Butterflies.

Tuesday, Sept. 14. I preached in Lelan about one, and in the evening near the Quay at St. Ives. Two or three pretty butterflies came, and looked, and smiled, and went away; but all the rest of the numerous congregation behaved with the utmost seriousness.

How Believers suffer Loss.

Wednesday, Sept. 15. We had our quarterly meeting. The next day I appointed the children to meet; I expected twenty, but I suppose we had fourscore, all of them wanting, many desiring, instruction. The more I converse with the believers in Cornwall the more I am convinced that they have sustained great loss for want of hearing the doctrine of Christian perfection clearly and strongly enforced. I see wherever this is not done the believers grow dead and cold. Nor can this be prevented but by keeping up in them an hourly expectation of being perfected in love. I say an hourly expectation, for to expect it at death, or some time hence, is much the same as not expecting it at all.

No more Cheating the King.

September. The night came on soon after we were on horseback, and we had eight miles to ride. In about half an hour it was so dark I could not see my hand, and it rained incessantly. However, a little after eight God brought us safe to Cubert. I preached at the Church Town the next day, and on *Tuesday*, 21, rode on to Port Isaac. Here the stewards of the eastern circuit met. What a change is wrought in one year's time! The detestable practice of cheating the King is no more found in our societies. And since that accursed thing has been put away, the work of God has every-where increased. This society in particular is more than doubled, and they are all alive to God.

Wesley Guided by his own Conscience.

Monday, Nov. 8. I began visiting the classes, in many of which we had hot spirits to deal with. Some were vehement for, some against, the meetings for prayer, which were in several parts of the town. I said little, being afraid of taking any step which I might afterward repent of. One I heard of on Friday, and five on Saturday, who, if I did not act as they thought best, would leave the society. I cannot help it; I must still be guided by my own conscience.

Lives of eminent Romish Saints.

Monday, Nov. 29. I retired to transcribe my answer to Bishop Warburton. My fragments of time I employed in reading and carefully considering the Lives of Magdalen de Pazzi, and some other eminent Romish saints. I could not but observe, 1. That many things related therein are highly improbable. I fear the relators did not scruple lying for the Church, or for the credit of their order; 2. That many of their reputed virtues were really no virtues at all, being no fruits of the love of God or man, and no part of the mind which was in Christ Jesus; 3. That many of their applauded actions were neither commendable or imitable; 4. That what was really good in their tempers or lives was so deeply tinctured with enthusiasm, that most readers would be far more likely to receive hurt than good from these accounts of them.

Review of the Year.

Friday, Dec. 31. I now stood and looked back on the past year, a year of uncommon trials and uncommon blessings. Abundance have been convinced of sin, very many have found peace with God, and in London only, I believe, full two hundred have been brought into glorious liberty. And yet I have had more care and trouble in six months than in several years preceding. What the end will be I know not, but it is enough that God knoweth.

A Beautiful Reply.

Saturday, Jan. 1, 1763. A woman told me, "Sir, I employ several men. Now, if one of my servants will not follow my direction, is it not right for me to discard him at once? Pray, do you apply this to Mr. Bell?" I answered, "It is right to discard such a servant; but what would you do if he were your son?"

The World to End that Night.

Monday, Feb. 28. Preaching in the evening at Spitalfields on "Prepare to meet thy God," I largely showed the utter absurdity of the supposition that the world was to end that night. But notwithstanding all I could say many were afraid to go to bed, and some wandered about in the fields, being persuaded that if the world did not end, at least London would be swallowed up by an earthquake. I went to bed at my usual time, and was fast asleep about ten o'clock.

A brief Interview with Mr. Whitefield.

May. I went on at leisure, and came to Edinburgh on *Saturday, May* 21. The next day I had the satisfaction of spending a little time with Mr. Whitefield. Humanly speaking, he is worn out; but we have to do with Him who hath all power in heaven and earth.

Monday, May 23, I rode to Forfar, and on *Tuesday,* 24, rode on to Aberdeen.

A Congregation of Ministers, Nobility, and Gentry.

Sunday, May 29. I preached at seven in the High School-yard at Edinburgh. It being the time of the General Assembly, which drew together not the ministers only, but abundance of the nobility and gentry, many of both were present; but abundantly more at five in the afternoon. I spoke as plain as ever I did in my life. But I never knew any in Scotland offended at plain dealing. In this respect the North Britons are a pattern to all mankind.

The Right Construction.

Tuesday, June 6. So deep and general was the impression now made upon the people, that even at five in the morning I was obliged to preach abroad, by the numbers who flocked to hear, although the northerly wind made the air exceeding sharp. A little after preaching, one came to me who believed God had just set her soul at full liberty. She had been clearly justified long before; but said the change she now experienced was extremely different from what she experienced then, as different as the noon-day light from that of daybreak; that she now felt her soul all love, and quite swallowed up in God. Now suppose, ten weeks or ten months hence, this person should be cold or dead, shall I say, "She *deceived* herself; this was merely the work of her own imagination?" Not at all. I have no right so to judge, nor authority so to speak. I will rather say, "She was *unfaithful* to the grace of God, and so *cast away* what was *really given.*" Therefore that way of talking, which has been very common, of staying "to see if the gift be really given," which some take to be exceedingly wise, I take to be exceedingly foolish. If a man says, "I now feel nothing but love," and I know him to be an honest man, I believe him. What then should I stay to see? Not whether he *has* such a blessing, but whether he will keep it.

A new Error Counteracted.

Saturday, June 11. I rode to Epworth, and preached at seven in the market-place.

Sunday, June 12. I preached at the room in the morning; in the afternoon, at the market-place; and about one the congregation gathered from all parts in Haxey parish, near Westwood-side. At every place I endeavored to settle the minds of the poor people, who had been not a little harassed by a new doctrine which honest Jonathan C—— and his converts had industriously propagated among them, that "there is no sin in believers." I trust that this plague is also stayed; but how ought these unstable ones to be ashamed who are so easily "tossed about with every wind of doctrine!"

Association and Training Necessary.

Wednesday, Aug. 24. I rode over to Haverfordwest. Finding it was the Assize week, I was afraid the bulk of the people would be too busy to think about hearing sermons. But I was mistaken; I have not seen so numerous a congregation since I set out of London; and they were, one and all, deeply attentive. Surely some will bring forth fruit.

Thursday, Aug. 25. I was more convinced than ever that the preaching like an apostle, without joining together those that are awakened, and training them up in the ways of God, is only begetting children for the murderer. How much preaching has there been for these twenty years all over Pembrokeshire! But no regular societies, no discipline, no order or connection; and the consequence is, that nine in ten of the once-awakened are now faster asleep than ever.

Satan makes Use of Honest, but Ignorant Christians.

Saturday, Aug. 27. I preached at seven to one or two hundred people, many of whom seemed full of good desires. But as there is no society, I expect no deep or lasting work. Mr. Evans now gave me an account from his own knowledge of what has made a great noise in Wales: "It is common in the congregations attended by Mr. W. W., and one or two other clergymen, after the preaching is over, for any one that has a mind, to give out a verse of a hymn. This they sing over and over with all their might, perhaps above thirty, yea, forty times. Meanwhile the bodies of two or three, sometimes ten or twelve, are violently agitated, and they leap up and down, in all manner of postures, frequently for hours together."

I think there needs no great penetration to understand this. They are honest, upright men, who really feel the love of God in their hearts. But they have little experience, either of the ways of God or the devices of Satan. So he serves himself of their simplicity in order to wear them out, and to bring a discredit on the work of God. About two I preached at Cowbridge in the Assembly-room, and then went on to Llandaff. The congregation was waiting, so I began without delay, explaining to them the righteousness of faith. A man had need to be all fire who comes into these parts, where almost every one is cold as ice; yet God is able to warm their hearts and make rivers run in the dry places.

The Poison of Mysticism.

Sunday, Aug. 28. I preached once more in W—— Church, but it was hard work. Mr. H. read the prayers (not as he did once, with such fervor and solemnity as struck almost every hearer, but) like one reading an old song, in a cold, dry, careless manner, and there was no singing at all. Thence I rode to Cardiff, and found the society in as ruinous a condition as the castle. The same poison of Mysticism has well-nigh extinguished the last spark of life here also. I preached in the Town Hall on "Now God commanded all men every-where to repent." There was a little shaking among the dry bones; possibly some of them may yet "come together and live."

No other Way to Reach the Outcasts.

Sunday, Sept. 4. I preached on the quay, when multitudes attended who would not have come to the other end of the city. In the afternoon I preached near the new square. I find no other way to reach the outcasts of men. And this way God has owned, and does still own, both by the conviction and conversion of sinners.

Saturday, Sept. 17. I preached on the Green at Bedminster. I am apt to think that many of the hearers scarce ever heard a Methodist before, or perhaps any other preacher. What but field preaching could reach these poor sinners? And are not their souls also precious in the sight of God?

Renewing the Covenant.

Monday, Dec. 26. I began preaching at a large commodious place in Bartholomew Close. I preached there again on *Wednesday*, and at both times with peculiar liberty of spirit. At every place this week I endeavored to prepare our brethren for renewing their covenant with God.

Sunday, Jan. 1, 1764. We met in the evening for that solemn purpose. I believe the number of those that met was considerably larger than it was last year. And so was the blessing: truly the consolations of God were not small with us. Many were filled with peace and joy, many with holy fear, and several backsliders were healed. On some of the following days I visited the little societies near London.

Thursday, Jan. 12. I preached at Mitcham, and in the afternoon rode to Dorking. But the gentleman to whose house I was invited seemed to have no desire I should preach. So that evening I had nothing to do.

Friday, Jan. 13. I went at noon into the street, and in a broad place, not far from the market-place, proclaimed "the grace of our Lord Jesus Christ." At first two or three little children were the whole of my congregation; but it quickly increased, though the air was sharp and the ground exceedingly wet, and all behaved well but three or four grumbling men, who stood so far off that they disturbed none but themselves. I had purposed to preach there again in the morning; but a violent storm made it impracticable. So, after preaching at Mitcham in the way, I rode back to London.

Wesley preaches the Terrors of the Lord.

Thursday, Jan. 19. I rode through Oxford to Henley. The people here bear no resemblance to those of Witney. I found a wild, staring congregation, many of them void both of common sense and common decency. I spoke exceedingly plain to them all, and reproved some of them sharply.

Friday, Jan. 20. I took (probably my final) leave of Henley, and returned to London.

Monday, Jan. 23. I rode to Sundon, and preached in the evening to a very quiet and very stupid people. How plain is it, that even to enlighten the understanding is beyond the power of man! After all our preaching here, even those who have constantly attended no more understand us than if he had preached in Greek.

Thursday, Jan. 26. Returning from Bedford, I tried another way to reach them. I preached on "Where their worm dieth not, and the fire is not quenched;" and set before them the terrors of the Lord in the strongest manner I was able. It seemed to be the very thing they wanted. They not only listened with the deepest attention, but appeared to be more affected than I had ever seen them by any discourse whatever.

Wesley's Objection to the Mystic Writers.

Sunday, Feb. 5. I began Mr. Hartley's ingenious "Defense of the Mystic Writers." But it does not satisfy me. I must still object, 1. To their sentiment. The chief of them do not appear to me to have any conception of Church communion. Again, they slight not only works of piety, the ordinances of God, but even works of mercy. And yet most of them, yea, all that I have seen, hold justification by works. In general, they are "wise above what is written," indulging themselves in many unscriptural speculations. I object, 2. To their spirit, that most of them are of a dark, shy, reserved, unsociable temper; and that they are apt to despise all who differ from them, as carnal unenlightened men. I object, 3. To their whole phraseology. It is both unscriptural and affectedly mysterious. I say affectedly, for this does not necessarily result from the nature of the things spoken of. St. John speaks as high and as deep things as Jacob Behmen. Why, then, does not Jacob speak as plain as him?

Criticism on an Oratorio.

Friday, Feb. 24. I returned to London.

Wednesday, Feb. 29. I heard "Judith," an Oratorio, performed at the Lock. Some parts of it were exceeding fine; but there are two things in all modern pieces of music which I could never reconcile to common sense: one is, singing the same words ten times over; the other, singing different words by different persons, at one and the same time. And this in the most solemn addresses to God, whether by way of prayer or thanksgiving. This can never be defended by all the musicians of Europe till reason is quite out of date.

A Token for Good.

Monday, March 26. I was desired to preach at Walsal. James Jones was alarmed at the motion, apprehending there would be much disturbance. However, I determined to make the trial. Coming into the house, I met with a token for good. A woman was telling her neighbor why she came: "I had a desire," said she, "to hear this man, yet I durst not, because I heard so much ill of him; but this morning I dreamed I was praying earnestly, and I heard a voice saying, 'See the eighth verse of the first chapter of St. John.' I waked, and got my Bible and read, 'He was not that light, but was sent to bear witness of that light.' I got up, and came away with all my heart."

An Odd Circumstance.

Saturday, March 31. An odd circumstance occurred during the morning preaching. It was well only serious persons were present. An ass walked gravely in at the gate, came up to the door of the house, lifted up his head, and stood stock still in a position of deep attention. Might not "the dumb beast reprove" many who have far less decency and not much more understanding?

A Wise Choice.

Thursday, April 5. About eleven I preached at Elsham. The two persons who are the most zealous and active here are the steward and gardener of a gentleman whom the minister persuaded to turn them off unless they would leave "his way." He gave them a week to consider of it; at the end of which they answered, "Sir, we choose rather to want bread here than to want 'a drop of water' hereafter." He replied, "Then follow your own conscience, so you do my business as well as formerly."

Wesley thrown from his Horse.

Friday, April 6. I preached at Ferry at nine in the morning and in the evening, and about noon in Sir N. H.'s hall at Gainsborough. Almost as soon as I began to speak a cock began to crow over my head; but he was quickly dislodged, and the whole congregation, rich and poor, were quiet and attentive.

Sunday, April 8. I set out for Misterton, though the common road was impassable, being all under water; but we found a way to ride round. I preached at eight, and I saw not one inattentive hearer. In our return, my mare, rushing violently through a gate, struck my heel against the gate-post, and left me behind her in an instant, laid on my back at full length. She stood still till I rose and mounted again; and neither of us was hurt at all.

High time to Prophesy on the Dry Bones.

Wednesday, April 11. Between eight and nine I began preaching at Beverley, in a room which is newly taken. It was filled from end to end, and that with serious hearers. Perhaps even these may know the day of their visitation. About one I began at Pocklington. Here, likewise, all were quiet, and listened with deep attention. When I came to York, at five in the afternoon, I was fresher than at seven in the morning. During the preaching many were not a little comforted; and one old follower of Christ, more than seventy years of age, was now first enabled to call him Lord by the Holy Ghost. I found that a most remarkable deadness had overspread this people, insomuch that not one had received remission of sins for several months last past. Then it is high time for us to prophesy on these dry bones, that they may live. At this I more immediately pointed in all my following discourses, and I have reason to believe God spoke in his word. To him be all the glory!

A Cold Reception explained.

April 17. In consequence of repeated invitations I rode to Helmsley. When I came Mr. Conyers was not at home; but, his housekeeper faintly asking me, I went in. By the books lying in the window and on the table, I easily perceived how he came to be so cold now who was so warm a year ago. Not one of ours, either verse or prose, was to be seen, but several of another kind. O that our brethren were as zealous to make *Christians* as they are to make *Calvinists!* He came home before dinner, and soon convinced me that the Philistines had been upon him. They had taken huge pains to prejudice him against me, and so successfully, that he did not even ask me to preach, so I had thoughts of going on; but in the afternoon he altered his purpose, and I preached in the evening to a large congregation. He seemed quite surprised, and was convinced *for the present* that things had been misrepresented. But how long will the conviction last? Perhaps till next month.

Christian Resignation.

Saturday, April 21. I visited one who was ill in bed; and, after having buried seven of her family in six months, had just heard that the eighth, her beloved husband, was cast away at sea. I asked, "Do not you fret at any of those things?" She said, with a lovely smile upon her pale cheek, "O no! How can I fret at any thing which is the will of God? Let him take all besides: he has given me himself. I love, I praise him every moment." Let any that doubts of Christian Perfection look on such a spectacle as this! One in such circumstances rejoicing evermore, and continually giving thanks.

Beginning at the Wrong End.

Monday, May 21. I took my leave of Newcastle, and about noon preached in the market-place at Morpeth. A few of the hearers were a little ludicrous at first; but their mirth was quickly spoiled. In the evening I preached in the court-house at Alnwick, where I rested the next day.

Wednesday, May 23. I rode over the sands to Holy Island, once the famous seat of a Bishop, now the residence of a few poor families, who live chiefly by fishing. At one side of the town are the ruins of a cathedral, with an adjoining monastery. It appears to have been a lofty and elegant building, the middle aisle being almost entire. I preached, in what was once the market-place, to almost all the inhabitants of the island, and distributed some little books among them, for which they were exceeding thankful. In the evening I preached at Berwick-upon-Tweed; the next evening at Dunbar; and on *Friday, May* 25, about ten, at Haddington, in Provost D.'s yard, to a very elegant congregation. But I expect little good will be done here, for we begin at the wrong end; religion must not go from the greatest to the least, or the power would appear to be of men. In the evening I preached at Musselborough, and the next on the Calton Hill at Edinburgh. It being the time of the General Assembly, many of the ministers were there. The wind was high and sharp, and blew away a few delicate ones. But most of the congregation did not stir till I had concluded.

Edinburgh General Assembly.

Monday, May 28. I spent some hours at the General Assembly, composed of about a hundred and fifty ministers. I was surprised to find, 1. That any one was admitted, even lads, twelve or fourteen years old. 2. That the chief speakers were lawyers, six or seven on one side only. 3. That a single question took up the whole time, which, when I went away, seemed to be as far from a conclusion as ever, namely, "Shall Mr. Lindsay be removed to Kilmarnock parish or not?" The argument for it was, "He has a large family, and this living is twice as good as his own." The argument against it was, "The people are resolved not to hear him, and will leave the kirk if he comes." If, then, the real point in view had been, as their law directs, *majus bonum Ecclesiæ,* [the greater good of the Church,] instead of taking up five hours, the debate might have been determined in five minutes. On *Monday* and *Tuesday* I spoke to the members of the society severally.

Thursday, May 31. I rode to Dundee, and, about half an hour after six, preached on the side of a meadow near the town. Poor and rich attended. Indeed, there is seldom fear of wanting a congregation in Scotland. But the misfortune is, they know every thing; so they learn nothing.

Wesley's Treatment of Bankrupts.

Monday, July 2. I gave a fair hearing to two of our brethren who had proved bankrupts. Such we immediately exclude from our society, unless it plainly appears not to be their own fault. Both these were in a prosperous way till they fell into that wretched trade of bill-broking, wherein no man continues long without being wholly ruined. By this means, not being sufficiently accurate in their accounts, they ran back without being sensible of it. Yet it was quite clear that J— R— is an honest man. I would hope the same concerning the other.

A Peculiarity in Mr. Wesley.

Tuesday, July 3. I was reflecting on an odd circumstance, which I cannot account for. I never relish a tune at first hearing, not till I have almost learned to sing it; and, as I learn it more perfectly, I gradually lose my relish for it. I observe something similar in poetry; yea, in all the objects of imagination. I seldom relish verses at first hearing; till I have heard them over and over, they give me no pleasure; and they give next to none when I have heard them a few times more, so as to be quite familiar. Just so, a face or a picture which does not strike me at first becomes more pleasing as I grow more acquainted with it; but only to a certain point, for when I am too much acquainted it is no longer pleasing. O how imperfectly do we understand even the machine which we carry about us!

A Sharp Appeal to a Retreating Hearer.

Thursday, July 5. I had the comfort of leaving our brethren at Leeds united in peace and love. About one I preached in a meadow at Wakefield. At first the sun was inconvenient; but it was not many minutes before that inconvenience was removed by the clouds coming between. We had not only a larger, but a far more attentive, congregation than ever was seen here before. One, indeed, a kind of gentleman, was walking away with great unconcern, when I spoke aloud, "Does Gallio care for none of these things? But where will you go, with the wrath of God on your head, and the curse of God on your back?" He stopped short, stood still, and went no further till the sermon was ended.

Wesley preaches three times a Day for ten Days in succession.

Saturday, July 7. I rode to Huddersfield, and preached between eleven and twelve. At half after one we took horse. The sun shone burning hot, and the wind was in our back; but very soon the sky was overcast, and the wind changed and blew just in our face all the way to Manchester. It was with difficulty that I preached in the evening, my voice being exceedingly weak; as I had preached three times a day for ten days, and many of the times abroad.

Danger of Riches.

Wednesday, July 11. I gave all our brethren a solemn warning not to love the world or the things of the world. This is one way whereby Satan will surely endeavor to overthrow the present work of God. Riches swiftly increase on many Methodists, so called; what but the mighty power of God can hinder them setting their hearts upon them? and if so, the life of God vanishes away.

Nothing in the House but a Dram of Gin.

July 31. Gower is a large tract of land bounded by Brecknockshire on the northeast, the sea on the southwest, and rivers on the other sides. Here all the people talk English, and are in general the most plain and loving people in Wales. It is, therefore. no wonder that they received "the word with all readiness of mind." Knowing that they were scattered up and down, I had sent two persons on Sunday, that they might be there early on Monday, and so sent notice of my coming all over the country; but they came to Oxwych scarce a quarter of an hour before me, so that the poor people had no notice at all; nor was there any to take us in, the person with whom the preacher used to lodge being three miles out of town. After I had stayed a while in the street, (for there was no public house,) a poor woman gave me house room. Having had nothing since breakfast, I was very willing to eat or drink; but she simply told me she had nothing in the house but a dram of gin. However, I afterward procured a dish of tea at another house, and was much refreshed. About seven I preached to a little company, and again in the morning. They were all attention, so that even for the sake of this handful of people I did not regret my labor.

English Law on Church Consecration.

Monday, Aug. 20. I went to Canterbury, and opened our new chapel by preaching on "One thing is needful." How is it that many Protestants, even in England, do not know that no other consecration of church or chapel is allowed, much less required, in England than the performance of public worship therein? This is the only consecration of any church in Great Britain which is necessary, or even lawful. It is true, Archbishop Laud composed a form of consecration; but it was never allowed, much less established, in England. Let this be remembered by all who talk so idly of preaching in unconsecrated places!

Wesley hooked into a little Dispute.

Tuesday, Oct. 9. I was desired to meet Mr. B., and we had a good deal of conversation together. He seems to be a person of middling sense, but a most unpleasing address. I would hope he has some little experience of religion, but it does not appear to advantage, as he is extremely hot, impetuous, overbearing, and impatient of contradiction. He hooked me, unawares, into a little dispute; but I cut it short as soon as possible, knowing neither was likely to convince the other. So we met and parted in peace.

Transitions in the Norwich Society.

Friday, Oct. 12. I returned to Norwich and inquired into the state of the society. I have seen no people in all England or Ireland so changeable as this. This society, in 1755, consisted of eighty-three members; two years after, of a hundred and thirty-four; in 1758 it was shrunk to a hundred and ten. In March, 1759, we took the Tabernacle, and within a month the society was increased to above seven hundred and sixty. But nearly five hundred of these had formerly been with James Wheatley, and having been scattered abroad, now ran together, they hardly knew why. Few of them were thoroughly awakened, most deeply ignorant; all bullocks unaccustomed to the yoke, having never had any rule or order among them, but every man doing what was right in his own eyes. It was not therefore strange that the next year only five hundred and seven of these were left. In 1761 they were further reduced, namely, to four hundred and twelve. I cannot tell how it was that, in 1762, they were increased again to six hundred and thirty. But the moon soon changed, so that, in 1763, they were shrunk to three hundred and ten. This large reduction was owing to the withdrawing the sacrament, to which they had been accustomed from the time the Tabernacle was built. They are now sunk to a hundred and seventy-four, and now probably the tide will turn again.

The right kind of Pupils.

Thursday, Nov. 8. At ten (and so every morning) I met the preachers that were in town, and read over with them the "Survey of the Wisdom of God in the Creation." Many pupils I had at the University, and I took some pains with them, but to what effect? What is become of them now? How many of them think either of their tutor or their God? But, blessed be God! I have had some pupils since who well reward me for my labor. Now "I live;" for "ye stand fast in the Lord."

The Power of Prejudice.

Monday, Nov. 12. I retired to Hoxton to answer what was personal in the letters ascribed to Mr. Hervey. How amazing is the power of prejudice! Were it not for this, every one who knew him and me would have cried out with indignation, "Whatever Mr. W. was, none can commend or excuse Mr. H. Such bitterness he ought not to have shown to his most cruel enemy; how much less to the guide of his youth, to one he owns to have been his 'father and his friend!'"

"As so many drops of Blood."

Monday, Nov. 19, and the other afternoons of this week, I took up my cross, and went in person to the principal persons in our society in every part of the town. By this means, within six days, near six hundred pounds were subscribed toward the public debt; and what was done, was done with the utmost cheerfulness. I remember but one exception; only one gentleman squeezed out ten shillings, as so many drops of blood.

Majestic in Decay.

Saturday, Dec. 8. I saw one who, many years ago, was a "minister of God to us for good" in repressing the madness of the people: Sir John Gonson, who was near fifty years a magistrate, and has lived more than ninety. He is majestic in decay, having few wrinkles, and not stooping at all, though just dropping into the grave, having no strength, and little memory or understanding. Well might that good man, Bishop Stratford, pray, "Lord, let me not live to be useless!" And he had his desire; he was struck with a palsy in the evening, praised God all night, and died in the morning.

Monday, Dec. 10, and the three following days, I visited Canterbury, Dover, and Sandwich, and returned to London on *Friday*, 14. In the machine I read Mr. Baxter's book upon apparitions. It contains several well-attested accounts, but there are some which I cannot subscribe to. How hard is it to keep the middle way; not to believe too little or too much!

Three Young Men Prostrated.

Monday, March 18, 1765. I rode to Stroud, and in the evening preached in the new house. But a considerable part of the congregation were obliged to stand without. Toward the close of the sermon a young man dropped down and vehemently cried to God. This occasioned a little hurry at first, but it was soon over, and all was quiet as before. After supper I was speaking a little, when a young gentleman cried out, "I am damned!" and fell to the ground. A second did so quickly after, and was much convulsed, and yet quite sensible. We joined in prayer, but had not time (it growing late) to wrestle with God for their full deliverance.

Afraid of Honor.

Sunday, May 12. At eight I preached in Derry to a large number of people. About eleven Mr. Knox went with me to church, and led me to a pew where

I was placed next the Mayor. What is this? What have I to do with honor? Lord, let me always *fear*, not *desire* it. The afternoon service was not over till about half an hour past six. At seven I preached to near all the inhabitants of the city. I think there was scarce one who did not feel that God was there. So general an impression upon a congregation I have hardly seen in any place.

Monday, May 13, and the following days, I had leisure to go on with the Notes on the Old Testament. But I wondered at the situation I was in, in the midst of rich and honorable men! Whilst this lasts it is well. And it will be well too when any or all of them change their countenance,

"And wonder at the strange man's face
As one they ne'er had known."

Extract from a Letter on Perfection.

May. But how came this opinion into my mind? I will tell you with all simplicity. In 1725 I met with Bishop Taylor's "Rules of Holy Living and Dying." I was struck particularly with the chapter upon *intention*, and felt a fixed intention "to give myself up to God." In this I was much confirmed soon after by the "Christian Pattern," and longed to give God all my heart. This is just what I mean by Perfection now; I sought after it from that hour.

In 1727 I read Mr. Law's "Christian Perfection" and "Serious Call," and more explicitly resolved to be all devoted to God in body, soul, and spirit. In 1730 I began to be *homo unius libri*, [a man of One Book;] to study (comparatively) no book but the Bible. I then saw, in a stronger light than ever before, that only one thing is needful, even faith that worketh by the love of God and man, all inward and outward holiness; and I groaned to love God with all my heart, and to serve him with all my strength.

January 1, 1733, I preached the sermon on the Circumcision of the Heart, which contains all that I now teach concerning salvation from all sin, and loving God with an undivided heart. In the same year I printed, (the first time I ventured to print any thing,) for the use of my pupils, 'A Collection of Forms of Prayer;' and in this I spoke explicitly of giving "the whole heart and the whole life to God." This was then, as it is now, my idea of Perfection, though I should have started at the word.

In 1735 I preached my farewell sermon at Epworth, in Lincolnshire. In this likewise I spoke with the utmost clearness of having one design, one desire, one love, and of pursuing the one end of our life in all our words and actions.

In January, 1738, I expressed my desire in these words:

> "O grant that nothing in my soul
>   May dwell but thy pure love alone!
> O may thy love possess me whole,
>   My joy, my treasure, and my crown!
> Strange flames far from my heart remove:
> My every act, word, thought, be love."

And I am still persuaded this is what the Lord Jesus hath bought for me with his own blood.

Now, whether you desire and expect this blessing or not, is it not an astonishing thing that you, or any man living, should be disgusted at me for expecting it; and that they should persuade one another that this hope is "subversive of the very foundations of

Christian experience?" Why, then, whoever retains it cannot possibly have any Christian experience at all. Then my brother, Mr. Fletcher, and I, and twenty thousand more, who seem to fear and to love God, are, in reality, children of the devil, and in the road to eternal damnation!

In God's name I entreat you make me sensible of this! Show me by plain, strong reasons what dishonor this hope does to Christ, wherein it opposes justification by faith, or any fundamental truth of religion. But do not wrest, and wire-draw, and color my words, as Mr. Hervey (or Cudworth) has done, in such a manner, that when I look in that glass I do not know my own face! "Shall I call you," says Mr. Hervey, "my father or my friend? For you have been both to me." So I was, and you have as well requited me! It is well my reward is with the Most High.

Wishing all happiness to you and yours, I am, dear sir, your affectionate brother and servant,

JOHN WESLEY.

Mr. Seed's Sermons.

Thursday, May 23. Lighting on a volume of Mr. Seed's sermons, I was utterly surprised. Where did this man lie hid, that I never heard of him all the time I was at Oxford? His language is pure in the highest degree, his apprehension clear, his judgment strong. And for true manly wit, and exquisite turns of thought, I know not if this century has produced his equal.

Honor and Dishonor balance each other.

Tuesday, May 28. We breakfasted at Ballyshannon, I believe the largest and pleasantest town in the county. Beyond it a good-natured man overtook me, with whom I talked largely and closely. He seemed much affected ; if it continues, well ; if not, I am clear of his blood. About twelve we stopped at a little house, but a cloud of smoke soon drove us out of the first room into another, where the landlord lay with a grievously bruised and swelled leg. I directed him how to cure it, and thence took occasion to give him some further advice. Several eagerly listened as well as himself. Perhaps some will remember it.

In the evening I took my usual stand in the market-house, at Sligo; but here how was the scene changed! I have seen nothing like this since my first entrance into the kingdom. Such a total want of good sense, of good manners, yea, of common decency, was shown by not a few of the hearers! It is good to visit Sligo after Londonderry ; honor and dishonor balance each other.

"Every bullet has its billet."

Thursday, June 6. I was brought on my way by Lieutenant Cook, who was in all the actions at Fort William Henry, at Louisbourg, Quebec, Martinico, and the Havannah, and gave a more distinct account of those eminent scenes of providence than ever I heard before. Although he was so often in the front of the battle, both against Indians, French, and Spaniards, and in the hottest fire, both advancing and retreating, he never received one wound. So true is the odd saying of King William, that "every bullet has its billet." Between five and six we reached Ennis, after a warm day, which much exhausted my strength ; but it was soon repaired, and the serious, well-behaved congregation (though many of them were people of fortune) made amends for the turbulent one at Galway. Such is the checker-work of life!

All the Town begs for a Sermon.

Tuesday, June 18. The town seemed to be all alive a little after four o'clock; so, finding the congregation ready, I began a little before five. A cry soon arose of young and old, on the right hand and on the left, but in many it was not so much the voice of sorrow as of joy and triumph. A fair beginning this! But who can tell what the end will be? About nine we rode through Doneraile, one of the pleasantest towns in the kingdom; but a man came galloping after us and said, "All the town begs you will stop and give them a sermon." I turned back, and took my stand in the main street. Men, women, and children flocked from all sides. There was no disturbance of any kind, while I declared "the grace of our Lord Jesus Christ." Fair blossoms again! And who knows but some of these may bring forth fruit unto perfection? In the evening I came to Cork, and at seven was surprised at the unusual largeness of the congregation. I had often been grieved at the smallness of the congregation here, and it could be no other while we cooped ourselves up in the house. But now the alarm is sounded abroad, people flock from all quarters. So plain it is that field-preaching is the most effectual way of overturning Satan's kingdom.

Sir Richard Cox's History of Ireland.

Wednesday, July 10. I preached at Clara about noon, and in the evening at Athlone. The two next evenings I preached in the market-house for the sake of the Papists, who durst not come to the room.

Saturday, July 13. I read Sir Richard Cox's "History of Ireland." I suppose it is accounted as authentic as any that is extant. But surely never was there the like in the habitable world! Such a series of robberies, murders, and burning of houses, towns, and countries, did I never hear or read of before. I do not now wonder Ireland is thinly inhabited, but that it has any inhabitants at all! Probably it had been wholly desolate before now, had not the English come and prevented the implacable wretches from going on till they had swept each other from the earth.

A Popish Miller turns Preacher.

July. In the afternoon I rode to Aghrim, and preached about seven to a deeply serious congregation, most of whom were present again at eight in the morning. On *Sunday*, 14, about five, I began in my usual place at Athlone, on the Connaught side of the river. I believe the congregation (both of Protestants and Papists) was never so large before. Some were displeased at this, and several pieces of turf were thrown over the houses, with some stones; but neither one nor the other could in the least interrupt the attention of the people. Then a Popish miller (prompted by his betters, so called) got up to preach over against me; but some of his comrades throwing a little dirt in his face, he leaped down in haste to fight them. This bred a fray, in which he was so roughly handled that he was glad to get off with only a bloody nose.

Wesley's broad Charity.

Wednesday, July 17. I preached in the Grove at Edinderry. Many of the Quakers were there, (it being the time of their general meeting,) and many of all sorts. I met here with the Journal of William Edmundson, one of their preachers in the last century. If the original equaled the picture, (which I see no reason to doubt,) what an amiable man was this! His opinions I leave, but what a spirit was here! What faith, love, gentleness, long-suffering! Could mistake send such a man as this to hell? Not so. I am so far from believing this that I scruple not to say, "Let my soul be with the soul of William Edmundson!"

The Deepest Part of the Holy Scripture.

Thursday, July 18. The wind in our face tempering the heat of the sun, we had a pleasant ride to Dublin. In the evening I began expounding the deepest part of the Holy Scripture, namely, the First Epistle of St. John, by which, above all other, even inspired writings, I advise every young preacher to form his style. Here are sublimity and simplicity together, the strongest sense and the plainest language! How can any one, that would "speak as the oracles of God," use harder words than are found here?

Wesley's Picture taken.

Wednesday, July 31. At the earnest desire of a friend, I suffered Mr. Hunter to take my picture. I sat only once, from about ten o'clock to half an hour after one, and in that time he began and ended the face, and with a most striking likeness.

A new House—A new Blessing.

Friday, Aug. 16. I rode over to Chester and preached to as many as the new house would well contain. We had likewise a numerous congregation on *Saturday* morning as well as evening. How the grace of God concurs with his providence! A new house not only brings a new congregation, but likewise (what we have observed again and again) a new blessing from God. And no wonder, if every labor of love finds even a present reward.

"The Dogs wiser than the Men."

Wednesday, Sept. 4. I rode on to North Tawton, a village where several of our preachers had preached occasionally. About six I went to the door of our inn, but I had hardly ended the psalm when a clergyman came with two or three (by the courtesy of England called) gentlemen. After I had named my text, I said, "There may be some truths which concern some men only, but this concerns all mankind." The minister cried out, "That is false doctrine! that is predestination!" Then the roar began, to second which they had brought a huntsman with his hounds; but the dogs were wiser than the men, for they could not bring them to make any noise at all. One of the gentlemen supplied their place. He assured us he was such, or none would have suspected it; for his language was as base, foul, and porterly as ever was heard at Billingsgate. Dog, rascal, puppy, and the like terms, adorned almost every sentence. Finding there was no probability of a quiet hearing, I left him the field, and withdrew to my lodging.

Sound Advice.

Wednesday, Sept. 18. I set out for Plymouth Dock. In the way we called on one of our friends near Liskeard, and found his wife, once strong in faith, in the very depth of despair. I could not but admire the providence of God which sent us so seasonably thither. We cried strongly to God in her behalf, and left her not a little comforted. The society at the Dock had been for some time in a miserable condition. Disputes had run so high concerning a worthless man, that every one's sword was set, as it were, against his brother. I showed them how Satan had desired to have them, that he might sift them as wheat; and afterward told them there was but one way to take, to pass an absolute act of oblivion; not to mention, on any pretense whatever, any thing that had been said or done on either side. They fully determined so to do. If they keep that resolution, God will return to them.

Physical Contrast between Mr. Wesley and Mr. Whitefield.

Sunday, Oct. 20. I preached a funeral sermon at Kingswood, over the remains of Susanna Flook, who, a few days before, rose up and said, "I am dying," and dropped down dead. So little security is there in youth or health! Be ye therefore likewise ready.

Monday, Oct. 21. I went in the coach to Salisbury, and on *Thursday*, 24, came to London.

Monday, Oct. 28. I breakfasted with Mr. Whitefield, who seemed to be an old, old man, being fairly worn out in his Master's service, though he has hardly seen fifty years; and yet it pleases God that I, who am now in my sixty-third year, find no disorder, no weakness, no decay, no difference from what I was at five-and-twenty, only that I have fewer teeth and more gray hairs.

"We will have peace."

Wednesday, Dec. 4. I preached about noon at Sandwich, and in the evening at Margate. A few people here also join in helping each other to work out their salvation. But the minister of the parish earnestly opposes them, and thinks he is doing God service!

Thursday, Dec. 5. I rode back to Feversham. Here I was quickly informed that the mob and the magistrates had agreed together to drive Methodism, so called, out of the town. After preaching, I told them what we had been constrained to do by the magistrate at Rolvenden—who, perhaps, would have been richer by some hundred pounds had he never meddled with the Methodists—concluding, "Since we have both God and the law on our side, if we can have peace by fair means, we had much rather; we should be exceeding glad; but if not, we *will* have peace."

Much Bruised by falling off his Horse.

Wednesday, Dec. 18. Riding through the borough, all my mare's feet flew up, and she fell with my leg under her. A gentleman stepping out lifted me up, and helped me into his shop. I was exceedingly sick, but was presently relieved by a little hartshorn and water. After resting a few minutes I took a coach, but when I was cold found myself much worse ; being bruised on my right arm, my breast, my knee, leg, and ankle, which swelled exceedingly. However, I went on to Shoreham ; where, by applying treacle twice a day, all the soreness was removed, and I recovered some strength, so as to be able to walk a little on plain ground. The word of God does at length bear fruit here also, and Mr. P. is comforted over all his trouble.

Saturday, Dec. 21. Being not yet able to ride, I returned in a chariot to London.

Whitefield no Bigot.

Friday, Jan. 24, 1766. I returned to London.

Tuesday, Jan. 28. Our brethren met together to consider our temporal affairs. One proposed that we should in the first place pay off the debt of the society, which was five hundred pounds. Toward this a hundred and seveny were subscribed immediately. At a second meeting this was enlarged to three hundred and twenty. Surely God will supply the rest!

Friday, Jan. 31. Mr. Whitefield called upon me. He breathes nothing but peace and love. Bigotry cannot stand before him, but hides its head wherever he comes.

A timely Supply and Relief.

Sunday, Feb. 2. I dined with W. Welsh, the father of the late Society for Reformation of Manners. But that excellent design is at a fuli stop. They have indeed convicted the wretch who, by willful perjury, carried the cause against them in Westminster Hall ; but they could never recover the expense of that suit. Lord, how long shall the ungodly triumph!

Wednesday, Feb. 5. One called upon me who had

been cheated out of a large fortune, and was now perishing for want of bread. I had a desire to clothe him and send him back to his own country, but was short of money. However, I appointed him to call again in an hour. He did so; but, before he came, one from whom I expected nothing less put twenty guineas into my hand; so I ordered him to be clothed from head to foot, and sent him straight away to Dublin.

The London Society suffers from Bell and Maxfield.

Monday, Feb. 10, and the four following days, I wrote a catalogue of the society, now reduced from eight-and-twenty hundred to about two-and-twenty. Such is the fruit of George Bell's enthusiasm and Thomas Maxfield's gratitude!

"A Christian School, or none at all."

Sunday, March 9. In the evening I went to Knightsbridge; and in the morning took the machine for Bristol, where I preached (as I had appointed) on *Tuesday* evening, and met the society.

Wednesday, March 12. I rode over to Kingswood; and, having told my whole mind to the masters and servants, spoke to the children in a far stronger manner than ever I did before. I will kill or cure, I will have one or the other—a Christian school, or none at all.

Sunday, March 16. I preached in Princes-street, at eight, on "Awake, thou that sleepest;" and at the square in the evening, to a listening multitude, on "Come, Lord Jesus!" At Kingswood we had such a congregation at ten as has not been there for several years, and I had the satiafaction to find four of our children again rejoicing in the love of God.

Wesley's Objections to the Liverpool Deed.

Thursday, April 10. I looked over the wonderful deed which was lately made here, on which I observed: 1. It takes up three large skins of parchment, and so could not cost less than six guineas; whereas our own deed, transcribed by a friend, would not have cost six shillings. 2. It is verbose beyond all sense and reason, and withal so ambiguously worded, that one passage only might find matter for a suit of ten or twelve years in chancery. 3. It everywhere calls the house a meeting-house, a name which I particularly object to. 4. It leaves no power either to the assistant or me, so much as to place or displace a steward. 5. Neither I, nor all the Conference, have power to send the same preacher two years together. To crown all, 6. If a preacher is not appointed at the Conference, the Trustees and the congregation are to choose one by most votes! And can any one wonder I dislike this deed, which tears the Methodist discipline up by the roots? Is it not strange, that any who have the least regard either for me or our discipline, should scruple to alter this uncouth deed?

Horse and Rider struggling in the Bogs.

Tuesday, June 24. Before eight we reached Dumfries, and after a short bait pushed on, in hopes of reaching Solway Frith before the sea was come in. Designing to call at an inn by the Frith side we inquired the way, and were directed to leave the main road and go straight to the house, which we saw before us. In ten minutes Duncan Wright was embogged; however, the horse plunged on and got through. I was inclined to turn back; but Duncan telling me I needed only go a little to the left, I did so, and sunk at once to my horse's shoulders. He sprung up twice, and twice sunk again, each time deeper than before. At the third plunge he threw me on one side, and we both made shift to scramble out. I was covered with fine, soft mud, from my feet to the crown of my head; yet, blessed be God! not hurt at all. But we could not cross till between seven and eight o'clock. An honest man crossed with us, who went two miles out of his way to guide us over the sands to Skilburness, where we found a little, clean house, and passed a comfortable night.

A long White Beard.

July. In the evening I preached near the preaching-house at Paddiham, and strongly insisted on communion with God, as the only religion that would avail us. At the close of the sermon came Mr. M. His long, white beard showed that his present disorder was of some continuance. In all other respects, he was quite sensible; but he told me, with much concern, "You can have no place in heaven without a beard! Therefore, I beg, let yours grow immediately."

The Wesleys confer with Mr. Whitefield.

Sunday, Aug. 17. After preaching in Leeds at seven, I rode to Bristol, and heard a sound, useful sermon on "Come unto me, all ye that labor and are heavy laden." At one I preached, to an immense multitude, on "Come, Lord Jesus!" I then set out for Rotherham; but the next day I turned off from the road I had designed to take, and, going on to Leicester that night, on *Wednesday* reached London. It was at the earnest request of ——, whose heart God has turned again, without any expectation of mine, that I came hither so suddenly; and, if no other good result from it but our firm union with Mr. Whitefield, it is an abundant recompense for my labor. My brother and I conferred with him every day; and, let the honorable men do what they please, we resolved, by the grace of God, to go on, hand in hand, through honor and dishonor.

A Heavy Load off his Shoulders.

Wednesday, Aug. 27. I rode to Bristol, and the next day delivered the management of Kingswood House to stewards on whom I could depend. So I have cast a heavy load off my shoulders. Blessed be God for able and faithful men, who will do his work without any temporal reward!

Wesley protected by Court of King's Bench.

Saturday, Aug. 30. We rode to Stallbridge, long the seat of war by a senseless, insolent mob, encouraged by their betters, so called, to outrage their quiet neighbors. For what? Why, they were mad; they were Methodists. So, to bring them to their senses, they would beat their brains out. They broke their windows, leaving not one whole pane of glass, spoiled their goods, and assaulted their persons with dirt, and rotten eggs, and stones whenever they appeared in the street. But no magistrate, though they applied to several, would show them either mercy or justice. At length they wrote to me. I ordered a lawyer to write to the rioters. He did so; but they set him at nought. We then moved the Court of King's Bench. By various artifices, they got the trial put off from one assizes to another for eighteen months. But it fell so much the heavier on themselves when they were found guilty; and, from that time, finding there is law for Methodists, they have suffered them to be at peace.

Twenty Thousand Hearers at Gwennap.

Sunday, Sept. 14. I preached in St. Agnes at eight. The congregation in Redruth, at one, was the largest I ever had seen there, but small compared to that which assembled at five in the natural amphitheater at Gwennap; far the finest I know in the kingdom. It is a round, green hollow, gently shelving down, about fifty feet deep; but I suppose it is two hundred across one way, and near three hundred the other. I believe there were full twenty thousand people; and, the evening being calm, all could hear.

Wesley rides Twenty-five Miles to see a Dying Man.

Thursday, Sept. 18. I rode to Collumpton, preached at six, and then went on to Tiverton.

Friday, Sept. 19, came a messenger from Jo. Magor, dangerously ill at Sidmouth, four or five-and-twenty miles off, to tell me he could not die in peace till he had seen me. So the next morning, after preaching, I set out, spent an hour with him, by which he was exceedingly refreshed, and returned to Tiverton time enough to rest a little before the evening preaching.

Wesley preaches on the Education of Children.

Sunday, Sept. 28. I preached in Princes-street at eight, in Kingswood at two, and at five near the new square. The last especially was an acceptable time, particularly while I was explaining, "Neither can they die any more; but are the children of God, being children of the resurrection." In the following days I preached at Pensford, Paulton, Coleford, Buckland, Frome, Beckington, Freshford, and Bradford.

Sunday, Oct. 5. At eight I administered the sacrament at Lady H—'s chapel in Bath. At eleven I preached there on those words in the Gospel for the day, "Thou shalt love thy neighbor as thyself." The word was quick and powerful, and I trust many even of the rich and great felt themselves sinners before God. Several evenings this week I preached at Bristol on the education of children. Some answered all by that poor, lame, miserable shift, "O, he has no children of his own!" But many of a nobler spirit, owned the truth, and pleaded guilty before God.

Playing with Edged Tools.

Monday, May 4, 1767. We rode to Castlebar, thirty old Irish, and about fifty-six English miles. Between six and seven I began preaching in the Court-house; but few of the rich were there. Many of these dare not hear me above once; they find it is playing with edged tools. Many of the poor were present at five in the morning, and many more, both rich and poor, in the evening. And "the power of the Lord was present to heal;" but how many rejected his "counsel against themselves?"

"He is the best Physician who performs the most cures."

Saturday, May 9. I rode to Ennis, but found the preaching had been discontinued, and the society was vanished away. So, having no business there, I left it in the morning, preached at Clare about eight, and in the evening at Limerick. The continued rain kept me from preaching abroad this week, and I was scandalized at the smallness of the congregation in the house. I am afraid my glorying, touching many of these societies, is at an end. Almost throughout the province of Ulster I found the work of God increasing; and not a little in Connaught, particularly at Sligo, Castlebar, and Galway. But in Munster, a land flowing with milk and honey, how widely is the case altered! At Ennis, the god of this world has wholly prevailed; at Clare there is but a spark left; and at Limerick itself, I find only the remembrance of the fire which was kindled two years ago. And yet one of the two preachers who was here last was almost universally admired! But, alas! how little does this avail! "He is the best physician," said a sensible man, "not who talks best, or who writes best, but who performs the most cures."

Obliged to be in Genteel Company.

Monday, June 15. I rode through a pleasant and well-cultivated country to Aghrim. For many years I have not seen so large a congregation here, and so remarkably well behaved. At the prayer, both before and after sermon, all of them kneeled upon the grass. A few of the poor Papists only remained standing, at a distance from the rest of the people. These would come in droves at every place, if the priests, as well as the King, would grant liberty of conscience. At the desire of the good old widow, Mrs. M——, I went with Mr. S—— to C——. Lord and Lady M—— were there before us, to whom I was probably

"A not-expected, much-unwelcome guest."

But whatsoever it was to them, it was a heavy afternoon to me; as I had no place to retire to, and so was obliged to be in genteel company for two or three hours together. O what a dull thing is life without religion! I do not wonder that time hangs heavy upon the hands of all who know not God, unless they are perpetually drunk with noise and hurry of some kind or another.

Power of Prayer.

Thursday, June 25. I was desired to look at the monument lately erected for the Earl of Charleville. It observes that he was the last of his family, the great Moores of Croghan. But how little did riches profit either him, who died in the strength of his years, or his heir, who was literally overwhelmed by them; being so full of care that sleep departed from him, and he was restless by day and night, till, after a few months, life was a burden, and an untimely death closed the scene! In the evening I preached at Mount Mellick, near the market-house. The congregation was exceeding large, and God made his word "quick and powerful, and sharper than a two-edged sword."

Friday, June 26. Finding some of the most earnest persons in the society were deeply prejudiced against each other, I desired them to come face to face, and labored much to remove their prejudice. I used both argument and persuasion ; but it was all in vain. Perceiving that reasoning profited nothing, we betook ourselves to prayer. On a sudden the mighty power of God broke in upon them. The angry ones on both sides burst into tears, and fell on each other's necks. All anger and prejudice vanished away, and they were as cordially united as ever.

A solemn Watch-night.

Wednesday, July 22. On *Wednesday* and *Thursday* we had our little Conference at Dublin. *Friday* we observed as a day of fasting and prayer, and concluded it with the most solemn watch-night that I ever remember in this kingdom. I was much tired between seven and eight o'clock, but less and less so as the service went on ; and at the conclusion, a little after twelve, I was fresher than at six in the morning.

Effects of Denunciatory Preaching at Edinburgh.

Sunday, Aug. 2. I was sorry to find both the society and the congregations smaller than when I was here last. I impute this chiefly to the manner of preaching which has been generally used. The people have been told, frequently and strongly, of their coldness, deadness, heaviness, and littleness of faith, but very rarely of any thing that would move thankfulness. Hereby many were driven away, and those that remained were kept cold and dead. I encouraged them strongly at eight in the morning ; and about noon preached upon the Castle Hill on "There is joy in heaven over one sinner that repenteth." The sun shone exceeding hot upon my head; but all was well, for God was in the midst of us. In the evening I preached on Luke xx, 34, etc., and many were comforted; especially while I was enlarging on those deep words, "Neither can they die any more, but are equal to the angels, and are the children of God, being the children of the resurrection."

Wesley travels One Hundred and Ten Miles in a Day!

Wednesday, Aug. 12. I took coach. The next day we reached Grantham, and London about seven on *Friday* evening, having run that day a hundred and ten miles. On the road I read over Seller's "History of Palmyra," and Norden's "Travels in Egypt and Abyssinia," two as dry and unsatisfying books as I ever read in my life.

Whitefield at Conference.

Tuesday, Aug. 18. I met in Conference with our assistants and a select number of preachers. To these were added, on *Thursday* and *Friday*, Mr. Whitefield, Howell Harris, and many stewards and local preachers. Love and harmony reigned from the beginning to the end; but we have all need of more love and holiness; and, in order thereto, of crying continually, "Lord, increase our faith." Having finished my work in London for the present, on *Monday*, 24, I rode to Wycomb, and preached in the evening to a numerous and deeply attentive congregation.

Refreshed as a Giant with new Wine.

Monday, Aug. 31. I rode to Carmarthen, and a little before six went down to the Green. The congregation was near as large as that at Brecknock, but nothing so gay; being almost all poor or middling people. To these, therefore, I directly preached the Gospel. They heard it with greediness; and though I was faint and weary when I began, I was soon as a giant refreshed with wine.

Prejudice and Bigotry give way.

Monday, Sept. 7. I rode to Carmarthen, and preached on the Green on "Is there a balm in Gilead?" In the afternoon, finding none that could direct us to Oxwych, we were obliged to ride round by Swansea. The next morning we came to Oxwych, and found George Story there, who had come to Swansea the day before in his way to Cork. Hearing I was near, he came over just in season to preach to the congregation who waited for me. At noon I preached to, I suppose, all the inhabitants of the town, and then rode to Neath. I had designed to preach abroad, but the rain would not permit. The preaching-house was much crowded, and the power of God was in the midst of the congregation. Prejudice sunk down before it, and the innumerable lies which most of them had heard of me vanished into air. The same power rested upon them early in the morning. The bigots on all sides were ashamed, and felt that, in Christ Jesus, nothing avails but the "faith that worketh by love."

Labor Lost.

Friday, Sept. 25. I was desired to preach at Freshford; but the people durst not come to the house because of the small-pox, of which Joseph Allen, "an Israelite indeed," had died the day before. So they placed a table near the church-yard. But I had no sooner begun to speak than the bells began to ring, by the procurement of a neighboring gentleman. However, it was labor lost; for my voice prevailed, and the people heard me distinctly; nay, a person extremely deaf, who had not been able to hear a sermon for several years, told his neighbors, with great joy, that he heard and understood all, from the beginning to the end.

The Way to Overturn Satan's Kingdom.

Wednesday, Sept. 30. I preached to a large and very serious congregation on Redcliff Hill. This is the way to overturn Satan's kingdom. In field-preaching, more than any other means, God is found of them that sought him not. By this, death, heaven, and hell come to the ears, if not the hearts, of them that "care for none of these things."

Friday, Oct. 2, and some days in the week, I visited the other societies round Bristol.

Sunday, Oct. 11. I preached at eight in Princes-street, and a little before five near the new square, where, notwithstanding the keenness of the wind, the congregation was exceeding large. I permitted all of Mr. Whitefield's society that pleased to be present at the love-feast that followed. I hope we shall "not know war any more," unless with the world, the flesh, and the devil.

A venerable Monument of Antiquity.

Saturday, March 19, 1768. We rode to Birmingham. The tumults which subsisted here so many years are now wholly suppressed by a resolute magistrate.

After preaching, I was pleased to see a venerable monument of antiquity, George Bridgins, in the one hundred and seventh year of his age. He can still walk to the preaching, and retains his senses and understanding tolerably well. But what a dream will even a life of a hundred years appear to him the moment he awakes in eternity!

"No children of his own."

Tuesday, March 29. I preached in Stockport at noon, and Manchester in the evening.

Wednesday, March 30. I rode to a little town called New Mills, in the High Peak of Derbyshire. I preached at noon in their large new chapel, which (in consideration that preaching-houses have need of air) has a casement in every window three inches square! That is the custom of the country! In the evening and the following morning I brought strange things to the ears of many in Manchester concerning the government of their families and the education of their children. But some still made that very silly answer, "O, he has no children of his own!" Neither had St. Paul, nor (that we know) any of the Apostles. What then? Were they therefore unable to instruct parents? Not so. They were able to instruct every one that has a soul to be saved.

Bishop Butler's "Analogy."

Friday, May 20. I went on in reading that fine book, Bishop Butler's "Analogy." But I doubt it is too hard for most of those for whom it is chiefly intended. *Free-thinkers*, so called, are seldom *close-thinkers*. They will not be at the pains of reading such a book as this. One that would profit them must dilute his sense, or they will neither swallow nor digest it.

Wesley disgusted with the Singing

Tuesday, Aug. 9. I took a full view of the castle, situate on the top of a steep hill, and commanding a various and extensive prospect both by sea and land. The building itself is far the loftiest which I have seen in Wales. What a taste had they who removed from hence to bury themselves in a hole at Margam! When we came to Neath, I was a little surprised to hear I was to preach in the church, of which the churchwardens had the disposal, the minister being just dead. I began reading prayers at six, but was greatly disgusted at the manner of singing. 1. Twelve or fourteen persons kept it to themselves, and quite shut out the congregation. 2. These repeated the same words, contrary to all sense and reason, six or eight or ten times over. 3. According to the shocking custom of modern music, different persons sung different words at one and the same moment, an intolerable insult on common sense, and utterly incompatible with any devotion.

He hastens to see his Sick Wife.

Sunday, Aug. 14. Hearing my wife was dangerously ill, I took chaise immediately, and reached the Foundery before one in the morning. Finding the fever was turned and the danger over, about two I set out again, and in the afternoon came (not at all tired) to Bristol. Our Conference began on *Tuesday*, and ended on *Friday*, 19. O what can we do for more laborers? We can only cry to "the Lord of the harvest."

Wesley Preaches to an Aged Saint.

Friday, Sept. 2. I preached at noon to an earnest company at Zennor, and in the evening to a far larger at St. Just. Here being informed that one of our sisters in the next parish, Morva, who entertained the preachers formerly, was now decrepit, and had not heard a sermon for many years, I went on *Saturday,* 3, at noon, to Alice Daniel's, and preached near the house on "They who shall be accounted worthy to obtain that world, and the resurrection from the dead, are equal unto the angels, and are the children of God, being the children of the resurrection." I have always thought there is something venerable in persons worn out with age, especially when they retain their understanding, and walk in the ways of God.

At his favorite work—Field-preaching.

Wednesday, Sept. 7. After the early preaching the select society met; such a company of lively believers, full of faith and love, as I never found in this country before. This, and the three following days, I preached at as many places as I could, though I was at first in doubt whether I could preach eight days together, mostly in the open air, three or four times a day. But my strength was as my work; I hardly felt any weariness first or last.

Sunday, Sept. 11. About nine I preached at St. Agnes, and again between one and two. At five I took my old stand at Gwennap, in the natural amphitheater. I suppose no human voice could have commanded such an audience on plain ground ; but the ground rising all round, gave me such an advantage, that I believe all could hear distinctly.

The Singing of the Methodists like that of the Ancients.

Saturday, Oct. 22. I was much surprised on reading an "Essay on Music," wrote by one who is a thorough master of the subject, to find that the music of the ancients was as simple as that of the Methodists ; that their music wholly consisted of melody, or the arrangement of single notes ; that what is now called harmony, singing in parts, the whole of counterpoint and fugues, is quite novel, being never known in the world till the Popedom of Leo the Tenth. He further observes, that as the singing different words by different persons at the very same time necessarily prevents attention to the sense, so it frequently destroys melody for the sake of harmony ; meantime it destroys the very end of music, which is to affect the passions.

To reprove well requires more than Human Wisdom.

Thursday, Dec. 1. The storm was ready to bear away both man and beast. But it abated about noon ; so that, after preaching at Margate, I had a pleasant ride to Canterbury. I made an odd observation here, which I recommend to all our preachers. The people of Canterbury have been so often reproved (and frequently without a cause) for being dead and cold that it has utterly discouraged them, and made them cold as stones. How delicate a thing is it to reprove ! To do it well requires more than human wisdom.

Friday, Dec. 2. Those who are called Mr. Whitefield's society, at Chatham, offered me the use of their preaching-house, which I suppose is nearly four times as large as that at the barracks. In the morning I walked on, ordering my servant to overtake me with my carriage, and he did so, but not till I had walked seven or eight miles.

A Profitable Hour with Mr. Whitefield.

Monday, Jan. 9, 1769. I spent a comfortable and profitable hour with Mr. Whitefield in calling to mind the former times, and the manner wherein God prepared us for a work which it had not then entered into our hearts to conceive.

Tuesday, Jan. 17. I rode to Chesham. Our own room being neither so large nor so convenient, Mr. Spooner, the Dissenting minister, gave me the use of his meeting. There was a great many hearers; they were very attentive, and I doubt that was all.

Wesley's Grandfather Annesley.

Monday, Feb. 6. I spent an hour with a venerable woman near ninety years of age, who retains her health, her senses, her understanding, and even her memory, to a good degree. In the last century she belonged to my Grandfather Annesley's congregation, at whose house her father and she used to dine every Thursday, and whom she remembers to have frequently seen in his study at the top of the house, with his window open, and without any fire winter or summer. He lived seventy-seven years, and would probably have lived longer, had he not began water-drinking at seventy.

Threescore Miles to Yarmouth.

Monday, Feb. 13. I rode to Colchester, and had the satisfaction of seeing such a congregation, both this evening and the following, as I never saw in that house before.

Wednesday, Feb. 15. I rode to Bury, and found not only an attentive audience, but a little society athirst for God.

Thursday, Feb. 16. Supposing we had but five-and-forty miles to Yarmouth, I did not set out till near seven, but it proved threescore; likewise it rained all day, and part of the road was very bad. However, God strengthened both man and beast, so we reached it before six in the evening. As we were both throughly wet, I was a little afraid for my companion, who was much older than me, though he had not lived so many years. But neither of us was any worse. The congregation was the largest I ever saw at Yarmouth, and I spoke far more plainly (if not roughly) than ever I did before. But I doubt if, after all the stumbling-blocks laid in their way, any thing will sink into their hearts.

Wesley's Motive in Writing Books.

Friday, Feb. 17. I abridged Dr. Watts's pretty "Treatise on the Passions." His hundred and seventy-seven pages will make a useful tract of four-and-twenty. Why do persons who treat the same subjects with me write so much larger books? Of many reasons is not this the chief: we do not write with the same view? Their *principal end* is to get money; my *only one* to do good.

Whitefield Vigorous in Soul, but Failing in Body.

Saturday, Feb. 25. I went on to London.

Monday, Feb. 27, I had one more agreeable conversation with my old friend and fellow-laborer, George Whitefield. His soul appeared to be vigorous still, but his body was sinking apace; and unless God interposes with his mighty hand he must soon finish his labors.

Wesley at work Three Days as a Peace-maker.

Thursday, March 21. I went to Parkgate, and about eleven embarked on board the King George. We had mild weather and smooth water all day. The next day the wind blew fresh. Yet about five we were in Dublin Bay, where we procured a fishing boat, which took us to Dunleary. Here we took a chaise, and got to Dublin about eight o'clock. On *Thursday, Friday,* and *Saturday* I labored to allay the ferment which still remained in the society. I heard the preachers face to face once and again, and endeavored to remove their little misunderstandings. And they did come a little nearer to each other, but still a jealousy was left, without an entire removal of which there can be no cordial agreement.

March 26. (Being *Easter-Day,*) many felt the power of the spirit which raised Jesus from the dead. On *Monday* and *Tuesday* I visited the classes, and the result of my closest observation was, 1. That out of five hundred members whom I left here, only four hundred and fifty remained ; 2. That near half of the believers had suffered loss, and many quite given up their faith ; 3. That the rest were more established than ever, and some swiftly growing in grace. So that, considering the heavy storm they had gone through, if there was cause of humiliation on the one hand, there was, on the other, more abundant cause of thankfulness to Him who had saved so many when all the waves went over them.

Wesley Preaches in a Stable.

Monday, April 17. In the evening, and twice on *Tuesday*, I preached to a genteel yet serious audience in Mr. M'Gough's avenue, at Armagh. But God only can reach the heart.

Wednesday, April 19. As it rained, I choose rather to preach in M'Gough's yard. The rain increasing, we retired into one of his buildings. This was the first time that I preached in a stable, and I believe more good was done by this than all the other sermons I have preached at Armagh.

He Officiates in Place of the Archdeacon.

April. We took horse about ten, being desired to call at Kinnard, (ten or eleven miles out of the way,) where a little society had been lately formed who were much alive to God. At the town end I was met by a messenger from Archdeacon C——e, who desired I would take a bed with him; and soon after by another, who told me the Archdeacon desired I would alight at his door. I did so, and found an old friend whom I had not seen for four or five-and-thirty years. He received me with the most cordial affection, and after a time said, "We have been building a new church, which my neighbors expected me to open; but, if you please to do it, it will be as well."

Hearing the bell, the people flocked together from all parts of the town, and "received the word with all readiness of mind." I saw the hand of God was in this for the strengthening of this loving people, several of whom believe that the blood of Christ has "cleansed" them "from all sin."

A Brilliant Congregation at Londonderry.

April 20. We took the new road to Dungiven. But it was hard work.

"Nigh founder'd, on we fared,
Treading the crude consistence."

We were near five hours going fourteen miles, partly on horseback, partly on foot. We had, as usual, a full house at Londonderry in the evening, and again at eight on *Sunday* morning. In the afternoon we had a brilliant congregation. But such a sight gives me no great pleasure, as I have very little hope of doing them good, only "with God all things are possible." Both this evening and the next I spoke exceeding plain to the members of the society. In no other place in Ireland has more pains been taken by the most able of our preachers. And to how little purpose! Bands they have none; four-and-forty persons in the society! The greater part of these heartless and cold. The audience in general dead as stones. However, we are to deliver our message, and let our Lord do as seemeth him good.

Tuesday, April 25. I fixed again the meeting of the singers and of the children, both which had been discontinued. Indeed, a general remissness had prevailed since the morning preaching was given up. No wonder wherever this is given up the glory is departed from us.

Papist Hearers.

Thursday, May 4. I found near Swadlinbar as artless, as earnest, and as loving a people as even at Tonny Lommon. About six I preached at the town's end, the very Papists appearing as attentive as the Protestants; and I doubt not thousands of these would soon be zealous Christians, were it not for their wretched priests, who will not enter into the kingdom of God themselves, and diligently hinder those that would.

An Eminent Beauty.

Thursday, May 25. I rode to Bandon. Since I was here before several have gone home rejoicing, but others are come in their place; so that the society contains just as many members as when I left; and most of the believers seem much alive, particularly the young men, maidens, and children. In the evening we were obliged to be in the house; but the next *Friday*, 26, I stood in the main street and cried to a numerous congregation, "Fear God and keep his commandments, for this is the whole duty of man." Afterward I visited one that a year or two ago was in high life, an eminent beauty, adored by her husband, admired and caressed by some of the first men in the nation. She was now without husband, without friend, without fortune, confined to her bed, in constant pain and in black despair, believing herself forsaken of God, and possessed by a legion of devils! Yet I found great liberty in praying for her, and a strong hope that she will die in peace.

A Money-loving People.

Tuesday, June 20. I went on to Aghrim, and spoke as plain as I possibly could to a money-loving people on "God said unto him, Thou fool!" But I am afraid many of them are sermon proof. Yet God has all power, and sometimes he sends, when and where it pleases him,

"O'erwhelming showers of saving grace."

But I have never observed these to last long; and in all the intervals of them he acts by his standing rule, "unto him that hath," and uses what he hath, "shall be given, and he shall have more abundantly; but from him that hath not," uses it not, "shall be taken away even that he hath."

What Wesley means by Christian Perfection.

June. By Christian perfection I mean, 1. Loving God with all our heart. Do you object to this? I mean, 2. A heart and life all devoted to God. Do you desire less? I mean, 3. Regaining the whole image of God. What objection to this? I mean, 4. Having all the mind that was in Christ. Is this going too far? I mean, 5. Walking uniformly as Christ walked. And this surely no Christian will object to. If any one means any thing more, or any thing else by perfection, I have no concern with it.

Preachers and Money sent to America.

Sunday, July 30. Mr. Crook being out of order, I read prayers and preached at Hunslet church both morning and afternoon. At five I preached at Leeds, and on *Monday*, 31, prepared all things for the ensuing Conference.

Tuesday, Aug. 1. It began, and a more loving one we never had. On *Thursday* I mentioned the case of our brethren at New York who had built the first Methodist preaching-house in America, and were in great want of money, but much more of preachers. Two of our preachers, Richard Boardman and Joseph Pillmoor, willingly offered themselves for the service; by whom we determined to send them fifty pounds, as a token of our brotherly love.

In answer to a Mother's Prayers.

Wednesday, Aug. 16. I examined the members of the society, (Haverford west,) now the most lively one in Wales. Many of them are rejoicing in the love of God, and many groaning for full redemption. To-day I gave a second reading to that lively book, Mr. Newton's account of his own experience. There is something very extraordinary therein, but one may account for it without a jot of predestination. I doubt not but his, as well as Colonel Gardner's, conversion was an answer to a mother's prayers.

Celebrates Lady Huntingdon's Birthday.

Wednesday, Aug. 23. I went on to Trevecka. Here we found a concourse of people from all parts, come to celebrate the Countess of Huntingdon's birthday, and the anniversary of her school, which was opened on the twenty-fourth of August, last year. I preached in the evening to as many as her chapel could well contain, which is extremely neat, or rather elegant, as is the dining-room, the school, and all the house.

About nine Howel Harris desired me to give a short exhortation to his family. I did so, and then went back to my lady's, and laid me down in peace.

Thursday, Aug. 24. I administered the Lord's Supper to the family. At ten the public service began. Mr. Fletcher preached an exceeding lively sermon in the court, the chapel being far too small. After him Mr. William Williams preached in Welsh till between one and two o'clock. At two we dined. Meantime a large number of people had baskets of bread and meat carried to them in the court. At three I took my turn there, then Mr. Fletcher, and about five the congregation was dismissed. Between seven and eight the love-feast began, at which I believe many were comforted. In the evening several of us retired into the neighboring wood, which is exceeding pleasantly laid out in walks, one of which leads to a little mount raised in the midst of a meadow, that commands a delightful prospect. This is Howel Harris's work, who has likewise greatly enlarged and beautified his house, so that with the gardens, orchards, walks, and pieces of water that surround it, it is a kind of little paradise.

Wesley's Criticism on Homer's Odyssey.

Sept. Last week I read over, as I rode, great part of Homer's Odyssey. I always imagined it was like Milton's "Paradise Regained,"

> The last faint effort of an expiring Muse.

But how was I mistaken! How far has Homer's latter poem the pre-eminence over the former! It is not, indeed, without its blemishes; among which, perhaps, one might reckon his making Ulysses swim nine days and nine nights without sustenance; the incredible manner of his escape from Polyphemus, (unless the goat was as strong as an ox,) and the introducing Minerva at every turn without any *dignus vindice nodus*. [Difficulty worthy of such intervention.] But his numerous beauties make large amends for these. Was ever man so happy in his descriptions, so exact and consistent in his characters, and so natural in telling a story? He likewise continually inserts the finest strokes of morality, (which I cannot find in Virgil;) on all occasions recommending the fear of God, with justice, mercy, and truth. In this only he is inconsistent with himself; he makes his hero say,

> Wisdom never lies:

And,

> Him, on whate'er pretense, that lies can tell,
> My soul abhors him as the gates of hell.

Meantime he himself, on the slightest pretense, tells deliberate lies over and over; nay, and is highly commended for so doing, even by the goddess of wisdom!

Rotten Eggs broken in the Right Place.

Tuesday, Sept. 19. Between twelve and one I preached at Freshford, and on White Hills, near Bradford, in the evening. By this means many had an opportunity of hearing who would not have come to the room. I had designed to preach there again next evening, but a gentleman in the town desired me to preach at his door. The beasts of the people were tolerably quiet till I had nearly finished my sermon. They then lifted up their voice, especially one called a gentleman, who had filled his pocket with rotten eggs ; but a young man coming unawares, clapped his hands on each side and mashed them all at once. In an instant he was perfumed all over, though it was not so sweet as balsam.

A Thousand at Love-feast.

Thursday, Oct. 5. I had the satisfaction to find that two of our brethren, with whom I had taken much pains, had at length put an end to their chancery suit, and closed their debate by a reference.

Sunday, Oct. 8. I permitted all of Mr. Whitefield's society that desired it to be present at our love-feast. I suppose there were a thousand of us in all, and we were not sent empty away.

Guthrie's "History of Scotland."

Monday, Nov. 6, and the following days, I visited as many of the people, sick and well, as I possibly could ; and on *Friday*, 9, leaving them more united than they had been for many years, I took coach again, and the next afternoon came to London. In the coach, going and coming, I read several volumes of Mr. Guthrie's ingenious "History of Scotland ;" I suppose as impartial a one as any to be found, and as much to be depended upon. I never read any writer before who gave me so much light into the real character of that odd mixture, King James the First ; nor into that of Mary Queen of Scots, so totally misrepresented by Buchanan, Queen Elizabeth's pensioner, and her other hireling writers ; and not much less by Dr. Robertson. Them he effectually exposes, showing how grossly they contradict matter of fact and one another. He likewise points out the many and great mistakes of Dr. Robertson, such as seem to imply either great inattention or great partiality. Upon the whole, that much-injured queen appears to have been far the greatest woman of that age, exquisitely beautiful in her person, of a fine address, of a deep, unaffected piety, and of a stronger understanding even in youth than Queen Elizabeth had at threescore. And probably the despair wherein Queen Elizabeth died was owing to her death, rather than that of Lord Essex.

Letters from America.

Monday, Dec. 25, (being *Christmas-Day,*) we had such a congregation at four as I have not seen for many years. And from morning to evening we had abundant proof that God is visiting and redeeming his people.

Tuesday, Dec. 26. I read the letters from our preachers in America, informing us that God had begun a glorious work there; that both in New York and Philadelphia multitudes flock to hear, and behave with the deepest seriousness; and that the society in each place already contains above a hundred members.

Friday, Dec. 29, we observed as a day of fasting and prayer, partly on account of the confused state of public affairs, partly as preparatory to the solemn engagement which we were about to renew.

Dr. Burnet's Theory of the Earth.

Monday, Jan. 1, 1770. About eighteen hundred of us met together; it was a most solemn season. As we did openly "avouch the Lord to be our God, so did he avouch us to be his people."

Wednesday, Jan. 17. In a little journey which I took into Bedfordshire, I finished Dr. Burnet's "Theory of the Earth." He is doubtless one of the first-rate writers, both as to sense and style; his language is remarkably clear, unaffected, nervous, and elegant. And as to his theory, none can deny that it is ingenious, and consistent with itself. And it is highly probable, 1. That the earth arose out of the chaos in some such manner as he describes; 2. That the antediluvian earth was without high or abrupt mountains, and without sea, being one uniform crust, inclosing the great abyss; 3. That the flood was caused by the breaking of this crust, and its sinking into the abyss of waters; and, 4. That the present state of the earth, both internal and external, shows it to be the ruins of the former earth. This is the substance of his two former books, and thus far I can go with him. I have no objection to the substance of his third book upon the General Conflagration, but think it one of the noblest tracts which is extant in our language. And I do not much object to the fourth, concerning the new heavens and the new earth. The substance of it is highly probable.

Rousseau and Voltaire.

Saturday, Feb. 3, and at my leisure moments on several of the following days, I read with much expectation a celebrated book, Rousseau upon Education. But how was I disappointed! Sure a more consummate coxcomb never saw the sun! How amazingly full of himself! Whatever he speaks he pronounces as an oracle. But many of his oracles are as palpably false as that "young children never love old people."

No! Do they never love grandfathers and grandmothers? Frequently more than they do their own parents. Indeed they love all that love them, and that with more warmth and sincerity than when they come to riper years.

But I object to his temper more than to his judgment; he is a mere misanthrope; a cynic all over. So indeed is his brother-infidel, Voltaire, and well-nigh as great a coxcomb. But he hides both his doggedness and vanity a little better; whereas here it stares us in the face continually. As to his book, it is whimsical to the last degree; grounded neither upon reason nor experience. To cite particular passages would be endless; but any one may observe concerning the whole, the advices which are good are trite and common, only disguised under new expressions. And those which are new, which are really his own, are lighter than vanity itself. Such discoveries I always expect from those who are too wise to believe their Bibles.

Baron Swedenborg.

Wednesday, Feb. 28. I sat down to read and seriously consider some of the writings of Baron Swedenborg. I began with huge prejudice in his favor, knowing him to be a pious man, one of a strong understanding, of much learning, and one who thoroughly believed himself. But I could not hold out long. Any one of his visions puts his real character out of doubt. He is one of the most ingenious, lively, entertaining madmen that ever set pen to paper. But his waking dreams are so wild, so far remote both from Scripture and common sense, that one might as easily swallow the stories of "Tom Thumb," or "Jack the Giant Killer."

Wesley preaches in a Workshop.

Monday, March 5. I came to Newbury, where I had been much importuned to preach. But where? The Dissenters would not permit me to preach in their meeting-house. Some were then desirous to hire the old play-house; but the good Mayor would not suffer it to be so profaned, so I made use of a workshop—a large commodious place. But it would by no means contain the congregation. All that could hear behaved well, and I was in hopes God would have a people in this place also.

Riding with a slack rein.

March. In the following days I went on slowly, through Staffordshire and Chesire to Manchester. In this journey, as well as in many others, I observed a mistake that almost universally prevails, and I desire all travelers to take good notice of it, which may save them both from trouble and danger. Near thirty years ago I was thinking, "How is it that no horse ever stumbles while I am reading?" (History, poetry, and philosophy I commonly read on horse-back, having other employment at other times.) No account can possibly be given but this: Because then I throw the reins on his neck. I then set myself to observe; and I aver, that in riding above a hundred thousand miles, I scarce ever remember any horse (except two, that would fall head over heels any way) to fall, or make a considerable stumble, while I rode *with a slack rein.* To fancy, therefore, that a *tight rein* prevents stumbling is a capital blunder. I have repeated the trial more frequently than most men in the kingdom can do. A slack rein will prevent stumbling if any thing will. But in some horses nothing can.

Snow-Drifts fail to arrest Wesley's Progress.

Wednesday, April 25. Taking horse at five, we rode to Dunkeld, the first considerable town in the Highlands. We were agreeably surprised ; a pleasanter situation cannot be easily imagined. Afterward we went some miles on a smooth, delightful road, hanging over the river Tay, and then went on, winding through the mountains, to the Castle of Blair. The mountains for the next twenty miles were much higher, and covered with snow. In the evening we came to Dalwhinny, the dearest inn I have met with in North Britain. In the morning we were informed so much snow had fallen in the night that we could get no further. And, indeed, three young women, attempting to cross the mountain to Blair, were swallowed up in the snow. However, we resolved, with God's help, to go as far as we could. But about noon we were at a full stop ; the snow, driving together on the top of the mountain, had quite blocked up the road. We dismounted, and, striking out of the road warily, sometimes to the left, sometimes to the right, with many stumbles, but no hurt, we got on to Dalmagarry, and before sunset to Inverness. Benjamin and William Chappel, who had been here three months, were waiting for a vessel to return to London. They had met a few people every night to sing and pray together ; and their behavior, suitable to their profession, had removed much prejudice.

Highlands of Scotland.

Monday, May 14. After ten years' inquiry, I have learned what are the Highlands of Scotland. Some told me, "The Highlands begin when you cross the Tay;" others, "When you cross the North Esk;" and others, "When you cross the river Spey;" but all of them missed the mark. For the truth of the matter is, the Highlands are bounded by no river at all, but by cairns, or heaps of stones laid in a row, southwest and northeast from sea to sea. These formerly divided the kingdom of the Picts from that of the Caledonians, which included all the country north of the cairns, several whereof are still remaining. It takes in Argyleshire, most of Perthshire, Murrayshire, with all the northwest counties. This is called the Highlands, because a considerable part of it (though not the whole) is mountainous. But it is not more mountainous than North Wales, nor than many parts of England and Ireland; nor do I believe it has any mountain higher than Snowdon Hill, or the Skiddaw in Cumberland. Talking Erse, therefore, is not the thing that distinguishes these from the Lowlands. Neither is this or that river; both the Tay, the Esk, and the Spey running through the Highlands, not south of them.

A Busy Day at Whitby.

Sunday, June 17. I met the Select Society, consisting of sixty-five members. I believe all of these were saved from sin; most of them are still in glorious liberty. Many of them spake with admirable simplicity, and their words were like fire. Immediately the flame kindled, and spread from heart to heart. At eight I preached; at nine met the children, most of whom had known the love of God, and several of them were able still to rejoice in God their Saviour. Almost as soon as I began to speak God spoke to their hearts, and they were ill able to contain themselves. I observed one little maid in particular, who heaved and strove for some time, till at length she was constrained to yield, and to break out into strong cries and tears.

We had a poor sermon at church. However, I went again in the afternoon, remembering the words of Mr. Philip Henry, "If the preacher does not know his duty, I bless God that I know mine." Between one and two I met the bands, being near two thirds of the society. Their openness was quite surprising, as well as the spirit with which they spoke. One plain woman cried, and spoke, and cried again, so that they were in tears on every side. I suppose if I could have stayed so long, some or other would have spoke till night.

At five I preached in the market-place again to a far larger congregation than before. Our love-feast took up the next two hours, at which many were filled with solemn joy. Afterward I met a few of the children again, all of whom had tasted that the Lord is gracious.

Wesley in the Sixty-eighth Year of his Age!

June. I can hardly believe that I am this day entered into the sixty-eighth year of my age. How marvelous are the ways of God! How has he kept me even from a child! From ten to thirteen or fourteen I had little but bread to eat, and not great plenty of that. I believe this was so far from hurting me, that it laid the foundation of lasting health. When I grew up, in consequence of reading Dr. Cheyne I chose to eat sparingly, and drink water. This was another great means of continuing my health till I was about seven-and-twenty. I then began spitting of blood, which continued several years. A warm climate cured this. I was afterward brought to the brink of death by a fever; but it left me healthier than before. Eleven years after I was in the third stage of a consumption. In three months it pleased God to remove this also. Since that time I have known neither pain nor sickness, and am now healthier than I was forty years ago. This hath God wrought!

A Refreshing Scene.

Thursday, July 5. I preached at six at Daw Green, near Dewsbury. All things contributed to make it a refreshing season: the gently-declining sun, the stillness of the evening, the beauty of the meadows and fields, through which

The smooth clear "river drew its sinuous train,"

the opposite hills and woods, and the earnestness of the people, covering the top of the hill on which we stood, and, above all, the Day-spring from on high, the consolation of the Holy One!

Wesley adapts his Subjects to his Hearers.

Sunday, July 15. I preached at eight, and again at two, and then hastened away to Barrow. The people here much resembled those at Horncastle.

So I would not take them out of their depth, but explained and enforced these solemn words, "It is appointed unto men once to die."

Monday, July 16. At nine I preached in Awkborough to a people of quite another kind. So I spoke to them directly of "Christ crucified," and the salvation which is through him. About noon I preached to a people of the same spirit at Amcoats. In the evening, the house at Swinfleet not being able to contain a third of the congregation, I preached on a smooth, green place, sheltered from the wind, on Heb. vii, 25. Many rejoiced to hear of being "saved to the uttermost," the very thing which their souls longed after."

Long Sermons.

Friday, July 20, and *Saturday,* I spent at Epworth.

Sunday, July 22. About eight I preached at Misterton; at one about half a mile from Haxey Church, and at five on Epworth Cross, to the largest congregation in Lincolnshire, on "I am not ashamed of the Gospel of Christ."

Monday, July 23. I preached at Doncaster and Rotherham; on *Tuesday* and *Wednesday* at Sheffield. On *Wednesday* evening my heart was so enlarged that I knew not how to leave off. Do some say, "I preach longer than usual when I am barren?" It is quite the contrary with me. I never exceed, but when I am full of matter; and still I consider it may not be with my audience as with me. So that it is strange if I exceed my time above a quarter of an hour.

Lord Littleton's "Dialogues of the Dead."

Thursday, Aug. 30. I rode to Falmouth, and preached at two in the afternoon, near the church, to a greater number of people than I ever saw there before, except the mob, five-and-twenty years ago. I preached at Penryn in the evening; *Friday* noon in Crowan; in the evening at Treworgey, near Redruth. Here I met with an ingenious book, the late Lord Littleton's "Dialogues of the Dead." A great part of it I could heartily subscribe to, though not to every word. I believe Madame Guion was in several mistakes, speculative and practical too; yet I would no more dare to call her, than her friend, Archbishop Fénélon, "A distracted enthusiast." She was undoubtedly a woman of a very uncommon understanding, and of excellent piety. Nor was she any more a "lunatic" than she was a heretic.

Another of this lively writer's assertions is, "Martin has spawned a strange brood of fellows called Methodists, Moravians, Hutchinsonians, who are madder than Jack was in his worst days." I would ask any one who knows what good breeding means, is this language for a nobleman or a porter? But let the language be as it may, is the sentiment just? To say nothing of the Methodists, (although some of them too are not quite out of their senses,) could his lordship show me in England many more sensible men that Mr. Gambold and Mr. Okely? And yet both of these were called Moravians. Or could he point out many men of stronger and deeper understanding than Dr. Horne and Mr. William Jones? (if he could pardon them for believing the Trinity!)

And yet both of those are Hutchinsonians. What pity is it that so ingenious a man, like many others gone before him, should pass so peremptory a sentence in a cause which he does not understand! Indeed, how could he understand it? How much has he read upon the question? What sensible Methodist, Moravian, or Hutchinsonian did he ever calmly converse with? What does he know of them, but from the caricatures drawn by Bishop Lavington, or Bishop Warburton? And did he ever give himself the trouble of reading the answers to those warm, lively men? Why should a good-natured and a thinking man thus condemn whole bodies of men by the lump? In this I can neither read the gentleman, the scholar, nor the Christian. Since the writing of this, Lord Littleton is no more; he is mingled with common dust. But as his book survives, there still needs an answer to the unjust reflections contained therein.

Druid Altars.

Saturday, Sept. 1. I took a walk to the top of that celebrated hill, Carn Brae. Here are many monuments of remote antiquity, scarce to be found in any other part of Europe. Druid altars of enormous size, being only huge rocks, strangely suspended one upon the other; and rock basins, hollowed on the surface of the rock, it is supposed, to contain the holy water. It is probable these are at least coeval with Pompey's theater, if not with the pyramids of Egypt. And what are they the better for this? Of what consequence is it, either to the dead or the living, whether they have withstood the wastes of time for three thousand or three hundred years?

Twenty thousand Hearers.

Sunday, Sept. 2. At five in the morning I preached in the natural amphitheater at Gwennap. The people covered a circle of near fourscore yards, and could not be fewer than twenty thousand. Yet, upon inquiry, I found they all could hear distinctly, it being a calm, still evening.

The two Brothers administer the Lord's Supper at Bristol.

Monday, Oct. 1, and the following days, I preached at many of the towns round Bristol, and found the congregations increasing in every place.

Sunday, Oct. 7. My brother and I complied with the desire of many of our friends, and agreed to administer the Lord's Supper every other Sunday at Bristol. We judged it best to have the entire service, and so began at nine o'clock. After it was ended I rode to Kingswood, gave an exhortation to the children, and preached to as many as the house would contain. A little before five I began at the Square, and found no want of strength. At the conclusion of the morning service I was weak and weary, hardly able to speak. After preaching at Kingswood I was better, and at night quite fresh and well.

Knowledge necessary to Stability.

Sunday, Nov. 4. At seven I met the society at Norwich, and administered the Lord's Supper to about a hundred and fourscore persons.

Monday, Nov. 5. I met the leaders, and inquired into the state of the society. In all England I find no people like those of Norwich. They are eminently "unstable as water." Out of two hundred, whom I left here last year, sixty-nine are gone already! What a blessing is knowledge when it is sanctified! What stability can be expected without it? For let their affections be ever so lively for the present, yet what hold can you have upon a people who neither know books nor men; neither themselves nor the Bible; neither natural nor spiritual things?

Whitefield's Funeral Sermon.

Saturday, Nov. 10. I returned to London, and had the melancholy news of Mr. Whitefield's death confirmed by his executors, who desired me to preach his funeral sermon on *Sunday*, the 18th. In order to write this, I retired to Lewisham on *Monday*, and on the *Sunday* following went to the chapel in Tottenham-Court-Road. An immense multitude was gathered together from all corners of the town. I was at first afraid that a great part of the congregation would not be able to hear; but it pleased God so to strengthen my voice, that even those at the door heard distinctly. It was an awful season; all were still as night; most appeared to be deeply affected; and an impression was made on many which we would hope will not speedily be effaced.

The time appointed for my beginning at the Tabernacle was half hour after five; but it was quite filled at three—so I began at four. At first the noise was exceeding great; but it ceased when I began to speak, and my voice was again so strengthened that all who were within could hear, unless an accidental noise hindered here or there for a few moments. O that all may hear the voice of Him with whom are the issues of life and death; and who so loudly, by this unexpected stroke, calls all his children to love one another!

Friday, Nov. 23. Being desired by the Trustees of the Tabernacle at Greenwich to preach Mr. Whitefield's sermon there, I went over to-day for that purpose; but neither would this house contain the congregation. Those who could not get in made some noise at first; but in a little while all were silent. Here, likewise, I trust God has given a blow to that bigotry which has prevailed for many years.

"A full Day of Work."

Tuesday, Dec. 25. This was a day full of work; but blessed be God! not tiresome work. I began in the Foundery at four; the service at West-street began at nine. In the afternoon I met the children at three, preached at five, and then had a comfortable season with the society.

Monday, Dec. 31. We concluded the year at the chapel with the voice of praise and thanksgiving. How many blessings has God poured upon us this year! May the next be as this, and much more abundant!

The Annual Covenant renewed.

Tuesday, Jan. 1, 1771. A large congregation met at Spitalfields in the evening in order to renew, with one heart and one voice, the covenant with God. This was not in vain; the spirit of glory and of God, as usual, rested upon them.

Wednesday, Jan. 2. I preached in the evening, at Deptford a kind of funeral sermon for Mr. Whitefield. In every place I wish to show all possible respect to the memory of that great and good man.

Wesley's lost Time with an Infidel.

Thursday, Jan. 3. I spent an hour and a half in beating the air in reasoning with an infidel of the lowest class. He told me roundly, "I believe God is powerful and the Creator of all things; but I am nothing obliged to him for creating me, since he did it only for his own pleasure. Neither can I believe that he is good, since he can remove all the evil in the world if he will; and, therefore, it is God's fault, and no one's else, that there is any evil in the universe." I am afraid we could not deny this if we allowed that God had "from all eternity, unchangeably determined every thing, great and small, which comes to pass in time."

An Event.

Wednesday, Jan. 23. For what cause I know not to this day, —— set out for Newcastle, purposing "never to return." *Non eam reliqui: Non dimisi: Non revocabo.* [I have not left her: I have not dismissed her: I will not recall her.]

The Tombs of Westminster Abbey.

Monday, March 25. I showed a friend, coming out of the country, the tombs in Westminster Abbey. The two with which I still think none of the others worthy to be compared are that of Mrs. Nightingale, and that of the Admiral rising out of his tomb at the resurrection. But the vile flattery inscribed on many of them reminded me of that just reflection,

If on the sculptured marble you rely,
Pity that worth like his should ever die.
If credit to the real life you give,
Pity a wretch like him should ever live!

The Widow's House.

Saturday, April 6. I gave the sacrament, at the Widow's house, to four or five-and-twenty that are widows indeed ; all poor enough, several sick or infirm, three bedrid, one on the brink of eternity. But almost all know in whom they have believed, and walk worthy of their profession.

No Opposition.

Thursday, April 11. I preached at Loughan and Athlone ; *Friday*, 12, at Aghrim.

Satuɪday, April 13. I rode back to Athlone, where there is now no opposition either from rich or poor. The consequence of this is there is no zeal, while the people "dwell at ease." O what state upon earth is exempt from danger! When persecution arises, how many are offended! When it does not arise, how many grow cold and leave their "first love!" Some perish by the storm, but far more by the calm. "Lord, save, or we perish!"

Church Benefactors.

Sunday, April 14. I designed to preach abroad, but the storm drove us into the house. This house was built and given, with the ground on which it stands, by a single gentleman. In Cork, one person, Mr. Thomas Janes, gave between three and four hundred pounds toward the preaching-house. Toward that in Dublin, Mr. Lunel gave four hundred. I know no such benefactors among the Methodists in England.

Wesley reminded of his Father's House.

Wednesday, May 15. A gentleman desired me to visit his daughter. I found a lovely, sensible woman, in the bloom of youth, scarce one-and-twenty, in the last stage of a consumption. From that time I visited her every day. In two or three days she was considerably better. But, as I expected, when the hot weather came on the sweet flower withered away.

Saturday, May 18. I dined at Mr. ——'s. Such another family I have not seen in the kingdom. He and Mrs. —— are in person, in understanding, and in temper, made for each other. And their ten children are in such order as I have not seen for many years; indeed, never since I left my father's house. May they never depart from the good way!

Ancient Ruins of Castle and Abbey.

Wednesday, May 22. After preaching at Balligarane, I rode to Ashkayton. There are no ruins, I believe, in the kingdom of Ireland to be compared to these. The old Earl of Desmond's castle is very large, and has been exceeding strong. Not far from this, and formerly communicating with it by a gallery, is his great hall, or banqueting room. The walls are still firm and entire; and these, with the fine carvings of the window frames, (all of polished marble,) give some idea of what it was once. Its last master lived like a prince for many years, and rebelled over and over against Queen Elizabeth. After his last rebellion, his army being totally routed, he fled into the woods with two or three hundred men. But the pursuit was so hot that these were soon scattered from him, and he crept alone into a small cabin. He was sitting there, when a soldier came in and struck him. He rose and said, "I am the Earl of Desmond." The wretch, rejoicing that he had found so great a prize, cut off his head at once. Queen Elizabeth and King James allowed a pension to his relict for many years. I have seen a striking picture of her, in her widow's weeds, said to be taken when she was a hundred and forty years old.

At a small distance from the castle stands the old abbey, the finest ruin of the kind in the kingdom. Not only the walls of the church, and many of the apartments, but the whole cloisters are entire. They are built of black marble exquisitely polished, and vaulted over with the same; so that they are as firm now as when they were built, perhaps seven or eight hundred years ago; and if not purposely destroyed, (as most of the ancient buildings in Ireland have been,) may last these thousand years. But add these to the years they have stood already, and what is it to eternity? A moment!

A Gift not attained by Nature or Art.

Friday, May 31. Observing many fashionable people in the court-house at Castlebar, I spoke with such closeness and pungency as I cannot do but at some peculiar seasons. It is indeed the gift of God, and cannot be attained by all the efforts of nature and art united.

Seed Sown by the Way-side.

Saturday, June 8. We set out for Ruskey, a little town near Macquire's bridge. But before we had gone nine miles we found a congregation waiting in the street at Lismolaw, where I know not who had given notice that I was to preach. I at first thought of riding on, but, fearing it might hurt the poor people,

I alighted and preached immediately. They were all attention while I explained, "Ye are saved through faith." About noon I preached at Ruskey.

The Methodist Plan requires the Preacher's Heart and Hand.

Monday, June 17. I met the singers for the last time. I joined them together two years ago; but, as the preachers following took no care or thought about them, they of course flew asunder. And no wonder; for nothing will stand in the Methodist plan, unless the preacher has his heart and his hand in it. Every preacher, therefore, should consider it is not his business to mind this or that thing only, but every thing.

Kicked by a Horse.

Thursday, June 20. We went on to Castle Caulfield. As we were walking in the afternoon, a horse that was feeding turned short, and struck me on the small of my back. Had he been but an inch or two nearer, I should not have traveled any further. As it was, I was well again in a few days. In the evening I preached, on the lovely green before the castle, to a serious and large congregation.

"I am a Wonder to Myself."

Friday, June 28. I preached in the street at Portadown to a serious, well-behaved congregation; and in the evening, at Kilmararty, to the largest congregation I have seen since we left Armagh. This day I entered the sixty-ninth year of my age. I am still a wonder to myself. My voice and strength are the same as at nine-and-twenty. This also hath God wrought.

Heart Religion Branded as Fanaticism.

Monday, Aug. 12. I set out for Wales, and, after preaching at Chepstow and Brecknock on *Wednesday,* 14, came to the Hay. Here I met with Dr. Maclaine's translation of "Mosheim's Ecclesiastical History." Certainly he is a very sensible translator of a very sensible writer; but I dare not affirm that either one or the other was acquainted with inward religion. The translator mentions, without any blame, Mr. Shinstra's "Letter against Fanaticism;" which, if the reasoning were just, would fix the charge of fanaticism on our Lord himself and all his Apostles. In truth I cannot but fear Mr. Shinstra is in the same class with Dr. Conyers Middleton, and aims every blow, though he seems to look another way, at the fanatics who wrote the Bible. The very thing which Mr. Shinstra calls fanaticism is no other than heart religion; in other words, "righteousness, and peace, and joy in the Holy Ghost." These must be *felt,* or they have no being. All, therefore, who condemn inward feelings in the gross, leave no place either for joy, peace, or love in religion, and consequently reduce it to a dry, dead carcass.

A Cardinal's Tomb.

Thursday, Oct. 4. I found time to take a view of the Winchester Cathedral. Here the sight of that bad Cardinal's tomb, whom the sculptor has placed in a posture of prayer, brought to my mind those fine lines of Shakspeare which he put into the mouth of Henry the Sixth:

> Lord Cardinal,
> If thou hast any hope of Heaven's grace
> Give us a sign. He dies, and makes no sign.

The Place of Wesley's First Sermon.

Tuesday, Oct. 15. I went on to Witney. I am surprised at the plainness and artlessness of this people. Who would imagine that they lived within ten, yea, or fifty miles of Oxford?

Wednesday, Oct. 16. I preached at South Lye. Here it was that I preached my first sermon, six-and-forty years ago. One man was in my present audience who heard it. Most of the rest are gone to their long home. After preaching at Witney in the evening I met the believers apart, and was greatly refreshed among them. So simple a people I scarce ever saw. They did "open the window in their breast;" and it was easy to discern that God was there, filling them "with joy and peace in believing."

Hoole's Translation of Tasso.

Monday, Oct. 21. As I drove to Chatham I read Mr. Hoole's fine translation of Tasso's "Jerusalem Delivered;" allowed, I suppose, by most judges of poetry, to be not much inferior to the Æneid. But I wonder Mr. Hoole was so imprudently faithful as to present Protestants with all Tasso's Popish fooleries. Those excrescences might have been pared off without the least injury to the work. In the evening I preached to a crowded audience, ripe for all the promises of God. How good is it for fallen man to earn his food by the sweat of his brow? Every-where we find the laboring part of mankind the readiest to receive the Gospel.

The Poor Rich Man.

Tuesday, Nov. 5. In our way to Bury we called at Felsham, near which is the seat of the late Mr. Reynolds. The house is, I think, the best contrived and the most beautiful I ever saw. It has four fronts, and five rooms on a floor, elegantly though not sumptuously furnished. At a small distance stands a delightful grove. On every side of this the poor rich man, who had no hope beyond the grave, placed seats to enjoy life as long as he could. But being resolved none of his family should be "put into the ground," he built a structure in the midst of the grove, vaulted above and beneath, with niches for coffins, strong enough to stand for ages. In one of these he had soon the satisfaction of laying the remains of his only child; and, two years after, those of his wife. After two years more, in the year 1759, having eat, and drank, and forgotten God for eighty-four years, he went himself to give an account of his stewardship.

The late Duke of Cumberland.

Friday, Nov. 29. We viewed the improvements of that active and useful man, the late Duke of Cumberland. The most remarkable work is the triangular tower which he built on the edge of Windsor Park. It is surrounded with shrubberies and woods, having some straight, some serpentine walks in them, and commands a beautiful prospect all three ways; a very extensive one to the south-west. In the lower part is an alcove, which must be extremely pleasant in a summer evening. There is a little circular projection at each corner, one of which is filled by a geometrical staircase; the other two contain little apartments, one of which is a study. I was agreeably surprised to find many of the books not only religious, but admirably well chosen. Perhaps the great man spent many hours here, with only Him that seeth in secret; and who can say how deep that change went, which was so discernible in the latter part of his life? Hence we went to Mr. Bateman's house, the oddest I ever saw with my eyes. Every thing breathes antiquity; scarce a bedstead is to be seen that is not a hundred and fifty years old; and every thing is quite out of the common way; he scorns to have any thing like his neighbors. For six hours, I suppose, these elegant oddities would much delight a curious man; but after six months they would probably give him no more pleasure than a collection of feathers.

Something Noble in his Ravings.

Sunday, Dec. 8. I read a little more of that strange book, Baron Swedenborg's *Theologia Cœlestis.* It surely contains many excellent things. Yet I cannot but think the fever he had twenty years ago, when he supposes he was "introduced into the society of angels," really introduced him into the society of lunatics; but still there is something noble even in his ravings:

> His *mind* has not yet lost
> All its original brightness, but appears
> Majestic, though in ruin.

A Reflection.

Monday, Dec. 30. At my brother's request, I sat again for my picture. This melancholy employment always reminds me of that natural reflection:

> Behold, what frailty we in man may see!
> His shadow is less given to change than he.

A Sentimental Journey.

Tuesday, Feb. 11, 1772. I casually took a volume of what is called "A Sentimental Journey through France and Italy." *Sentimental!* what is that? It is not English; he might as well say *Continental.* It is not sense. It conveys no determinate idea; yet one fool makes many. And this nonsensical word (who would believe it?) is become a fashionable one. However, the book agrees full well with the title; for one is as queer as the other. For oddity, uncouthness, and unlikeness to all the world beside, I suppose the writer is without a rival.

"Sum of all Villainies."

Wednesday, Feb. 12. In returning I read a very different book, published by an honest Quaker, on that execrable sum of all villainies, commonly called the Slave-Trade. I read of nothing like it in the heathen world, whether ancient or modern; and it infinitely exceeds, in every instance of barbarity, whatever Christian slaves suffer in Mohammedan countries.

Friday, Feb. 14. I began to execute a design, which had long been in my thoughts, to print as accurate an edition of my Works as a bookseller would do. Surely I ought to be as exact for God's sake, as he would be for money.

Practical Sympathy.

Friday, Feb. 21. I met several of my friends who had begun a subscription to prevent my riding on horseback, which I cannot do quite so well since a hurt which I got some months ago. If they continue it, well; if not, I shall have strength according to my need.

Had been to Boarding-school.

Monday, April 6. In the afternoon I drank tea at Am. O. But how was I shocked! The children that used to cling about me, and drink in every word, had been at a boarding-school. There they had unlearned all religion, and even seriousness; and had learned pride, vanity, affectation, and whatever could guard them against the knowledge and love of God. Methodist parents who would send your girls headlong to hell, send them to a fashionable boarding-school!

A little piece of Stateliness.

Tuesday, April 14. I set out for Carlisle. A great part of the road was miserably bad. However, we reached it in the afternoon, and found a small company of plain, loving people. The place where they had appointed me to preach was out of the gate; yet it was tolerably filled with attentive hearers. Afterward, inquiring for the Glasgow road, I found it was not much round to go by Edinburgh; so I chose that road, and went five miles forward this evening to one of our friends' houses. Here we had a hearty welcome *sub lare parvulo,* [in an humble dwelling,] with sweet and quiet rest.

Wednesday, April 15. Though it was a lone house, we had a large congregation at five in the morning. Afterward we rode for upward of twenty miles through a most delightful country; the fruitful mountains rising on either hand, and the clear stream running beneath. In the afternoon we had a furious storm of rain and snow; however, we reached Selkirk safe. Here I observed a little piece of stateliness which was quite new to me; the maid came in, and said, "Sir, *the lord of the stable* waits to know if he should feed your horses." We call him *ostler* in England.

Presented with the Freedom of the City.

Tuesday, April 28. We walked through the Duke of Athol's gardens, in which was one thing I never saw before—a summer-house in the middle of a green-house, by means of which one might in the depth of winter enjoy the warmth of May, and sit surrounded with greens and flowers on every side. In the evening I preached once more at Perth, to a large and serious congregation. Afterward they did me an honor I never thought of—presented me with the freedom of the city.

Another Martyr to Screaming.

Thursday, May 7. I took Thomas Cherry away with me; but it was too late; he will hardly recover. Let all observe, (that no more preachers may murder themselves,) here is another martyr to screaming! We had a huge congregation in the evening at Dundee, it being the fast day before the sacrament. Never in my life did I speak more plain or close; let God apply it as pleaseth him.

Friday, May 8. I labored to reconcile those who (according to the custom of the place) were vehemently contending about nothing.

Saturday, May 9. I went to Edinburgh.

A Monument of the Reign of Charles the Second.

Thursday, May 21. I went to the Bass, seven miles from Dunbar, which, in the horrid reign of Charles the

Second, was the prison of those venerable men who suffered the loss of all things for a good conscience. It is a high rock surrounded by the sea, two or three miles in circumference, and about two miles from the shore. The strong east wind made the water so rough that the boat could hardly live; and when we came to the only landing-place, (the other sides being quite perpendicular,) it was with much difficulty that we got up, climbing on our hands and knees. The castle, as one may judge by what remains, was utterly inaccessible. The walls of the chapel, and the Governor's house, are tolerably entire. The garden walls are still seen near the top of the rock, with the well in the midst of it. How many prayers did the holy men confined here offer up in that evil day! And how many thanksgivings should we return for all the liberty, civil and religious, which we enjoy?

The Famous Roman Camp.

Friday, May 22. We took a view of the famous Roman camp, lying on a mountain two or three miles from the town. It is encompassed with two broad and deep ditches, and is not easy of approach on any side. Here lay General Lesley with his army, while Cromwell was starving below. He had no way to escape; but the enthusiastic fury of the Scots delivered him. When they marched into the valley to swallow him up, he mowed them down like grass.

Saturday, May 23. I went on to Alnwick, and preached in the Town Hall. What a difference between an English and a Scotch congregation! These judge themselves rather than the preacher; and their aim is, not only to know, but to love and obey.

"Is James Watson here?"

Friday, June 5. Upon examination, I found the society at Newcastle also smaller than it was two years since. This I can impute to nothing but the want of visiting from house to house, without which the people will hardly increase either in number or grace. In the following week I preached in many towns round Newcastle, and on *Saturday* went again to Sunderland. In the evening we mightily wrestled with God for an enlargement of his work. As we were concluding, an eminent backslider came strongly into my mind, and I broke out abruptly, "Lord, is Saul also among the prophets! Is James Watson here? If he be, show thy power!" Down dropped James Watson like a stone, and began crying for mercy.

> Here, Lord, let all his wand'rings end,
> And all his steps to theeward tend!

Field-preaching and Visiting from House to House a Cross.

Sunday, Sept. 6. I preached on the quay, at Kingswood, and near King's Square. To this day field-preaching is a cross to me. But I know my commission, and see no other way of "preaching the Gospel to every creature." In the following week I preached at Bath, Frome, Corsley, Bradford, and Keynshan; on *Tuesday, Sept.* 15, at Pensford. Thence I went to Publow, which is now what Leytonstone was once. Here is a family indeed. Such mistresses, and such a company of children as, I believe, all England cannot parallel!

Wednesday, Sept. 16. I spent an hour with them in exhortation and prayer, and was much comforted among them. I preached at Pensford at eight, Paulton about one, and Coleford in the evening.

Friday, Sept. 18. I preached very quietly at the Devizes. Scarce one of the old persecutors is alive. Very few of them lived out half their days; many were snatched away in an hour when they looked not for it.

Friday, Sept. 25. I went over to Kingswood again, and had much satisfaction with the children. On *Sunday* I talked with the elder children one by one, advising them as each had need; and it was easy to perceive that God is again working in many of their hearts.

Wednesday, Sept. 30. I began visiting the society from house to house, taking them from west to east. This will undoubtedly be a heavy cross, no way pleasing to flesh and blood. But I already saw how unspeakably useful it will be to many souls.

A Free and Full Salvation.

Sunday, Nov. 8. In discoursing on Psalm xv, 1, I was led to speak more strongly and explicitly than I had done for a long times before on the universal love of God. Perhaps in times past, from an earnest desire of living peaceably with all men, we have not declared, in this respect, the whole counsel of God. But since Mr. Hill and his allies have cut us off from this hope, and proclaimed an inexpiable war, we see it is our calling to go straight forward, declaring to all mankind that Christ tasted death for all to cleanse them from all sin.

Monday, Nov. 9. I began to expound (chiefly in

the mornings, as I did some years ago) that compendium of the Holy Scriptures, the first Epistle of St. John.

Wesley Revises his Letters.

Friday, Jan. 1, 1773. We (as usual) solemnly renewed our covenant with God.

Monday, Jan. 4. I began revising my letters and papers. One of them was wrote above a hundred and fifty years ago, (in 1619,) I suppose by my grandfather's father, to her he was to marry in a few days. Several were wrote by my brothers and me when at school, many while we were at the University; abundantly testifying (if it be worth knowing) what was our aim from our youth up.

We observed *Friday, Jan.* 8, as a day of fasting and prayer, on account of the general want of trade and scarcity of provisions. The next week I made an end of revising my letters; and from those I had both wrote and received I could not but make one remark—that for above these forty years, of all the friends who were once the most closely united, and afterward separated from me, every one had separated himself! He left me, not I him. And from both mine and their own letters, the steps whereby they did this are clear and undeniable.

Wesley's Estimate of Captain Webb.

Tuesday, Feb. 2. Captain Webb preached at the Foundery. I admire the wisdom of God in still raising up preachers according to the various tastes of men. The Captain is all life and fire; therefore, although he is not deep or regular, yet many who would not hear a better preacher flock together to hear him. And many are convinced under his preaching, some justified, a few built up in love.

A Physician to the Poor.

June 14. I preached in the evening at Lisburn. All the time I could spare here was taken up by poor patients. I generally asked, "What remedies have you used?" and was not a little surprised. What has fashion to do with physic? Why, (in Ireland, at least,) almost as much as with head-dress. Blisters, for any thing or nothing, were all the fashion when I was in Ireland last. Now the grand fashionable medicine for twenty diseases (who would imagine it?) is mercury sublimate! Why is it not a halter or a pistol? They would cure a *little* more speedily.

Wesley's first entire Night of Wakefulness.

Friday, June 25. I went on to Dublin. I left three hundred and seventy-eight members in the society, and found four hundred and twelve, many of whom were truly alive to God.

Saturday, July 3. I sent to the commanding officer to desire leave to preach in the barracks; but he replied he would have no innovations. No; whoredom, drunkenness, cursing and swearing forever!

Monday, July 5. About eleven we crossed Dublin bar, and were at Hoy Lake the next afternoon. This was the first night I ever lay awake in my life, though I was at ease in body and mind. I believe few can say this: in seventy years I never lost one night's sleep!

Dr. Leland's "History of Ireland."

July 5. In my passage I read Dr. Leland's "History of Ireland;" a fine writer, but unreasonably partial. I can easily believe that the Irish were originally Tartars or Scythians, though calling at Spain in their way; but not that they were a jot less barbarous than their descendants in Scotland, or that ever they were a civilized nation till they were civilized by the English; much less that Ireland was, in the seventh or eighth century, the grand seat of learning; that it had many famous colleges, in one of which only, Armagh, there were seven thousand students. All this, with St. Patrick's converting thirty thousand at one sermon, I rank with the history of "Bel and the Dragon."

Wesley's Loss by his Literary Labors.

Wednesday, July 21. We had our quarterly meeting at London, at which I was surprised to find that our income does not yet answer our expense. We were again near two hundred pounds bad. My private account I find still worse. I have labored as much as many writers, and all my labor has gained me in seventy years is a debt of five or six hundred pounds.

A Congregation of Thirty Thousand!

Saturday, Aug. 22. I preached in Illogan and at Redruth. *Sunday,* 23, in St. Agnes Church-town at eight; about one at Redruth; and at five in the amphitheater at Gwennap. The people both filled it and covered the ground round about to a considerable distance. So that, supposing the space to be fourscore yards square, and to contain five persons in a square yard, there must be above two-and-thirty thousand people; the largest assembly I ever preached to. Yet I found, upon inquiry, all could hear, even to the skirts of the congregation! Perhaps the first time that a man of seventy had been heard by thirty thousand persons at once!

Children's Prayer-meeting at Kingswood.

Friday, Sept. 10. I went over to Kingswood and inquired into the present state of the children; I found part of them had walked closely with God; part had not and were in heaviness. Hearing in the evening that they were got to prayer by themselves in the school, I went down; but not being willing to disturb them, stood by the window. Two or three had gone in first, then more and more, till above thirty were gathered together. Such a sight I never saw before nor since. Three or four stood and stared as if affrighted; the rest were all on their knees pouring out their souls before God in a manner not easy to be described. Sometimes one, sometimes more, prayed aloud; sometimes a cry went up from them all; till five or six of them, who were in doubts before, saw the clear light of God's countenance.

Wesley Disabled, but at Work.

Monday, Sept. 13. My cold remaining, I was ill able to speak. In the evening I was much worse, my palate and throat being greatly inflamed. However, I preached as I could, but I could then go no further. I could swallow neither liquids nor solids, and the windpipe seemed nearly closed. I lay down at my usual time, but the defluxion of rheum was so uninterrupted that I slept not a minute till near three in the morning. On the following nine days I grew better.

Friday, Sept. 17. I went to Kingswood, and found several of the children still alive to God.

Saturday, Sept. 18. I gave them a short exhortation, which tired but did not hurt me.

Sunday, Sept. 19. I thought myself able to speak to the congregation, which I did for half an hour; but afterward I found a pain in my left side and in my shoulder by turns, exactly as I did at Canterbury twenty years before. In the morning I could scarce lift my hand to my head; but, after being electrified, I was much better, so that I preached with tolerable ease in the evening, and the next evening read the letters, though my voice was weak. From this time I slowly recovered my voice and my strength, and on *Sunday* preached without any trouble.

An Important Branch of the Pastoral Office.

Tuesday, Jan. 12, 1774. I began at the east end of the town to visit the society from house to house. I know no branch of the pastoral office which is of greater importance than this. But it is so grievous to flesh and blood that I can prevail on few, even of our preachers, to undertake it.

Sunday, Jan. 23. Mr. Pentycross assisted me at chapel. O what a curse upon the poor sons of men is the confusion of opinions! Worse by many degrees than the curse of Babel, the confusion of tongues. What but this could prevent this amiable young man from joining heart and hand with us?

Monday, Jan. 24. I was desired by Mrs. Wright, of New York, to let her take my effigy in wax-work.

She has that of Mr. Whitefield and many others, but none of them, I think, comes up to a well-drawn picture.

Harvest from Seed Sown by the Way-side.

Sunday, April 24. It being a cold and stormy day, Haworth Church contained the people tolerably well. On *Monday, Tuesday,* and *Wednesday* I preached at Bingley and Yeadon; and on *Thursday* opened the new house at Wakefield. What a change is here, since our friend was afraid to let me preach in his house, lest the mob should pull it down! So I preached in the main street, and then was sown the first seed which has since borne so plenteous a harvest. Hence I went to Leeds, and on *Saturday,* 30, to Birstal. Here, on the top of the hill, was the standard first set up four-and-thirty years ago. And since that time what hath God wrought!

A Device of Satan.

Sunday, May 1. I preached at eight on that delicate device of Satan to destroy the whole religion of the heart, the telling men not to regard frames or feelings, but to live by naked faith; that is, in plain terms, not to regard either love, joy, peace, or any other fruit of the Spirit; not to regard whether they feel these, or the reverse; whether their souls be in a heavenly or hellish frame! At one I preached at the foot of the hill to many thousand hearers, and at Leeds to about the same number, whom I besought in strong terms not to receive "the grace of God in vain."

State of Things at Glasgow.

Thursday, May 12. I went in the stage coach to Glasgow, and on *Friday* and *Saturday* preached on the old green to a people, the greatest part of whom *hear* much, *know* every thing, and *feel* nothing.

Sunday, May 15. My spirit was moved within me at the sermons I heard both morning and afternoon. They contained much truth, but were no more likely to awaken one soul than an Italian opera. In the evening a multitude of people assembled on the green, to whom I earnestly applied these words: "Though I have all knowledge, though I have all faith, though I give all my goods to feed the poor," etc., "and have not love, I am nothing."

Monday, May 16. In the afternoon, as also at seven in the morning, I preached in the kirk at Port Glasgow. My subjects were death and judgment, and I spoke as home as I possibly could. The evening congregation at Greenock was exceeding large. I opened and enforced these awful words, "Strait is the gate, and narrow is the way, that leadeth unto life." I know not that ever I spoke more strongly. And some fruit of it quickly appeared, for the house, twice as large as that at Glasgow, was thoroughly filled at five in the morning.

Tuesday, May 17. In the evening I preached on the green at Glasgow once more, although the north wind was piercing cold. At five in the morning I commended our friends to God. How is it that there is no increase in this society? It is exceeding easy to answer. One preacher stays here two or three months at a time, preaching on Sunday mornings, and three or four evenings in a week. Can a Methodist preacher preserve either bodily health or spiritual life with this exercise? And if he is but half alive, what will the people be? Just so it is at Greenock too.

"Could not find the Way to their Hearts."

Saturday, May 21. I returned to Perth, and preached in the evening to a large congregation, but I could not find the way to their hearts. The generality of the people here are so wise that they need no more knowledge, and so good that they need no more religion! Who can warn them that are brimful of wisdom and goodness to flee from the wrath to come?

Lord K——'s Essay on Liberty and Necessity.

May 23. In the evening I preached at Dundee, and *Tuesday*, 24, went on to Arbroath. In the way I read Lord K——'s plausible "Essays on Morality and Natural Religion." Did ever man take so much pains to so little purpose, as he does in his Essay on Liberty and Necessity? *Cui bono?* What good would it do to mankind if he could convince them that they are a mere piece of clock-work? that they have no more share in directing their own actions than in directing the sea or the north wind? He owns that "if men saw themselves in this light, all sense of moral obligation, of right and wrong, of good or ill desert, would immediately cease." Well, my Lord sees himself in this light; consequently, if his own doctrine is true, he has no "sense of moral obligation, of right and wrong, of good or ill desert." Is he not then excellently well qualified for a judge? Will he condemn a man for not "holding the wind in his fist?"

Wesley Arrested by Sheriff's Warrant.

Saturday, June 4. I found uncommon liberty at Edinburgh in applying Ezekiel's vision of the dry bones. As I was walking home two men followed me, one of whom said, " Sir, you are my prisoner. I have a warrant from the Sheriff to carry you to the Tolbooth." At first I thought he jested; but finding the thing was serious, I desired one or two of our friends to go with me. When we were safe lodged in a house adjoining to the Tolbooth, I desired the officer to let me see his warrant. I found the prosecutor was one George Sutherland, once a member of the society. He had deposed, "That Hugh Saunderson, one of John Wesley's preachers, had taken from his wife one hundred pounds in money, and upward of thirty pounds in goods; and had, besides that, terrified her into madness; so that, through the want of her help and the loss of business, he was damaged five hundred pounds."

Before the Sheriff, Archibald Cockburn, Esq., he had deposed, " That the said John Wesley and Hugh Saunderson, to evade her pursuit, were preparing to fly the country; and therefore he desired his warrant to search for, seize, and incarcerate them in the Tolbooth till they should find security for their appearance." To this request the Sheriff had assented, and given his warrant for that purpose. But why does he incarcerate John Wesley? Nothing is laid against him, less or more. Hugh Saunderson preaches in connection with him. What then? Was not the Sheriff strangely overseen? Mr. Sutherland furiously insisted that the officer should carry us to the Tolbooth without delay. However, he waited till two or three of our friends came, and gave a bond for our appearance on the 24th instant. Mr. Sutherland did appear, the cause was heard, and the prosecutor fined one thousand pounds.

Wesley's Remarkable Preservation.

Monday, June 20. About nine I set out for Horsley, with Mr. Hopper and Mr. Smith. I took Mrs Smith and her two little girls in the chaise with me About two miles from the town, just on the brow of the hill, on a sudden both the horses set out, without any visible cause, and flew down the hill like an arrow out of a bow. In a minute John fell off the coach-box. The horses then went on full speed, sometimes to the edge of the ditch on the right, sometimes on the left. A cart came up against them; they avoided it as exactly as if the man had been on the box. A narrow bridge was at the foot of the hill. They went directly over the middle of it. They ran up the next hill with the same speed; many persons meeting us, but getting out of the way. Near the top of the hill was a gate, which led into a farmer's yard. It stood open. They turned short, and ran through it, without touching the gate on one side or the post on the other. I thought, "However, the gate which is on the other side of the yard, and is shut, will stop them;" but they rushed through it as if it had been a cobweb, and galloped on through the corn-field. The little girls cried out, "Grandpapa, save us!" I told them, "Nothing will hurt you; do not be afraid;" feeling no more fear or care, (blessed be God!) than if I had been sitting in my study. The horses ran on till they came to the edge of a very steep precipice. Just then Mr. Smith, who could not overtake us before, galloped in between. They stopped in a moment. Had they gone on ever so little, he and we must have gone down together!

I am persuaded both evil and good angels had a large share in this transaction how large we do not know now, but we shall know hereafter. I think some of the most remarkable circumstances were: 1. Both the horses, which were tame and quiet as could be, starting out in a moment just at the top of the hill, and running down full speed. 2. The coachman's being thrown on his head with such violence, and yet not hurt at all. 3. The chaise running again and again to the edge of each ditch, and yet not into it. 4. The avoiding the cart. 5. The keeping just the middle of the bridge. 6. The turning short through the first gate, in a manner that no coachman in England could have turned them when in full gallop. 7. The going through the second gate as if it had been but smoke, without slackening their pace at all. This would have been impossible had not the end of the chariot-pole struck exactly on the center of the gate, whence the whole, by the sudden, impetuous shock, was broke into small pieces. 8. That the little girl, who used to have fits, on my saying, "Nothing will hurt you," ceased crying, and was quite composed. Lastly, That Mr. Smith struck in just then. In a minute more we had been down the precipice, and had not the horses then stopped at once, they must have carried him and us down together. "Let those give thanks whom the Lord hath redeemed, and delivered from the hand of the enemy!"

Wesley's Seventy-second Birthday

Tuesday, June 28. This being my birthday, the first day of my seventy-second year, I was considering, How is this, that I find just the same strength as

I did thirty years ago? That my sight is considerably better now, and my nerves firmer than they were then? That I have none of the infirmities of old age, and have lost several I had in my youth? The grand cause is the good pleasure of God, who doeth whatsoever pleaseth him. The chief means are, 1. My constantly rising at four for about fifty years. 2. My generally preaching at five in the morning—one of the most healthy exercises in the world. 3. My never traveling less, by sea or land, than four thousand five hundred miles in a year. In the evening I preached at Yarn, about eleven the next day at Osmotherly, and in the evening at Thirsk.

Thursday, June 30. I preached at Hutton Rudby, and found still remaining a few sparks of the uncommon flame which was kindled there ten years ago. It was quenched chiefly by the silly, childish contentions of those who were real partakers of that great blessing.

"It is a Miracle if they do not."

Monday, July 25. I went on to Sheffield, and on *Tuesday* met the select society, but it was reduced from sixty to twenty, and but half of these retained all they once received! What a grievous error to think that those once saved from sin cannot lose what they have gained! It is a miracle if they do not, seeing all earth and hell are so enraged against them; while meantime so very few, even of the children of God, skillfully endeavor to strengthen their hands.

Good Advice to Electors.

Monday, Oct. 3, and on *Tuesday* and *Wednesday*, I examined the society.

Thursday, Oct. 6. I met those of our society who had votes in the ensuing election, and advised them, 1. To vote without fee or reward for the person they judged most worthy; 2. To speak no evil of the person they vote against; and, 3. To take care their spirits were not sharpened against those that voted on the other side.

John Downes, a Genius.

Monday, Oct. 31, and the following days, I visited the societies near London.

Friday, Nov. 5. In the afternoon John Downes (who had preached with us many years) was saying, "I feel such a love to the people at West-street that I could be content to die with them. I do not find myself very well, but I must be with them this evening." He went thither, and began preaching on "Come unto me, ye that are weary and heavy laden.'" After preaching ten or twelve minutes he sank down, and spake no more till his spirit returned to God.

I suppose he was by nature full as great a genius as Sir Isaac Newton. I will mention but two or three instances of it: When he was at school learning algebra, he came one day to his master and said, "Sir, I can prove this proposition a better way than it is proved in the book." His master thought it could not be, but upon trial acknowledged it to be so. Some time after his father sent him to Newcastle with a clock, which was to be mended. He observed the clock-maker's tools, and the manner how he took it to pieces and put it together again; and when he came home, first made himself tools, and then made a clock which went as true as any in the town. I suppose such strength of genius as this has scarce been known in Europe before.

Another proof of it was this: Thirty years ago, while I was shaving, he was whittling the top of a stick. I asked, "What are you doing?" He answered, "I am taking your face, which I intend to engrave on a copper plate." Accordingly, without any instruction, he first made himself tools, and then engraved the plate. The second picture which he engraved was that which was prefixed to the "Notes upon the New Testament." Such another instance I suppose not all England, or perhaps Europe, can produce. For several months past he had far deeper communion with God than ever he had had in his life; and for some days he had been frequently saying, "I am so happy that I scarce know how to live. I enjoy such fellowship with God as I thought could not be had on this side of heaven." And having now finished his course of fifty-two years, after a long conflict with pain, sickness, and poverty, he gloriously rested from his labors, and entered into the joy of his Lord.

Only Two Reasons allowed for not Attending Class.

Thursday, Nov. 17. About noon I preached at Lowestoft, where the little flock are remarkably lively. The evening congregation at Yarmouth was all attention, and truly the power of God was present to heal them. In the evening I returned to Norwich. Never was a poor society so neglected as this has been for the year past. The morning preaching was at an end, the bands suffered all to fall in pieces, and no care at all taken of the classes, so that whether they met or not it was all one; going to church and sacrament were forgotten, and the people rambled hither and thither as they listed.

On *Friday* evening I met the society, and told them plain I was resolved to have a regular society or none. I then read the rules, and desired every one to consider whether he was willing to walk by these rules or no. Those in particular of meeting their class every week, unless hindered by distance or sickness, (the only reasons for not meeting which I could allow,) and being constant at church and sacrament. I desired those who were so minded to meet me the next night, and the rest to stay away. The next night we had far the greater part, on whom I strongly enforced the same thing.

Sunday, Nov. 20. I spoke to every leader concerning every one under his care, and put out every person whom they could not recommend to me. After this was done, out of two hundred and four members, one hundred and seventy-four remained. And these points shall be carried if only fifty remain in the society.

A Very Small Boat.

Friday, Nov. 25. I set out between eight and nine in a one-horse chaise, the wind being high and cold enough. Much snow lay on the ground, and much fell as we crept along over the fen banks. Honest Mr. Tubbs would needs walk and lead the horse through water and mud up to his mid-leg, smiling and saying, "We fen-men do not mind a little dirt." When we had gone about four miles the road would not admit of a chaise, so I borrowed a horse and rode forward, but not far, for all the grounds were under water. Here, therefore, I procured a boat full twice as large as a kneading-trough. I was at one end and a boy at the other, who paddled me safe to Erith.

A Lovely Place and Family.

Monday, May 22, 1775. I spent two or three hours in one of the loveliest places, and with one of the loveliest families in the kingdom. Almost all I heard put me in mind of those beautiful lines of Prior:

> "The nymph did like the scene appear,
> Serenely pleasant, calmly fair;
> Soft fell her words, as flew the air."

How willingly could I have accepted the invitation to spend a few days here! Nay, at present I must be about my Father's business; but I trust to meet them in a still lovelier place.

Dr. Leibnitz Sharply Criticised.

May. Between Limerick and Castlebar I read over the famous controversy between Drs. Clarke and Leibnitz. And is this he whom the King of Prussia extols as something more than human? So poor a writer have I seldom read, either as to sentiments or temper. In sentiment he is a thorough fatalist, maintaining roundly and without reserve that God has absolutely decreed from all eternity whatever is done in time, and that no creature can do more good or less evil than God has peremptorily decreed. And his temper is just suitable to his sentiments. He is haughty, self-conceited, sour, impatient of contradiction, and holds his opponent in utter contempt, though in truth he is but a child in his hands.

"Up and Be Doing!"

Sunday, July 23. I again assisted at St. Patrick's in delivering the elements of the Lord's Supper. In the evening I embarked in the Nonpareil, and about ten on *Tuesday* morning landed at Park Gate.

Wednesday, July 26. I found one relic of my illness, my hand shook so that I could hardly write my name; but after I had been well electrified by driving four or five hours over very rugged, broken pavement, my complaint was removed, and my hand was as steady as when I was ten years old. About noon I preached in the shell of the house at Wigan. In the middle of the sermon came an impetuous storm of thunder, lightning, and rain, which added much to the solemnity of the occasion.

Thursday, July 27. I went on to Miss Bosanquet's and prepared for the Conference. How willingly could I spend the residue of a busy life in this delightful retirement! But,

> "Man was not born in shades to lie!"

Up and be doing! Labor on, till

> "Death sings a requiem to the parting soul."

Sunday, July 30. I preached under Birstal Hill, and the greater part of the huge audience could hear while I enforced, "When the breath of man goeth forth he turneth again to his dust, and then all his thoughts perish." I preached at Leeds in the evening, and found strength in proportion to my work

Examination of Character, and Conference.

Tuesday, Aug. 1. Our Conference began. Having received several letters intimating that many of the preachers were utterly unqualified for the work, having neither grace nor gifts sufficient for it, I determined to examine this weighty charge with all possible exactness. In order to this I read those letters to all the Conference, and begged that every one would freely propose and enforce whatever objection he had to any one. The objections proposed were considered at large; in two or three difficult cases committees were appointed for that purpose. In consequence of this we were all fully convinced that the charge advanced was without foundation; that God has really sent those laborers into his vineyard, and has qualified them for the work; and we were all more closely united together than we have been for many years.

The Amphitheater Wesley's Favorite Preaching-place.

Sunday, Sept. 3. I preached at eight in St. Agnes Church-town on "Believe on the Lord Jesus Christ and thou shalt be saved." A young woman followed me into the house weeping bitterly, and crying out, "I must have Christ; I will have Christ. Give me Christ or else I die!" Two or three of us claimed the promise in her behalf. She was soon filled with joy unspeakable, and burst out, "O let me die! Let me go to him now! How can I bear to stay here any longer!" We left her full of that peace which passeth all understanding. About eleven I preached at Redruth; at five in the evening in the amphitheater at Gwennap. I think this is the most magnificent spectacle which is to be seen on this side heaven. And no music is to be heard upon earth comparable to the sound of many thousand voices, when they are all harmoniously joined together, singing praises to God and the Lamb.

The Sentiments of Lord Chesterfield Denounced.

Thursday, Oct. 12. About noon I preached at Watlington, and in the evening at Oxford, in a large house formerly belonging to the Presbyterians; but it was not large enough; many could not get in. Such a congregation I have not seen at Oxford, either for seriousness or number, for more than twenty years. I borrowed here a volume of Lord Chesterfield's Letters, which I had heard very strongly commended. And what did I learn? That he was a man of much wit, middling sense, and some learning; but as absolutely void of virtue as any Jew, Turk, or Heathen that ever lived. I say not only void of all religion, (for I doubt whether he believed there is a God, though he tags most of his letters with the name, for better sound sake,) but even of virtue, of justice, and mercy, which he never once recommended to his son. And truth he sets at open defiance; he continually guards him against it. Half his letters inculcate deep dissimulation, as the most necessary of all accomplishments. Add to this his studiously instilling into the young man all the principles of debauchery when, himself was between seventy and eighty years old. Add his cruel censure of that amiable man, the Archbishop of Cambray, *(quantum dispar illi,)* [how unequal to him,] as a mere time-serving hypocrite! And this is the favorite of the age! Whereas, if justice and truth take place, if he is rewarded according to his desert, his name will stink to all generations.

Wesley's Motive for Writing His "Calm Address to the American Colonies."

Saturday, Nov. 11. I made some additions to the "Calm Address to our American Colonies." Need any one ask from what motive this was wrote? Let him look around: England is in a flame! A flame of malice and rage against the king and almost all that are in authority under him. I labor to put out this flame. Ought not every true patriot to do the same? If hireling writers on either side judge of me by themselves, that I cannot help.

Wesley Buys an Estate.

May, 1776. About noon I preached at the New Mills, nine miles from Banff, to a large congregation of plain, simple people. As we rode in the afternoon the heat overcame me, so that I was weary and faint before we came to Keith; but I no sooner stood up in the market-place than I forgot my weariness, such were the seriousness and attention of the whole congregation, though as numerous as that at Banff. Mr. Gordon, the minister of the parish, invited me to supper, and told me his kirk was at my service. A little society is formed here already, and is in a fair way of increasing; but they were just now in danger of losing their preaching-house, the owner being determined to sell it. I saw but one way to secure it for them, which was to buy it myself. So (who would have thought it?) I bought an estate consisting of two houses, a yard, a garden, with three acres of good land. But he told me flat, "Sir, I will take no less for it than sixteen pounds, ten shillings, to be paid, part now, part at Michaelmas, and the residue next May."

Wesley Seventy-three Years Old.

Friday, June 28. I am seventy-three years old, and far abler to preach than I was at three-and-twenty. What natural means has God used to produce so wonderful an effect? 1. Continual exercise and change of air, by traveling above four thousand miles in a year; 2. Constant rising at four; 3. The ability, if ever I want, to sleep immediately; 4. The never losing a night's sleep in my life; 5. Two violent fevers, and two deep consumptions. These, it is true, were rough medicines, but they were of admirable service, causing my flesh to come again as the flesh of a little child. May I add, lastly, evenness of temper? I feel and grieve, but by the grace of God I fret at nothing. But still "the help that is done upon earth he doeth it himself." And this he doeth in answer to many prayers.

Fasting and Prayer for the Brethren in America.

Tuesday, Aug. 6. Our Conference began and ended on *Friday*, 9, which we observed with fasting and prayer, as well for our own nation as for our brethren in America. In several Conferences we have had great love and unity; but in this there was, over and above, such a general seriousness and solemnity of spirit as we scarcely have had before.

Sunday, Aug. 11. About half an hour after four I set out, and at half an hour after eleven on *Monday* came to Bristol. I found Mr. Fletcher a little better, and proposed his taking a journey with me to Cornwall, nothing being so likely to restore his health as a journey of four or five hundred miles; but his physician would in no wise consent, so I gave up the point.

Wesley's First Interview with Dr. Coke.

Tuesday, Aug. 13. I preached at Taunton, and afterward went with Mr. Brown to Kingston. The large old parsonage is pleasantly situated close to the church-yard, just fit for a contemplative man. Here I found a clergyman, Dr. Coke, late Gentleman Commoner of Jesus College in Oxford, who came twenty miles on purpose. I had much conversation with him, and a union then began which I trust shall never end.

Why the Work of God does not Prosper.

Wednesday, Aug. 14. I preached at Tiverton, and on *Thursday* went on to Launceston. Here I found the plain reason why the work of God had gained no ground in this circuit all the year. The preachers had given up the Methodist testimony. Either they did not speak of perfection at all, (the peculiar doctrine committed to our trust,) or they spoke of it only in general terms, without urging the believers to "go on unto perfection," and to expect it every moment. And wherever this is not earnestly done, the work of God does not prosper.

Love Supplies all Defects.

Wednesday, Sept. 4. I was desired to call at Ottery, a large town eleven miles from Exeter. I preached in the market-house to abundance of people, who behaved with great decency. At five I preached in the market-place at Axminster to a still larger congregation. I have seldom heard people speak with more honesty and simplicity than many did at the love-feast which followed. I have not seen a more unpolished people than these; but love supplies all defects. It supplies all the essentials of good breeding, without the help of a dancing master.

Wesley Visits the Bristol Society from House to House.

Monday, Sept. 9. I began what I had long intended, visiting the society from house to house, setting apart at least two hours in a day for that purpose. I was surprised to find the simplicity with which one and all spoke, both of their temporal and spiritual state. Nor could I easily have known, by any other means, how great a work God has wrought among them. I found exceeding little to reprove, but much to praise God for.

Celebrated Gardens.

Wednesday, Sept. 11. I preached about one at Bath, and about six in a meadow near the preaching-house in Frome, besought a listening multitude "not to receive the grace of God in vain."

Thursday, Sept. 12. I spent about two hours in Mr. Hoare's gardens at Stourton. I have seen the most celebrated gardens in England, but these far exceed them all. 1. In the situation, being laid out on the sloping sides of a semicircular mountain. 2. In the vast basin of water inclosed between them, covering, I suppose, sixty acres of ground. 3. In the delightful interchange of shady groves and sunny glades, curiously mixed together. Above all, in the lovely grottoes, two of which excel every thing of the kind which I ever saw: the fountain grotto, made entirely of rock-work, admirably well imitating nature; and the castle grotto, into which you enter unawares beneath a heap of ruins. This is within totally built of roots of trees, wonderfully interwoven. On one side of it is a little hermitage, with a lamp, a chair, a table, and bones upon it.

Others were delighted with the temples, but I was not: 1. Because several of the statues about them were mean. 2. Because I cannot admire the images of devils, and we know the gods of the heathens are but devils. 3. Because I defy all mankind to reconcile statues with nudities, either to common sense or common decency. Returning from thence through Maiden Bradley, we saw the clumsy house of the Duke of Somerset, and afterward the grand and elegant one of Lord Weymouth, beautifully situated in a lovely park.

The Power of God Wesley's Strength.

Sunday, Sept. 22. After reading prayers, preaching, and administering the sacrament at Bristol, I hastened away to Kingswood, and preached under the trees to such a multitude as had not been lately seen there. I began in King's Square a little before five, where the word of God was quick and powerful. And I was no more tired at night than when I rose in the morning. Such is the power of God! After settling all things at Bristol and Kingswood, and visiting the rest of the societies in Somersetshire, Wiltshire, and Hants, I returned in October to London with Mr. Fletcher.

East Indies—Wesley Indignant.

Wednesday, Nov. 13. I set out with Mr. Fletcher to Norwich. I took coach at twelve, slept till six, and then spent the time very agreeably in conversation, singing, and reading. I read Mr. Bolt's account of the affairs in the East Indies, I suppose much the best that is extant. But what a scene is here opened! What consummate villains, what devils incarnate, were the managers there! What utter strangers to justice, mercy, and truth; to every sentiment of humanity! I believe no Heathen history contains a parallel. I remember none in all the annals of antiquity. Not even the divine Cato, or the virtuous Brutus, plundered the provinces committed to their charge with such merciless cruelty as the English have plundered the desolated provinces of Indostan.

No Intermission of the Work.

Tuesday, Dec. 31. We concluded the year with solemn praise to God for continuing his great work in our land. It has never been intermitted one year or one month since the year 1738, in which my brother and I began to preach that strange doctrine of salvation by faith.

Charmed with the Book of Ecclesiastes.

Wednesday, Jan. 1, 1777. We met, as usual, to renew our covenant with God. It was a solemn season, wherein many found his power present to heal, and were enabled to urge their way with strength renewed.

Thursday, Jan. 2. I began expounding, in order, the Book of Ecclesiastes. I never before had so clear a sight either of the meaning or the beauties of it. Neither did I imagine that the several parts of it were in so exquisite a manner connected together; all tending to prove that grand truth, that there is no happiness out of God.

Wesley Visits the Poor.

Wednesday, Jan. 15. I began visiting those of our society who lived in Bethnal Green hamlets. Many of them I found in such poverty as few can conceive without seeing it. O why do not all the rich that fear God constantly visit the poor! Can they spend part of their spare time better? Certainly not. So they will find in that day when "every man shall receive his own reward according to his own labor." Such another scene I saw the next day in visiting another part of the society. I have not found any such distress, no, not in the prison at Newgate. One poor man was just creeping out of his sick bed to his ragged wife and three children, who were more than half naked, and the very picture of famine; when, one bringing in a loaf of bread, they all ran, seizing upon it, and tore it in pieces in an instant. Who would not rejoice that there is another world?

Growing into an Honorable Man.

Sunday, Jan. 26. I preached again at Allhallows Church, morning and afternoon. I found great liberty of spirit, and the congregation seemed to be much affected. How is this? Do I yet please men? Is the offense of the cross ceased? It seems, after being scandalous near fifty years, I am at length growing into an honorable man!

Thursday, Jan. 30. I had a visit from Mr. B—, grown an old, feeble, decrepit man, hardly able to face a puff of wind, or creep down stairs! Such is the fruit of cooping one's self in a house, of sitting still day after day!

Wesley Visits Dr. Dodd.

Saturday, Feb. 15. At the third message I took up my cross and went to see Dr. Dodd, in the Compter. I was greatly surprised. He seemed, though deeply affected, yet thoroughly resigned to the will of God! Mrs. Dodd likewise behaved with the utmost propriety. I doubt not God will bring good out of this evil.

Tuesday, Feb. 18. I visited him again, and found him still in a desirable state of mind; calmly giving himself up to whatsoever God should determine concerning him.

Slave-ships Unemployed.

Friday, April 11. I preached at Stockport about ten, and at Manchester in the evening.

Monday, April 14. I preached about noon at Warrington, and in the evening at Liverpool, where many large ships are now laid up in the docks which had been employed for many years in buying or stealing poor Africans and selling them in America for slaves. The men-butchers have now nothing to do at this laudable occupation. Since the American war broke out there is no demand for human cattle; so the men of Africa, as well as Europe, may enjoy their native liberty.

Laying a Corner-stone at London.

Monday, April 21, was the day appointed for laying the foundation of the new chapel. The rain befriended us much by keeping away thousands who purposed to be there. But there were still such multitudes that it was with great difficulty I got through them to lay the first stone. Upon this was a plate of brass (covered with another stone) on which was engraved, "This was laid by Mr. John Wesley on April 1, 1777." Probably this will be seen no more by any human eye, but will remain there till the earth and the works thereof are burned up.

Sunday, April 27. The sun breaking out, I snatched the opportunity of preaching to many thousands in Moorfields. All were still as night while I showed how "the son of God was manifested to destroy the works of the devil."

"Pretty Fools."

Wednesday, May 14. At eleven I preached at Pocklington, with an eye to the death of that lovely woman, Mrs. Cross. A gay young gentleman with a young lady stepped in, stayed five minutes, and went out again, with as easy an unconcern as if they had been listening to a ballad-singer. I mentioned to the congregation the deep folly and ignorance implied in such behavior. These pretty fools never thought that for this very opportunity they are to give an account before men and angels! In the evening I preached at York. I would gladly have rested the next day, feeling my breast much out of order; but notice having been given of my preaching at Tadcaster, I set out at nine in the morning. About ten the chaise broke down. I borrowed a horse, but as he was none of the easiest, in riding three miles I was so thoroughly electrified that the pain in my breast was quite cured. I preached in the evening at York, on *Friday* took the diligence, and on *Saturday* afternoon came to London.

A Trip to the Isle of Man.

Friday, May 30. I went on to Whitehaven, where I found a little vessel waiting for me. After preaching in the evening, I went on board about eight o'clock, and before eight in the morning landed at Douglas, in the Isle of Man.

Douglas exceedingly resembles Newlyn in Cornwall, both in its situation, form, and buildings, only it is much larger, and has a few houses equal to most in Penzance. As soon as we landed I was challenged by Mr. Booth, who had seen me in Ireland, and whose brother has been for many years a member of the society in Coolylough. A chaise was provided to carry me to Castletown. I was greatly surprised at the country. All the way from Douglas to Castletown it is as pleasant and as well cultivated as most parts of England, with many gentlemen's seats. Castletown a good deal resembles Galway, only it is not so large. At six I preached near the Castle, I believe to all the inhabitants of the town. Two or three gay young women showed they knew nothing about religion; all the rest were deeply serious. Afterward I spent an hour very agreeably at Mrs. Wood's, the widow of the late Governor. I was much pressed to stay a little longer at Castletown, but my time was fixed.

Sunday, June 1. At six I preached in our own room, and, to my surprise, saw all the gentlewomen there. Young as well as old were now deeply affected, and would fain have had me stayed, were it but an hour or two; but I was forced to hasten away, in order to be at Peeltown before the service began. Mr.

Corbett said he would gladly have asked me to preach, but that the Bishop had forbidden him, who had also forbidden all his clergy to admit any Methodist preacher to the Lord's Supper. But is any clergyman obliged, either in law or conscience, to obey such a prohibition? By no means. The *will* even of the King does not bind any *English* subject, unless it be seconded by express law. How much less the will of a Bishop? "But did not you take an oath to obey him?" No, nor any clergyman in the three kingdoms. This is a mere vulgar error. Shame that it should prevail almost universally. As it rained, I retired after service into a large malt house. Most of the congregation followed, and devoured the word. It being far in the afternoon, the whole congregation stopped in the church-yard, and the word of God was with power. It was a happy opportunity.

Wesley Visits Dr. Dodd for the Last Time.

Saturday, June 21. I returned to London.

Wednesday, June 25. I saw Dr. Dodd for the last time. He was in exactly such a temper as I wished. He never at any time expressed the least murmuring or resentment at any one, but entirely and calmly gave himself up to the will of God. Such a prisoner I scarce ever saw before, much less such a condemned malefactor. I should think none could converse with him without acknowledging that God is with him.

Wesley Completes his Seventy-fourth Year.

Thursday, June 26. I read the truly wonderful performance of Mr. Rowland Hill. I stood amazed!

Compared to him, Mr. Toplady himself is a very civil, fair-spoken gentleman.

Friday, June 27. I wrote an answer to it, "Not rendering railing for railing," (I have not so learned Christ,) but "speaking the truth in love."

Saturday, June 28. I have now completed my seventy-fourth year, and, by the peculiar favor of God, I find my health and strength, and all my faculties of body and mind, just the same as they were at four-and-twenty.

Are the Methodists a Fallen People?

Tuesday, Aug. 5. Our yearly Conference began. I now particularly inquired (as that report had been spread far and wide) of every assistant, "Have you reason to believe, from your own observation, that the Methodists are a fallen people? Is there a decay or an increase in the work of God where you have been? Are the societies in general more dead or more alive to God than they were some years ago?" The almost universal answer was, "If we must 'know them by their fruits,' there is no decay in the work of God among the people in general. The societies are not dead to God; they are as much alive as they have been for many years. And we look on this report as a mere device of Satan to make our hands hang down."

"But how can this question be decided? You, and you, can judge no further than you see. You cannot judge of one part by another of the people of London, suppose, by those of Bristol. And none but myself has an opportunity of seeing them throughout the three kingdoms."

But to come to a short issue. In most places the Methodists are still a poor, despised people, laboring under reproach and many inconveniences ; therefore, wherever the power of God is not they decrease. By this, then, you may form a sure judgment. Do the Methodists in general decrease in number? Then they decrease in grace ; they are a fallen, or, at least, a falling people. But they do not decrease in number ; they continually increase ; therefore they are not a fallen people. The Conference concluded on *Friday*, as it began, in much love. But there was one jarring string ; John Hilton told us he must withdraw from our connection because he saw the Methodists were a fallen people. Some would have reasoned with him, but it was lost labor ; so we let him go in peace.

Dr. Coke Dismissed from his Curacy.

Tuesday, Aug. 19. I went forward to Taunton with Dr. Coke, who, being dismissed from his curacy, has bid adieu to his honorable name and determined to cast in his lot with us. In the evening I endeavored to guard all who love or fear God against that miserable bigotry which many of our mistaken brethren are advancing with all their might.

Wesley Visits the Classes in London.

Monday, Nov. 3. I began visiting the classes in London, in which I was fully employed for seven or eight days ; afterward I visited those in the neighboring towns, and found reason to rejoice over them.

Sunday, Nov. 16. I was desired to preach a charity sermon in St. Margaret's Church, Rood-lane. In the morning I desired my friends not to come; in the afternoon it was crowded sufficiently, and I believe many of them felt the word of God sharper than any two-edged sword.

Wesley Consents to Publish a Magazine.

Monday, Nov. 24. I spent the afternoon at Mr. Blackwell's with the B—— of ——. His whole behavior was worthy of a Christian Bishop, easy, affable, courteous; and yet all his conversation spoke the dignity which was suitable to his character. Having been many times desired for near forty years, to publish a magazine, I at length complied, and now began to collect materials for it. If it once begin I incline to think it will not end but with my life.

He Lays a Corner-stone at Bath.

Saturday, Dec. 13. Being strongly urged to lay the first stone of the house which was going to be built at Bath, on *Sunday, Dec.* 14, after preaching at West-street chapel in the morning, and at St. Paul's, Shadwell, in the afternoon, I went to Brentford. I preached at six, and, taking chaise at twelve on *Monday, Dec.* 15, easily reached Bath in the afternoon.

Tuesday, Dec. 16. I paid a short visit to Bristol; preached in the evening, and morning following, *Wednesday, Dec.* 17, and at one laid the foundation of the new chapel at Bath. The wind was piercing cold, yet scarce any of the congregation went away before the end of the sermon. After preaching in the room in the evening I took chaise, and the next afternoon reached London. Just at this time there was a combination among many of the post-chaise drivers on the Bath road, especially those that drove in the night, to deliver their passengers into each other's hands. One driver stopped at the spot they had appointed, when another waited to attack the chaise. In consequence of this many were robbed, but I had a good Protector still. I have traveled all roads by day and by night for these forty years, and never was interrupted yet.

A Good Word for the Local Preachers.

Wednesday, Dec. 31. We concluded the old year and began the new with prayer and thanksgiving. Four or five of the Local Preachers assisted me. I was agreeably surprised, their manner of praying being so artless and unlabored, and yet rational and scriptural both as to sense and expression.

Thursday, Jan. 1, 1778. We had a very solemn opportunity of renewing our covenant with God.

Wesley Writes a Serious Address to the Inhabitants of England.

Tuesday, Feb. 17. I wrote "A Serious Address to the Inhabitants of England" with regard to the present state of the nation—So strangely misrepresented both by ignorant and designing men—to remove, if possible, the apprehensions which have been so diligently spread, as if it were on the brink of ruin.

Panic in Bristol.

Sunday, March 1. I preached at Brentford in the evening; *Monday, March* 2, at Newbury, and the next evening at Bath.

Wednesday, March 4. I went on to Bristol. I found the panic had spread hither also, as if the nation were on the brink of ruin. Strange that those who love God should be so frightened at shadows! I can compare this only to the alarm which spread through the nation in King William's time that on that very night the Irish Papists were to cut the throats of all the Protestants in England.

Monday, March 9. On this and the following days I visited the society, and found a good increase. This year I myself (which I have seldom done) chose the preachers for Bristol; and these were plain men, and likely to do more good than has been done in one year for these twenty years.

How the Poor Man's Prayer was Answered.

Monday, May 18. There were two roads to Sligo, one of which was several miles shorter, but had some sloughs in it. However, having a good guide, we chose this. Two sloughs we got over well. On our approaching the third, seven or eight countrymen presently ran to help us. One of them carried me over on his shoulders, others got the horses through, and some carried the chaise. We then thought the difficulty was past; but in half an hour we came to another slough. Being helped over it, I walked on, leaving Mr. Delap, John Carr, Joseph Bradford, and Jesse Bugden, with the chaise, which was stuck fast in the slough. As none of them thought of unharnessing the horses, the traces were soon broke; at length they fastened ropes to the chaise and to the stronger horse; and the horse pulling, and the men thrusting at once, they thrust it through the slough to the firm land. In an hour or two after we all met at Ballinacurrah. While I was walking a poor man overtook me, who appeared to be in deep distress; he said he owed his landlord twenty shillings rent, for which he had turned him and his family out of doors, and that he had been down with his relations to beg their help, but they would do nothing. Upon my giving him a guinea he would needs kneel down in the road to pray for me, and then cried out, "O, I shall have a house! I shall have a house over my head!" So, perhaps, God answered that poor man's prayer by the sticking fast of the chaise in the slough!

Massacre at Sligo.

Tuesday, May 19. In the evening I preached at Sligo in the old Court-house, an exceeding spacious building. I know not that ever I saw so large a congregation here before, nor (considering their number) so well behaved. Will God revive his work even in this sink of wickedness, and after so many deadly stumbling-blocks? Upon inquiry I found there had been for some time a real revival of religion here. The congregations have considerably increased, and the society is nearly doubled. We had in the evening a larger congregation than before, among whom were most of the gentry of the town, and all but one or two young gentlemen (so-called) were remarkably serious and attentive. I now received an intelligible account of the famous massacre at Sligo. A little before the Revolution, one Mr. Morris, a Popish gentleman, invited all the chief Protestants to an entertainment, at the close of which, on a signal given, the men he had prepared fell upon them and left not one of them alive. As soon as King William prevailed he quitted Sligo. But venturing thither about twenty years after, supposing no one then knew him, he was discovered, and used according to his deserts.

An Extraordinary Congregation.

Saturday, May 23. I was desired to preach once more at Coote Hill, which I had not seen for many years. The use of the Presbyterian meeting-house being procured, I had a very extraordinary congregation. To many Church people were added Seceders, Arians, Moravians, and what not; however I went straight forward, insisting that "without holiness no man shall see the Lord."

Giant's Causeway.

Saturday, June 6. I was desired to take a ride to the celebrated Giant's Causeway. It lies eleven English miles from Coleraine. When we came to the edge of a precipice three or four poor boys were ready to hold our horses and show us the way down. It being dead low-water we could go anywhere, and see every thing to the best advantage. It is doubtless the effect of subterraneous fire. This manifestly appears from many of the stones which composed the pillars that are now fallen down; these evidently bear the mark of fire, being burned black on one or the other surface. It appears likewise from numerous pumice stones scattered among the pillars; just such pillars and pumices are found in every country which is, or ever was, subject to volcanoes.

Largest Congregation in Ireland.

Tuesday, June 9. We rode through a small village, wherein was a little society. One desiring me to step into a house there, it was filled presently, and the poor people were all ear while I gave a short exhortation and spent a few minutes in prayer. In the evening, as the Town-hall at Carrickfergus could not contain the congregation, I preached in the market-house, on "Fear God and keep his commandments, for this is the whole [*duty*] of man." The people in general appeared to be more serious, and the society more earnest than they had been for many years. Thence we went to Belfast, the largest town in Ulster, said to contain thirty thousand souls. The streets are well laid out; are broad, straight, and well built. The poor-house stands on an eminence fronting the main street, and having a beautiful prospect on every side over the whole country; the old men, the old women, the male and the female children, are all employed according to their strength; and all their apartments are airy, sweet, and clean, equal to any thing of the kind I have seen in England. I preached in the evening, on one side of the new church, to far the largest congregation I have seen in Ireland; but I doubt the bulk of them were nearly concerned in my text, "And Gallio cared for none of these things."

Wesley Seventy-five Years Old.

Sunday, June 28. I am this day seventy-five years old, and I do not find myself, blessed be God! any weaker than I was at five-and-twenty. This also hath God wrought! All this week I visited as many as I could, and endeavored to confirm their love to each other, and I have not known the society for many years so united as it is now.

A Consummate Enthusiast.

Saturday, July 4. A remarkable piece was put into my hands, the "Life of Mr. Morsay," and I saw no reason to alter the judgment which I had formed of him forty years ago. He was a man of uncommon understanding, and greatly devoted to God. But he was a consummate enthusiast. Not the word of God, but his own imaginations, which he took for Divine inspirations, were the sole rule both of his words and actions. Hence arose his marvelous instability, taking such huge strides backward and forward; hence his frequent darkness of soul; for when he departed from God's word God departed from him. Upon the whole I do not know that ever I read a more dangerous writer, one who so wonderfully blends together truth and falsehood, solid piety, and wild enthusiasm.

Discussions at the Dublin Conference.

Tuesday, July 7. Our little Conference began, at which about twenty preachers were present. On *Wednesday* we heard one of our friends at large upon the duty of leaving the Church; but, after a full discussion of the point, we all remained firm in our judgment that it is our duty not to leave the Church wherein God has blessed us and does bless us still.

Sunday, July 12. After I had several times explained the nature of it, we solemnly renewed our covenant with God. It was a time never to be forgotten; God poured down upon the assembly "the spirit of grace and supplication;" especially in singing that verse of the concluding hymn,

> "To us the covenant blood apply,
> Which takes our sins away;
> And register our names on high,
> And keep us to that day.

The Largest Conference yet Held.

Sunday, Aug. 2. At one I preached at the foot of Birstal Hill to the largest congregation that ever was seen there. It was supposed there were twelve or fourteen thousand, but there were some thousands more at Leeds. I think it was the largest congregation that I have seen for many years, except that at Gwennap in Cornwall.

Tuesday, Aug. 4. Our Conference began; so large a number of preachers never met at a Conference before. I preached morning and evening till *Thursday* night, then my voice began to fail; so I desired two of our preachers to supply my place the next day. On *Saturday* the Conference ended.

Old Sermons.

Tuesday, Sept. 1. I went to Tiverton; I was musing here on what I heard a good man say long since, "Once in seven years I burn all my sermons; for it is a shame if I cannot write better sermons now than I could seven years ago." Whatever others can do, I really cannot. I cannot write a better sermon on the Good Steward than I did seven years ago; I cannot write a better on the Great Assize than I did twenty years ago; I cannot write a better on the Use of Money than I did near thirty years ago; nay, I know not that I can write a better on the Circumcision of the Heart than I did five-and-forty years ago. Perhaps, indeed, I may have read five or six hundred books more than I had then, and may know a little more history or natural philosophy than I did, but I am not sensible that this has made any essential addition to my knowledge in divinity. Forty years ago I knew and preached every Christian doctrine which I preach now.

Wesley Preaches under a Tree of his Own Planting.

Friday, Sept. 4. I spent some time in the evening, and an hour in the morning, with the lovely children at Publow. Such another company of them I never saw since Miss Bosanquet removed from Leytonstone.

Saturday, Sept. 5. I returned to Bristol.

Sunday, Sept. 6. At eight I preached near the Drawbridge; at two near Kingswood school, under the tree which I planted for the use of the next generation; and at five near King's Square, to a very numerous and exceeding serious congregation.

Called Gentlemen by Courtesy.

Tuesday, Sept. 8. In the evening I stood on one side of the market-place of Frome, and declared to a very numerous congregation, "His commandments are not grievous." They stood as quiet as those at Bristol, a very few excepted, most of whom were, by the courtesy of England, called gentlemen. How much inferior to the keelmen and colliers!

Voltaire and his Physician.

Sept. On *Monday, Tuesday,* and *Wednesday,* on meeting the classes, I carefully examined whether there was any truth in the assertion that above a hundred in our society were concerned in unlawful distilling. The result was that I found two persons, and no more, that were concerned therein. I now procured a copy of part of Mr. Fletcher's late letter to Mr. Ireland, which I think it my duty to publish as a full answer to the lying accounts which have been published concerning that bad man, "Mr. Voltaire, [who,] finding himself ill, sent for Dr. Tronchin, first physician to the Duke of Orleans, one of his converts to infidelity, and said to him, 'Sir, I desire you will save my life; I will give you half my fortune if you will lengthen out my days only six months; if not, I shall go to the devil and carry you with me.'"

Wesley Preaches at the Poor-house.

Saturday, Oct. 3. Visiting one at the poor-house, I was much moved to see such a company of poor, maimed, halt, and blind, who seemed to have no one caring for their souls. So I appointed to be there the next day, and at two o'clock had all that could get out of bed, young and old, in the great hall. My heart was greatly enlarged toward them, and many blessed God for the consolation.

He Opens the New Chapel in City Road

Sunday, Nov. 1, was the day appointed for opening the new chapel in the City Road. It is perfectly neat, but not fine, and contains far more people than the Foundery; I believe, together with the morning chapel, as many as the Tabernacle. Many were afraid that the multitudes crowding from all parts would have occasioned much disturbance, but they were happily disappointed; there was none at all; all was quietness, decency, and order. I preached on part of Solomon's prayer at the dedication of the Temple; and both in the morning and afternoon (when I preached on the hundred forty and four thousand standing with the Lamb on Mount Zion) God was eminently present in the midst of the congregation.

Wesley Outwalks the Stage.

Wednesday, Nov. 4. I took a view of the old church at Minster, once a spacious and elegant building. It stands pleasantly on the top of a hill, and commands all the country round. We went from thence to Queensborough, which contains above fifty houses, and sends two members to Parliament. Surely the whole Isle of Sheppey is now but a shadow of what it was once.

Thursday, Nov. 5. I returned to Chatham, and on the following morning set out in the stage-coach for London. At the end of Stroud I chose to walk up the hill, leaving the coach to follow me. But it was in no great haste; it did not overtake me till I had walked above five miles. I cared not if it had been ten; the more I walk, the sounder I sleep.

Is the Scandal of the Cross Ceased?

Sunday, Nov. 29. I was desired to preach a charity sermon in St. Luke's Church, Old-street. I doubt whether it was ever so crowded before, and the fear of God seemed to possess the whole audience. In the afternoon I preached at the new chapel, and at seven in St. Margaret's, Rood-lane, full as much crowded as St. Luke's. Is then the scandal of the cross ceased?

"Honest Silas Told."

Sunday, Dec. 20. I buried what was mortal of honest Silas Told. For many years he attended the malefactors in Newgate without fee or reward; and I suppose no man for this hundred years has been so successful in that melancholy office. God had given him peculiar talents for it, and he had amazing success therein. The greatest part of those whom he attended died in peace, and many of them in the triumph of faith

A Christmas-Day's Work.

Friday, Dec. 25, (being *Christmas-Day*,) our service began at four, as usual, in the new chapel. I expected Mr. Richardson to read prayers at West-street chapel, but he did not come; so I read prayers myself, and preached, and administered the sacrament to several hundred people. In the afternoon I preached at the new chapel, thoroughly filled in every corner; and in the evening at St. Sepulchre's, one of the largest parish churches in London. It was warm enough, being sufficiently filled, yet I felt no weakness or weariness, but was stronger after I had preached my fourth sermon than I was after the first.

Thursday, Dec. 31. We concluded the old year with a solemn watch-night, and began the new with praise and thanksgiving. We had a violent storm at night; the roaring of the wind was like loud thunder; it kept me awake half an hour; I then slept in peace.

Wesley requires Accuracy in Statistics.

Sunday, Feb. 21, 1779. I returned to Norwich and took an exact account of the society. I wish all our preachers would be accurate in their accounts, and rather speak under than above the truth. I have heard again and again of the increase of their society, and what is the naked truth? Why, I left in it two hundred and two members, and I find one hundred and seventy-nine!

Essay on Taste—Criticism.

March. After preaching at Wednesbury, Darlaston, Dudley, and Wolverhampton, on *Wednesday*, 24, I went on to Madeley. In the way I finished a celebrated "Essay on Taste." And is this the treatise that gained the premium? It is lively and pretty, but neither deep nor strong. Scarce any of the terms are accurately defined; indeed, defining is not this author's talent. He has not by any means a clear apprehension; and it is through this capital defect that he jumbles together true and false propositions in every chapter and on every page. To this essay three extracts are subjoined. The first is much to the purpose. The second is a superficial, empty thing. Is this a specimen of the great M. D'Alembert? But I was most surprised at the third. What! is this extracted from the famous Montesquieu? It has neither strength nor clearness, nor justness of thought! And is this the writer so admired all over Europe? He is no more to be compared to Lord Forbes, or Dr. Beattie, than a mouse to an elephant.

A Just Reflection.

Monday, April 5. I preached at Northwich. I used to go on from hence to Little Leigh, but since Mr Barker has gone hence that place knows us no more.

I cannot but wonder at the infatuation of men that really love and fear God, and yet leave great part of, if not all, their substance to men that neither love nor fear him! Surely if I did little good with my money while living, I would at least do good with it when I could live no longer.

Smollet s History of England.

Thursday, April 22. I was a little surprised at a passage in Dr. Smollet's "History of England," vol. xv, pp. 121, 122:

"Imposture and fanaticism still hang upon the skirts of religion. Weak minds were seduced by the delusions of a superstition styled Methodism, raised upon the affectation of superior sanctity and pretensions to divine illumination. Many thousands were infected with this enthusiasm by the endeavors of a few obscure preachers such as Whitefield and the two Wesleys, who found means to lay the whole kingdom under contribution."

Poor Dr. Smollet! Thus to transmit to all succeeding generations a whole heap of notorious falsehoods! "Imposture and fanaticism!" Neither one nor the other had any share in the late revival of scriptural religion, which is no other than the love of God and man, gratitude to our Creator, and good-will to our fellow-creatures. Is this delusion and superstition? No, it is real wisdom; it is solid virtue. Does this fanaticism "hang upon the skirts of religion?" Nay, it is the very essence of it. Does the Doctor call this enthusiasm? Why? Because he knows nothing about it. Who told him that these "obscure preachers" made "pretensions to divine illumination?" How often has that silly calumny been refuted to the satisfaction of all candid men! However, they "found means to lay the whole kingdom under contribution." So does this frontless man, blind and bold, stumble on without the least shadow of truth! Meantime, what faith can be given to his history? What credit can any man of reason give to any fact upon *his* authority?

Swedenborg's Heaven and Hell.

April. In traveling this week I looked over Baron Swedenborg's "Account of Heaven and Hell." He was a man of piety, of a strong understanding and most lively imagination; but he had a violent fever when he was five-and-fifty years old, which quite overturned his understanding. Nor did he ever recover it; but it continued "majestic, though in ruins." From that time he was exactly in the state of that gentleman at Argos,

Qui se credebat miros audire tragœdos,
In vacuo lætus sessor plausorque theatro.

Who wondrous tragedies was wont to hear,
Sitting alone in the empty theater.

His words, therefore, from that time were *ægri somnia*, the dreams of a disordered imagination; just as authentic as Quevedo's "Visions of Hell." Of this work in particular I must observe, that the doctrine contained therein is not only quite unproved, quite precarious from beginning to end as depending entirely on the assertion of a single brain-sick man, but that, in many instances, it is contradictory to

Scripture, to reason, and to itself. But, over and above this, it contains many sentiments that are essentially and dangerously wrong. Such is that concerning the Trinity, for he roundly affirms God to be only one person, who was crucified; so that he revives and openly asserts the long-exploded heresy of the Sabellians and Patripassians, yea, and that of the Anthropomorphites, affirming that God constantly appears in heaven in the form of a man. And the worst is he flatly affirms, "None can go to heaven who believes three persons in the Godhead;" which is more than the most violent Arian or Socinian ever affirmed before.

Add to this that his ideas of heaven are low, groveling, just suiting a Mohammedan paradise, and his account of it has a natural tendency to sink our conceptions both of the glory of heaven and of the inhabitants of it, whom he describes as far inferior both in holiness and happiness to Gregory Lopez, or Monsieur De Renty. And his account of hell leaves nothing terrible in it; for, first, he quenches the unquenchable fire. He assures us there is no fire there; only he allows that the governor of it, the devil, sometimes orders the spirits that behave ill to be "laid on a bed of hot ashes." And, secondly, he informs you that all the damned enjoy their favorite pleasures. He that delights in filth is to have his filth, yea, and his harlot too! Now, how dreadful a tendency must this have in such an age and nation as this! I wish those pious men, Mr. Clowes and Mr. Clotworthy, would calmly consider these things before they usher into the world any more of this madman's dreams.

Not Suited to the Meridian of Edinburgh.

Monday, June 14. I preached again at Arbroath; *Tuesday, June* 15, at Dundee; and *Wednesday, June* 16, at Edinburgh.

Thursday, June 17. I examined the society. In five years I found five members had been gained! ninety-nine being increased to a hundred and four. What then have our preachers been doing all this time? 1. They have preached four evenings in the week, and on *Sunday* morning; the other mornings they have fairly given up. 2. They have taken great care not to speak too plain lest they should give offense. 3. When Mr. Drackenbury preached the old Methodist doctrine, one of them said, "You must not preach such doctrine here. The doctrine of perfection is not calculated for the meridian of Edinburgh." Waiving, then, all other hinderances, is it any wonder that the work of God has not prospered here?

Stripling Preachers.

Thursday, July 1. This was the first of eighteen or twenty days full as hot as any I remember in Georgia, and yet the season is remarkably healthy. I preached in Beverly at noon, and at Hull in the evening.

Saturday, July 3. I reached Grimsby, and found a little trial. In this and many other parts of the kingdom, those striplings who call themselves Lady Huntingdon's preachers have greatly hindered the work of God. They have neither sense, courage, nor grace to go and beat up the devil's quarters in any place where Christ has not been named; but wherever we have entered as by storm and gathered a few souls, often at the peril of our lives, they creep in and, by doubtful disputations, set every one's sword against his brother. One of these has just crept into Grimsby, and is striving to divide the poor little flock; but I hope his labor will be in vain, and they will still hold "the unity of the spirit in the bond of peace."

Good Alice Shadford.

Sunday, July 11. About eight I preached at Misterton, and about one at Overthorpe. But good Alice Shadford was not there. She was long "a mother in Israel," a burning and shining light, an unexceptionable instance of perfect love. After spending near a hundred years on earth, she was some months since transplanted to paradise.

Legacy of a Minister to his Parishioners.

Monday, July 12. I preached at Crowle, and afterward searched the church-yard to find the tomb of Mr. Ashbourn. We could find nothing of it there. At length we found a large flat stone in the church, but the inscription was utterly illegible, the letters being filled up with dust. However, we made a shift to pick it out, and then read as follows:

HERE LIES THE BODY OF MR. SOLOMON ASHBOURN.
HE DIED IN 1711,
AND SOLEMNLY BEQUEATHED THE FOLLOWING VERSES TO HIS PARISHIONERS.

"Ye stiff-necked and uncircumcised in heart and ears, ye do always resist the Holy Ghost; as your fathers did so do ye." Acts vii, 51.

"I have labored in vain, I have spent my strength for naught, and in vain; yet surely my judgment is with the Lord, and my work with my God." Isa. xlix, 4.

A Dancing-master has the Preference.

Wednesday, July 21. The house was filled at five, and we had another solemn opportunity. About eight, calling at Hinckley, I was desired to preach; as also at Forcell, ten or twelve miles further. When I came to Coventry I found notice had been given for my preaching in the park, but the heavy rain prevented. I sent to the Mayor, desiring the use of the Town Hall. He refused, but the same day gave the use of it to a dancing-master. I then went to the women's market. Many soon gathered together, and listened with all seriousness. I preached there again the next morning, *Thursday*, 22, and again in the evening. Then I took coach for London. I was nobly attended; behind the coach were ten convicted felons, loudly blaspheming and rattling their chains; by my side sat a man with a loaded blunderbuss, and another upon the coach.

The last Night at the Foundery.

Sunday, July 25. Both the chapels were full enough. On *Monday* I retired to Lewisham to write.

Tuesday, Aug. 3. Our Conference began, which continued and ended in peace and love.

Sunday, Aug. 8. I was at West-street in the morning, and at the new chapel in the evening, when I took a solemn leave of the affectionate congregation. This was the last night which I spent at the Foundery. What hath God wrought there in one-and-forty years!

In Charge of Angels.

Friday, Aug. 13. As I was going down a steep pair of stairs my foot slipped and I fell down several steps.

Falling on the edge of one of them, it broke the case of an almanac which was in my pocket all to pieces. The edge of another stair met my right buckle, and snapped the steel chape of it in two, but I was not hurt. So doth our good Master give his angels charge over us! In the evening I preached at Brecknock, and leaving my brother there, on *Saturday*, 14, went forward to Carmarthen. This evening, and in the morning, *Sunday*, 15, the new preaching-house contained the congregation; but in the afternoon we had, I think, the largest congregation I ever saw in Wales. I preached on the Gospel for the day, the story of the Pharisee and the Publican; and I believe many were constrained to cry out for the present, "God be merciful to me a sinner!"

Wesley Preaches to American Prisoners.

Saturday, Aug. 21. I went to Pembroke. Understanding that a large number of American prisoners were here, in the evening I took my stand over against the place where they were confined, so that they all could hear distinctly. Many of them seemed much affected. O that God may set their souls at liberty!

Well Repaid.

Friday, Aug. 27. I preached at Cardiff about noon, and at six in the evening. We then went on to Newport, and, setting out early in the morning, reached Bristol in the afternoon.

Sunday, Aug. 29. I had a very large number of communicants. It was one of the hottest days I have known in England. The thermometer rose to eighty degrees, as high as it usually rises in Jamaica. Being desired to visit a dying man on Kingsdown, I had no time but at two o'clock. The sun shone without a cloud, so that I had a warm journey. But I was well repaid, for the poor sinner found peace. At five I preached to an immense multitude in the Square, and God comforted many drooping souls.

Make your Will before you Sleep.

Thursday, Sept. 23. In the evening one sat behind me in the pulpit at Bristol who was one of our first masters at Kingswood. A little after he left the school he likewise left the society. Riches then flowed in upon him, with which, having no relations, Mr. Spencer designed to do much good after his death. "But God said unto him, thou fool!" Two hours after he died intestate, and left his money to be scrambled for! Reader, if you have not done it already, make your will before you sleep!

Wesley's Prerogative called in Question.

Monday, Nov. 22. My brother and I set out for Bath on a very extraordinary occasion. Some time since Mr. Smyth, a clergyman, whose labors God had greatly blessed in the north of Ireland, brought his wife over to Bath, who had been for some time in a declining state of health. I desired him to preach every Sunday evening in our chapel while he remained there. But as soon as I was gone, Mr. M'Nab, one of our preachers, vehemently opposed that, affirming it was the common cause of all the lay preachers; that they were appointed by the Conference, not by me, and would not suffer the clergy to ride over their heads, Mr. Smyth in particular, of whom he said all manner of evil. Others warmly defended him. Hence the society was torn in pieces, and thrown into the utmost confusion.

Tuesday, Nov. 23. I read to the society a paper which I wrote near twenty years ago on a like occasion. Herein I observed that "the rules of our preachers were fixed by me before any Conference existed," particularly the twelfth: "Above all, you are to preach when and where I appoint." By obstinately opposing which rule, Mr. M'Nab has made all this uproar. In the morning, at a meeting of the preachers, I informed Mr. M'Nab that, as he did not agree to our fundamental rule, I could not receive him as one of our preachers till he was of another mind.

Dr. Warner's History of Ireland.

Friday, Nov. 26. I took coach again, and on *Saturday* reached London. In this journey I read Dr. Warner's History of Ireland, from its first settlement to the English conquest; and, after calm deliberation, I make no scruple to pronounce it a mere senseless romance. I do not believe one leaf of it is true, from the beginning to the end. I totally reject the authorities on which he builds; I will not take Flagherty's or Keating's word for a farthing. I doubt not Ireland was, before the Christian era, full as barbarous as Scotland or England. Indeed, it appears from their own accounts that the Irish in general were continually plundering and murdering each other from the earliest ages to that period; and so they were ever since, by the account of Dr. Warner himself, till they were restrained by the English. How then were they converted by St. Patrick? Cousin-german to St. George! To what religion? Not to Christianity. Neither in his age nor the following had they the least savor of Christianity either in their lives or their tempers.

The Mansion of Ancient Kings.

Saturday, May 20, 1780. I took one more walk through Holyrood House, the mansion of ancient kings. But how melancholy an appearance does it make now! The stately rooms are dirty as stables; the colors of the tapestry are quite faded; several of the pictures are cut and defaced. The roof of the royal chapel is fallen in, and the bones of James the Fifth, and the once beautiful Lord Darnley, are scattered about like those of sheep or oxen. Such is human greatness! Is not "a living dog better than a dead lion?"

Sunday, May 21. The rain hindered me from preaching at noon upon the Castle Hill. In the evening the house was well filled, and I was enabled to speak strong words. But I am not a preacher for the people of Edinburgh. Hugh Saunderson and Michael Fenwick are more to their taste.

An Angel Climbing a Ladder.

Wednesday, May 31. I went to Mr. Parker's, at Shincliff, near Durham. The congregation being far too large to get into the house, I stood near his door. It seemed as if the whole village were ready to receive the truth in the love thereof. Perhaps their earnestness may provoke the people of Durham to jealousy.

In the afternoon we took a view of the castle at Durham, the residence of the Bishop. The situation is wonderfully fine, surrounded by the river, and commanding all the country; and many of the apartments are large and stately, but the furniture is mean beyond imagination! I know not where I have seen such in a gentleman's house, or a man of five hundred a year, except that of the Lord Lieutenant in Dublin. In the largest chambers the tapestry is quite faded; besides that, it is coarse and ill-judged. Take but one instance: in Jacob's Vision you see, on the one side, a little paltry ladder, and an angel climbing it in the attitude of a chimney sweeper; and, on the other side, Jacob staring at him from under a large silver-laced hat!

Wesley Pensioned for Defending the King.

Monday, June 5. About noon I preached at Tockwith, and then went on to York. I was surprised to find a general faintness here; one proof of which was, that the morning preaching was given up.

Tuesday, June 6, was the quarterly meeting, the most numerous I ever saw. At two was the lovefeast, at which several instances of the mighty power of God were repeated, by which it appears that his work is still increasing in several parts of the circuit. An arch news-writer published a paragraph to-day, probably designed for wit, concerning the large pension which the famous Wesley received for defending the King. This so increased the congregation in the evening, that scores were obliged to go away. And God applied that word to many hearts, "I will not destroy the city for ten's sake!"

Wednesday, June 7. I preached at Pocklington and Swinfleet.

Thursday, June 8. I preached on the green at Thorne to a listening multitude. Only two or three were much diverted at the thought of seeing the dead, small and great, standing before God!

Wesley enters the Seventy-eighth Year of his Age.

Wednesday, May 28. I went to Sheffield, but the house was not ready, so I preached in the Square. I can hardly think I am entered this day into the seventy-eighth year of my age. By the blessing of God I am just the same as when I entered the twenty-eighth. This hath God wrought, chiefly by my constant exercise, my rising early, and preaching morning and evening.

The Celebrated Cartoons.

Sunday, July 23. I preached (after reading prayers) at ten, at half-hour past two, and in the evening. Very many heard; I hope some felt what was spoken. We have sown, O may God give the increase!

Monday, July 24. I went on to Bristol. While I was at Bath I narrowly observed and considered the celebrated cartoons, the three first in particular. What a poor designer was one of the finest painters in the world! 1. Here are two men in a boat, each of them more than half as long as the boat itself. 2. Our Lord, saying to Peter, "Feed my sheep," points to three or four sheep standing by him. 3. While Peter and John heal the lame man, two naked boys stand by them. For what? O pity that so fine a painter should be utterly without common sense!

In the evening I saw one of the greatest curiosities

in the vegetable creation, the nightly cereus. About four in the afternoon the dry stem began to swell; about six it gradually opened, and about eight it was in its full glory. I think the inner part of this flower, which was snow white, was about five inches diameter; the yellow rays which surrounded it, I judged, were in diameter nine or ten inches. About twelve it began to droop, being covered with a cold sweat; at four it died away.

The Duke of Dorset's Seat.

Monday, Oct. 16. I went to Tunbridge Wells, and preached to a serious congregation on Rev. xx, 12.

Tuesday, Oct. 17. I came back to Sevenoaks, and in the afternoon walked over to the Duke of Dorset's seat. The park is the pleasantest I ever saw, the trees are so elegantly disposed. The house, which is at least two hundred years old, is immensely large. It consists of two squares, considerably bigger than the two quadrangles in Lincoln College. I believe we were shown above thirty rooms, besides the hall, the chapels, and three galleries. The pictures are innumerable; I think four times as many as in the castle at Blenheim. Into one of the galleries opens the king's bed-chamber, ornamented above all the rest. The bed-curtains are cloth-of-gold, and so richly wrought that it requires some strength to draw them. The tables, the chairs, the frames of the looking-glasses, are all plated over with silver. The tapestry, representing the whole history of Nebuchadnezzar, is as fresh as if newly woven. But the bed-curtains are exceeding dirty, and look more like copper than gold. The silver on the tables, chairs, and glass looks as dull as lead. And, to complete all, King Nebuchadnezzar among the beasts, together with his eagle's claws, has a large crown upon his head, and is clothed in scarlet and gold.

Three Services, but not Tired!

Sunday, Feb. 25, 1781. My brother, Mr. Richardson, and Mr. Buckingham being ill, I went through the service at Spitalfields alone. The congregation was much larger than usual, but my strength was as my day, both here, at the new chapel, and afterward at St. Antholin's Church. The service lasted till near nine, but I was no more tired than at nine in the morning.

Wesley Opens the New Chapel at Manchester.

March. After preaching at Congleton, Macclesfield, and Stockport, in my way, on *Friday,* 30, I opened the new chapel at Manchester, about the size of that in London. The whole congregation behaved with the utmost seriousness. I trust much good will be done in this place.

Sunday, April 1. I began reading prayers at ten o'clock. Our country friends flocked in from all sides. At the communion was such a sight as I am persuaded was never seen at Manchester before; eleven or twelve hundred communicants at once, and all of them fearing God.

Tuesday, April 3. I took a solemn leave of our affectionate friends here, and went on to Bolton. The society here are true, original Methodists. They are not conformed to the world, either in its maxims, its spirit, or its fashions, but are simple followers of the

Lamb; consequently, they increase both in grace and number.

Just in Time.

Saturday, April 7. At noon I preached at Preston-on-the-Hill, and in the evening at Warrington.

Sunday, April 8. The service was at the usual hours. I came just in time to put a stop to a bad custom which was creeping in here; a few men, who had fine voices, sang a Psalm which no one knew, in a tune fit for an opera, wherein three, four, or five persons sung different words at the same time! What an insult upon common sense! What a burlesque upon public worship! No custom can excuse such a mixture of profaneness and absurdity.

Another Visit to the Isle of Man.

Wednesday, May 30. I embarked on board the packet-boat for the Isle of Man. We had a dead calm for many hours; however, we landed at Douglas on *Friday* morning. Both the preachers met me here, and gave me a comfortable account of the still-increasing work of God. Before dinner we took a walk in a garden near the town, wherein any of the inhabitants of it may walk. It is wonderfully pleasant, yet not so pleasant as the gardens of the nunnery, (so it is still called,) which are not far from it. These are delightfully laid out, and yield to few places of the size in England. At six I preached in the market-place to a large congregation, all of whom, except a few children and two or three giddy young women, were seriously attentive

Description of the Island and of Methodism.

Thursday, June 7. I met our little body of preachers. They were two-and-twenty in all. I never saw in England so many stout, well-looking preachers together. If their spirit be answerable to their look, I know not what can stand before them. In the afternoon I rode over to Dawby, and preached to a very large and very serious congregation.

Friday, June 8. Having now visited the island round, east, south, north, and west, I was thoroughly convinced that we have no such circuit as this either in England, Scotland, or Ireland. It is shut up from the world, and, having little trade, is visited by scarce any strangers. Here are no Papists, no Dissenters of any kind, no Calvinists, no disputers. Here is no opposition, either from the Governor, (a mild, humane man,) from the Bishop, (a good man,) or from the bulk of the clergy. One or two of them did oppose for a time, but they seem now to understand better; so that we have now rather too little than too much reproach; the scandal of the cross being, for the present, ceased. The natives are a plain, artless, simple people; unpolished, that is, unpolluted; few of them are rich or genteel, the far greater part moderately poor, and most of the strangers that settle among them are men that have seen affliction. The Local Preachers are men of faith and love, knit together in one mind and one judgment. They speak either Manx or English, and follow a regular plan, which the assistant gives them monthly. The isle is supposed to have thirty thousand inhabitants. Allowing half of them to be adults, and our societies to contain one-or-two-and-twenty hundred members, what a fair proportion is this! What has been seen like this in any part either of Great Britain or Ireland?

Wesley Enters his Seventy-ninth Year.

Thursday, June 28. I preached at eleven, in the main street at Selby, to a large and quiet congregation, and in the evening at Thorne. This day I enter into my seventy-ninth year, and, by the grace of God, I feel no more of the infirmities of old age than I did at twenty-nine.

Friday, June 29. I preached at Crowle and at Epworh. I have now preached thrice a day for seven days following, but it is just the same as if it had been but once.

Dr. Robertson's History of America.

July 6. To-day I finished the second volume of Dr. Robertson's "History of America." His language is always clear and strong, and frequently elegant; and I suppose his history is preferable to any history of America which has appeared in the English tongue. But I cannot admire, first, his intolerable prolixity in this history, as well as his "History of Charles the Fifth." He promises eight books of the History of America, and fills four of them with critical dissertations. True, the dissertations are sensible, but they have lost their way—they are not history, they are swelled beyond all proportion, doubtless for the benefit of the author and the book-seller rather than the reader. I cannot admire, secondly, a Christian divine writing a history with so very little of Christianity in it. Nay, he seems studiously to avoid saying any thing which might imply that he believes the Bible. I can still less admire, thirdly, his speaking so honorably of a professed Infidel; yea, and referring to his masterpiece of Infidelity, "Sketches of the History of Man," as artful, as unfair, as disingenuous a book as even Toland's "Nazarenus." Least of all can I admire, fourthly, his copying after Dr. Hawkesworth, (who once professed better things,) in totally excluding the Creator from governing the world. Was it not enough never to mention the providence of God, where there was the fairest occasion, without saying expressly, "The *fortune* of Certiz," or "chance," did thus or thus! So far as fortune or chance governs the world God has no place in it.

The poor American, though not pretending to be a Christian, knew better than this. When the Indian was asked, "Why do you think the beloved ones take care of *you?*" he answered, "When I was in the battle the bullet went on this side, and on that side, and this man died, and that man died, and I am alive! So I know the beloved ones take care of *me*." It is true, the doctrine of a particular providence (and any but a *particular* providence is no providence at all) is absolutely out of fashion in England, and a prudent author might write this to gain the favor of his gentle readers. Yet I will not say this is real prudence, because he may lose hereby more than he gains, as the majority, even of Britons, to this day, retain some sort of respect for the Bible.

Mr. Fletcher and Dr. Coke present at the Leeds Conference.

Monday, Aug. 6. I desired Mr. Fletcher, Dr. Coke, and four more of our brethren, to meet every evening, that we might consult together on any difficulty that occurred. On *Tuesday* our Conference began, at which were present about seventy preachers, whom I had severally invited to come and assist me with their advice in carrying on the great work of God.

Wednesday, Aug. 8. I desired Mr. Fletcher to preach. I do not wonder he should be so popular, not only because he preaches with all his might, but because the power of God attends both his preaching and prayer. On *Monday* and *Tuesday* we finished the remaining business of the Conference, and ended it with solemn prayer and thanksgiving.

Wesley's Ne Plus Ultra.

Sunday, Sept. 5. About five in the evening I preached at Gwennap. I believe two-or-three-and-twenty thousand were present, and I believe God enabled me so to speak that even those who stood furthest off could hear distinctly. I think this is my *ne plus ultra.* [Utmost limit.] I shall scarce see a larger congregation till we meet in the air.

"I can plan, but who will execute?"

Friday, Sept. 8. I went over to Kingswood, and made a particular inquiry into the management of the school. I found some of the rules had not been observed at all, particularly that of rising in the morning. Surely Satan has a peculiar spite at this school! What trouble has it cost me for above these thirty years! I can *plan,* but who will *execute?* I know not; God help me!

Sunday, Sept. 9. In the calm, sunshiny evening I preached near King's Square. I know nothing more solemn than such a congregation praising God with one heart and one voice. Surely they who talk of the indecency of field-preaching never saw such a sight as this.

Wesley Preaches to Condemned Criminals.

Thursday, Oct. 4. I was importuned to preach the condemned sermon at Bristol. I did so, though with little hope of doing good, the criminals being eminently impenitent. Yet they were, for the present, melted into tears, and they were not out of God's reach.

A Young People's Prayer-Meeting.

Monday, Nov. 5. I began visiting the classes, and found a considerable increase in the society. This I impute chiefly to a small company of young persons who have kept a prayer-meeting at five every morning. In the following week I visited most of the country societies, and found them increasing.

A Successful Organizer.

March, 1782. Both Mr. and Mrs. Fletcher complained that, after all the pains they had taken, they could not prevail on the people to join in society, no, not even to meet in a class. Resolving to try, I preached to a crowded audience on "I am not ashamed of the Gospel of Christ." I followed the blow in the afternoon by strongly applying those words, "Awake, thou that sleepest," and then enforcing the necessity of Christian fellowship on all who desired either to awake or keep awake. I then desired those that were willing to join together for this purpose, to call upon Mr. Fletcher and me after service. Ninety-four or ninety-five persons did so—about as many men as women. We explained to them the nature of a Christian society, and they willingly joined therein.

"If decreed they cannot help it."

Thursday, March 28. Coming to Congleton, I found the Calvinists were just breaking in, and striving to make havoc of the flock. Is this brotherly love? Is this doing as we would be done to? No more than robbing on the highway. But if it is *decreed*, they cannot help it, so we cannot blame them.

Work of God at Epworth.

Friday, May 10. I preached at Sheffield; *Saturday*, 11, at noon, at Doncaster, and in the evening at Epworth. I found the accounts I had received of the work of God here were not at all exaggerated. Here is a little country town containing a little more than eight or nine hundred grown people, and there has been such a work among them as we have not seen in so short a time either at Leeds, Bristol, or London.

Sunday, May 12. About eight I preached at Misterton; about one at Overthorpe. Many of the Epworth children were there, and their spirit spread to all around them. But the huge congregation was in the market-place at Epworth, and the Lord in the midst of them. The love-feast which followed exceeded all. I never knew such a one here before. As soon as one had done speaking another began. Several of them were children, but they spoke with the wisdom of the aged though with the fire of youth. So out of the mouth of babes and sucklings did God perfect praise.

Monday, May 13. I preached at Thorne. Never did I see such a congregation here before. The flame of Epworth had spread hither also. In seven weeks fifty persons have found peace with God.

Tuesday, May 14. Some years ago four factories for spinning and weaving were set up at Epworth. In these a large number of young women and boys and girls were employed. The whole conversation of these was profane and loose to the last degree. But some of these stumbling in at the prayer-meeting were suddenly cut to the heart. These never rested till they had gained their companions. The whole scene was changed. In three of the factories no more lewdness or profaneness were found, for God had put a new song in their mouth, and blasphemies were turned to praise. Those three I visited to-day, and found religion had taken deep root in them. No trifling word was heard among them, and they watch over each other in love. I found it exceeding good to be there, and we rejoiced together in the God of our salvation.

Lady Maxwell and her Poor Children.

Friday, May 31. As I lodged with Lady Maxwell at Saughton Hall, (a good old mansion-house three miles from Edinburgh,) she desired me to give a short discourse to a few of her poor neighbors. I did so at four in the afternoon, on the story of Dives and Lazarus. About seven I preached in our house at Edinburgh, and fully delivered my own soul.

Saturday, June 1. I spent a little time with forty

poor children, whom Lady Maxwell keeps at school. They are swiftly brought forward in reading and writing, and learn the principles of religion. But I observe in them all the *ambitiosa paupertas*. [Ostentatious poverty.] Be they ever so poor, they must have a scrap of finery. Many of them have not a shoe to their foot; but the girl in rags is not without her ruffles.

Scotch Hearers.

Sunday, June 2. Mr. Collins intended to have preached on the Castle Hill at twelve o'olock, but the dull minister kept us in the kirk till past one. At six the house was well filled, and I did not shun to declare the whole counsel of God. I almost wonder at myself. I seldom speak any where so roughly as in Scotland. And yet most of the people hear and hear, and are just what they were before.

A Comfortable Fall.

Saturday, June 15. As I was coming down stairs the carpet slipped from under my feet, which, I know not how, turned me round, and pitched me back with my head foremost for six or seven stairs. It was impossible to recover myself till I came to the bottom. My head rebounded once or twice from the edge of the stone stairs. But it felt to me exactly as if I had fallen on a cushion or pillow. Mr. Douglas ran out sufficiently affrighted. But he needed not. For I rose as well as ever, having received no damage but the loss of a little skin from one or two of my fingers. Doth not God give his angels charge over us to keep us in all our ways?

Wesley Enters his Eightieth Year.

Wednesday, June 26. I preached at Thirsk; *Thursday*, 27, at York.

Friday, June 28. I entered into my eightieth year, but, blessed be God! my time is not "labor and sorrow." I find no more pain or bodily infirmities than at five-and-twenty. This I still impute, 1. To the power of God fitting me for what he calls me to. 2. To my still traveling four or five thousand miles a year. 3. To my sleeping, night or day, whenever I want it. 4. To my rising at a set hour. And, 5. To my constant preaching, particularly in the morning.

Saturday, June 29. I went on to Leeds, and, after preaching, met the select society, consisting of about sixty members, most of whom can testify that "the blood of Jesus Christ cleanseth from all sin."

Dines with the Bishop of Exeter.

Thursday, Aug. 15. I set out for the west; preached at Taunton in the evening; *Friday* noon, at Collumpton, and in the evening at Exeter. Here poor Hugh Saunderson has pitched his standard, and declared open war. Part of the society have joined him; the rest go on their way quietly to make their calling and election sure.

Sunday, Aug. 18. I was much pleased with the decent behavior of the whole congregation at the cathedral, as also with the solemn music at the post-communion, one of the finest compositions I ever heard. The Bishop inviting me to dinner, I could not but observe, 1. The lovely situation of the palace, covered with trees, and as rural and retired as if it was quite in the country. 2. The plainness of the furniture, not costly or showy, but just fit for a Christian bishop. 3. The dinner sufficient, but not redundant—plain and good, but not delicate. 4. The propriety of the company—five clergymen and four of the aldermen; and, 5. The genuine, unaffected courtesy of the Bishop, who, I hope, will be a blessing to his whole diocese.

Wesley Rides in Haste to Visit the Dying Rector.

Monday, Sept. 2. I went on to Port Isaac.

Tuesday, Sept. 3. I preached in the street at Camelford. Being informed here that my old friend, Mr. Thompson, Rector of St. Gennis, was near death, and had expressed a particular desire to see me, I judged no time was to be lost. So, borrowing the best horse I could find, I set out and rode as fast as I could.

I found Mr. Thompson just alive, but quite sensible. It seemed to me as if none in the house but himself was very glad to see me. He had many doubts concerning his final state, and rather feared than desired to die; so that my whole business was to comfort him, and to increase and confirm his confidence in God. He desired me to administer the Lord's Supper, which I willingly did, and left him much happier than I found him, calmly waiting till his change should come.

Labors to Strengthen a Feeble Society.

Monday, Nov. 4. At five in the morning the congregation was exceeding large. That in the evening seemed so deeply affected that I hope Norwich will again lift up its head. At nine we took coach, and before eleven on *Tuesday, Nov.* 4, reached Colchester. In order to strengthen this poor feeble society I stayed with them till *Friday*, preaching morning and evening, and visiting in the day as many as I could, sick or well. I divided the classes anew, which had been strangely and irregularly jumbled together, appointed stewards, regulated temporal as well as spiritual things, and left them in a better way than they had been for several years.

Monday, Nov. 14, and the following days, I visited the societies in and about London.

Wesley's Salary.

Friday, Feb. 21, 1783. At our yearly meeting for that purpose we examined our yearly accounts, and found the money received (just answering the expense) was upward of three thousand pounds a year, but that is nothing to me; what I receive of it yearly is neither more nor less than thirty pounds.

Description of Rotterdam.

Saturday, June 14. I had much conversation with the two English ministers, sensible, well-bred, serious men. These, as well as Mr. Loyal, were very willing I should preach in their churches, but they thought it would be best for me to preach in the cathedral church. By our conversing freely together many prejudices were removed, and all our hearts seemed to be united together.

In the evening we again took a walk round the town, and I observed: 1. Many of the houses are higher than most in Edinburgh. It is true they have not so many stories, but each story is far loftier.

2. The streets, the outside and inside of their houses in every part, doors, windows, well-staircases, furniture, even floors, are kept so nicely clean that you cannot find a speck of dirt. 3. There is such a grandeur and elegance in the fronts of the large houses as I never saw elsewhere, and such a profusion of marble within, particularly in their lower floors and staircases, as I wonder other nations do not imitate. 4. The women and children (which I least of all expected) were in general the most beautiful I ever saw. They were surprisingly fair, and had an inexpressible air of innocence in their countenance. 5. This was wonderfully set off by their dress, which was *simplex munditiis,* plain and neat in the highest degree. 6. It has lately been observed that growing vegetables greatly resist putridity, so there is a use in their numerous rows of trees which was not thought of at first. The elms balance the canals, preventing the putrefaction which those otherwise might produce. One little circumstance I observed, which I suppose is peculiar to Holland: To most chamber windows a looking-glass is placed on the outside of the sash, so as to show the whole street with all the passengers. There is something very pleasing in these moving pictures. Are they found in no other country?

Wesley's Estimate of the Hollanders.

Wednesday, June 25. We took boat for Haerlem. The great church here is a noble structure, equaled by few cathedrals in England either in length, breadth, or height; the organ is the largest I ever saw, and is said to be the finest in Europe. Hence we went to Mr. Van K——'s, whose wife was convinced of sin and justified by reading Mr. Whitefield's sermons. Here we were as at home. Before dinner we took a walk in Haerlem Wood. It adjoins to the town, and is cut out in many shady walks, with lovely vistas shooting out every way. The walk from the Hague to Scheveling is pleasant, those near Amsterdam more so, but these exceed them all. We returned in the afternoon to Amsterdam, and in the evenign took leave of as many of our friends as we could. How entirely were we mistaken in the Hollanders, supposing them to be of a cold, phlegmatic, unfriendly temper! I have not met with a more warmly affectionate people in all Europe! No, not in Ireland!

Wesley Reaches Fourscore Years!

Saturday, June 28. I have this day lived fourscore years, and, by the mercy of God, my eyes are not waxed dim; and what little strength of body or mind I had thirty years since, just the same I have now. God grant I may never live to be useless! Rather may I

> My body with my charge lay down,
> And cease at once to work and live.

Pleased with his Visit to Holland.

Tuesday, July 1. I called on as many as I could of my friends, and we parted with much affection. We then hired a yacht, which brought us to Helvoetsluys about eleven the next day. At two we went on board, but the wind turning against us we did not reach Harwich till about nine on *Friday* morning. After a little rest we procured a carriage, and reached

London about eleven at night. I can by no means regret either the trouble or expense which attended this little journey. It opened me a way into, as it were, a new world, where the land, the buildings, the people, the customs, were all such as I had never seen before. But, as those with whom I conversed were of the same spirit with my friends in England, I was as much at home in Utrecht and Amsterdam as in Bristol and London.

Wesley Unwilling to be Idle.

Tuesday, Aug. 5. Early in the morning I was seized with a most impetuous flux. In a few hours it was joined by a violent and almost continual cramp; first in my feet, legs, thighs, then in my side and my throat. The case being judged extreme, a grain and a half of opium was given me in three doses. This speedily stopped the cramp, but at the same time took away my speech, hearing, and power of motion, and locked me up from head to foot, so that I lay a mere log. I then sent for Dr. Drummond, who from that time attended me twice a day. For some days I was worse and worse, till on *Friday* I was removed to Mr. Castleman's. Still my head was not affected, and I had no pain, although in a continual fever. But I continued slowly to recover, so that I could read or write an hour or two at a time. On *Wednesday, Aug.* 12, I took a vomit, which almost shook me to pieces, but, however, did me good.

Sunday, Aug. 17, and all the following week, my fever gradually abated, but I had a continual thirst, and little or no increase of strength; nevertheless, being unwilling to be idle, on *Saturday, Aug.* 23, I spent an hour with the penitents; and, finding myself no worse, on *Sunday, Aug.* 24, I preached at the new room morning and afternoon. Finding my strength was now in some measure restored, I determined to delay no longer, but, setting out on *Monday, Aug.* 25, reached Gloucester in the afternoon; in the evening I preached in the Town-hall, I believe not in vain.

Tuesday, Aug. 26. I went on to Worcester, where many young people are just setting out in the ways of God. I joined fifteen of them this afternoon to the society, all of them, I believe, athirst for salvation.

Wednesday, Aug. 27. I preached at Birmingham, and had a comfortable season.

Thursday, Aug. 28. I paid another visit to the amiable family at Hilton Hall.

Friday, Aug. 29. About ten I preached for the first time at Stafford to a large and deeply attentive congregation. It is now the day of small things here, but the grain of mustard-seed may grow up into a great tree.

Wesley Solicits and Distributes Relief to the Poor.

Saturday, Sept. 13, I reached Bristol. I had likewise good reward for my labor, in the recovery of my health by a journey of five or six hundred miles. On *Wednesday, Sept.* 17, and the two following days, I visited several of the country societies, and found most of them not only increasing in number, but in the knowledge and love of God.

Friday, Sept. 26. Observing the deep poverty of many of our brethren, I determined to do what I could for their relief. I spoke severally to some that were in good circumstances, and received about forty pounds. Next I inquired who were in the most pressing want, and visited them at their own houses. I was surprised to find no murmuring spirits among them, but many that were truly happy in God, and all of them appeared to be exceeding thankful for the scanty relief which they received.

Sunday, Sept. 28. It being a fair day, I snatched the opportunity of preaching abroad to twice or thrice as many as the room would have contained.

Wednesday, Oct. 1. I preached at Bath to such a congregation as I have not seen there of a long season. All my leisure hours this week I employed in visiting the remaining poor and begging for them. Having collected about fifty pounds more, I was enabled to relieve most of those that were in pressing distress.

Captain Webb's Path Luminous.

Monday, Oct. 6. Leaving the society in a more prosperous way than it had been for several years, I preached in the Devizes about noon, and at Sarum in the evening. Captain Webb lately kindled a flame here, and it is not yet gone out. Several persons were still rejoicing in God, and the people in general were much quickened.

Tuesday, Oct. 7. I found Captain Webb's preaching in the street at Winchester had been blessed greatly. Many were more or less convinced of sin, and several had found peace with God. I never saw the preaching-house so crowded before with serious and attentive hearers. So was that at Portsmouth also.

Wesley Visits the Isle of Wight.

Wednesday, Oct. 8. We took a wherry for the Isle of Wight. Before we were half over the sea rose, and the water washed over us. However, we got safe to Watton Bridge, and then walked on to Newport. There is much life among the people here, and they walk worthy of their profession.

Thursday, Oct. 9. I went to Newtown, (two miles from Newport,) supposed to be the oldest town in the isle, but its glory is past! The church lies in ruins, and the town has scarce six houses remaining. However, the preaching-house was thoroughly filled, and the people appeared to be all of one rank—none rich and none extremely poor, but all were extremely serious and attentive.

Wesley's Weight.

Wednesday, Nov. 19. I came once more to the lovely family at Shoreham. A little longer that venerable old man is permitted to remain here that the flock may not be scattered. When I was at Sevenoaks I made an odd remark. In the year 1769 I weighed a hundred and twenty-two pounds. In the year 1783 I weighed not a pound more or less. I doubt whether such another instance is to be found in Great Britain.

Wesley Attaches great importance to Morning Preaching.

Monday, March 15, 1784. Leaving Bristol after preaching at five, in the evening I preached at Stroud, where, to my surprise, I found the morning preaching was given up, as also in the neighboring places. If this be the case while I am alive, what must it be when

I am gone? Give up this, and Methodism too will degenerate into a mere sect, only distinguished by some opinions and modes of worship.

Wesley Walks Twelve Miles without fatigue.

Monday, May 10. I set out for Inverness. I had sent Mr. M'Allum before, on George Whitefield's horse, to give notice of my coming. Hereby I was obliged to take both George and Mrs. M'Allum with me in my chaise. To ease the horses we walked forward from Nairn, ordering Richard to follow us as soon as they were fed; he did so, but there were two roads. So, as we took one and he the other, we walked about twelve miles and a half of the way through heavy rain. We then found Richard waiting for us at a little ale-house, and drove on to Inverness. But, blessed be God! I was no more tired than when I set out from Nairn. I preached at seven to a far larger congregation than I had seen here since I preached in the kirk. And surely the labor was not in vain, for God sent a message to many hearts.

Hugh Blair.

Saturday, May 15. We set out early, and dined at Aberdeen. On the road I read Ewen Cameron's Translation of Fingal. I think he has proved the authenticity of it beyond all reasonable contradiction; but what a poet was Ossian! Little inferior to either Homer and Virgil; in some respects superior to both. And what a hero was Fingal! Far more humane than Hector himself, whom we cannot excuse for murdering one that lay upon the ground; and with whom Achilles, or even pious Æneas, is not worthy to be named. But who is this excellent translator, Ewen Cameron? Is not his other name Hugh Blair?

Another Interview with Lady Maxwell.

Saturday, May 22. I had some close conversation with L. M——, who appeared to be clearly saved from sin, although exceedingly depressed by the tottering tenement of clay. About noon I spent an hour with her poor scholars, forty of whom she has provided with a serious master, who takes pains to instruct them in the principles of religion as well as in reading and writing. A famous actress, just come down from London, which, for the honor of Scotland, just during the sitting of the Assembly, stole away a great part of the congregation to-night. How much wiser are these Scots than their forefathers!

Wesley Surrounded by Praying Children.

Tuesday, June 8. I came to Stockton-upon-Tees. Here I found an uncommon work of God among the children. Many of them from six to fourteen were under serious impressions, and earnestly desirous to save their souls. There were upward of sixty who constantly came to be examined, and appeared to be greatly awakened. I preached at noon on "The kingdom of heaven is at hand," and the people seemed to feel every word. As soon as I came down from the desk I was inclosed by a body of children, one of whom and another sank down upon their knees until they were all kneeling, so I kneeled down myself and began praying for them. Abundance of people ran back into the house. The fire kindled and ran from heart to heart, till few, if any, were unaffected. Is not this a new thing in the earth? God begins his work in children. Thus it has been also in Cornwall, Manchester, and Epworth. Thus the flame spreads to those of riper years, till at length they all know him, and praise him from the least unto the greatest.

Wesley Enters his Eighty-second Year!

Friday, June 28. To-day I entered on my eighty-second year, and found myself just as strong to labor, and as fit for any exercise of body or mind, as I was forty years ago. I do not impute this to second causes, but to the sovereign Lord of all. It is he who bids the sun of life stand still, so long as it pleaseth him. I am as strong at eighty-one as I was at twenty-one, but abundantly more healthy, being a stranger to the headache, toothache, and other bodily disorders which attended me in my youth. We can only say, "The Lord reigneth!" While we live let us live to him!

Preaches Three Times a Day.

Friday, July 9. I preached at Huddersfield in the morning, at Longwood House at noon, and in the evening at Halifax.

Sunday, July 11. I preached in the morning at Greetland House; at one, and in the evening, at Halifax. The house would in nowise contain the people; yet the wind was so high that I could not preach abroad.

Monday, July 12. Mr. Sutcliffe read prayers, and I preached at Heptonstall, where many poor souls were refreshed. Between one and two I preached in Todmorden Church, and at five in our own preaching-house, boldly situated on the steep ascent of a tall mountain.

Sunday-schools springing up Every-where.

Thursday, June 15. I retired to Otley, and rested two days.

Sunday, July 18. I preached morning and afternoon in Bingley Church, but it would not near contain the congregation. Before service I stepped into the Sunday-school, which contains two hundred and forty children, taught every Sunday by several masters, and superintended by the curate. So many children in one parish are restrained from open sin, and taught a little good manners, at least, as well as to read the Bible. I find these schools springing up wherever I go. Perhaps God may have a deeper end therein than men are aware of. Who knows but some of these schools may become nurseries for Christians?

Wesley Appoints Preachers to America.

Saturday, Aug. 28. Being informed the boat would pass at eight, we hastened to the New Passage, but we were time enough, for it did not set out till past six in the evening. However, we got into the boat about seven, and before nine reached Bristol.

Tuesday, Aug. 31. Dr. Coke, Mr. Whatcoat, and Mr. Vasey came down from London, in order to embark for America.

Wednesday, Sept. 1. Being now clear in my own mind, I took a step which I had long weighed in my mind, and appointed Mr. Whatcoat and Mr. Vasey to go and serve the desolate sheep in America.

Thursday, Sept. 2. I added to them three more, which I verily believe will be much to the glory of God.

Wesley Preaches under Trees he had Planted Forty Years before.

Sunday, Sept. 12. Dr. Coke read prayers and I preached, in the new room. Afterward I hastened to Kingswood, and preached under the shade of that double row of trees which I planted about forty years ago. How little did any one think then that they would answer such an intention! The sun shone as hot as it used to do even in Georgia; but his rays could not pierce our canopy, and our Lord, meantime, shone upon many souls, and refreshed them that were weary.

Wesley Visits Newgate Felons.

Monday, Nov. 8. This week I visited the societies near London; a very heavy, but necessary work.

Thursday, Nov. 18. I visited two persons in Newgate who were under sentence of death. They seemed to be in an excellent temper, calmly resigned to the will of God. But how much stress can be reasonably laid on such impressions it is hard to say; so often have I known them to vanish away as soon as ever the expectation of death was removed.

Burglars Unsuccessful.

Saturday, Nov. 20. At three in the morning two or three men broke into our house through the kitchen window. Thence they came up into the parlor and broke open Mr. Moore's bureau, where they found two or three pounds. The night before I had prevented his leaving there seventy pounds which he had just received. They next broke open the cupboard, and took away some silver spoons. Just at this time the alarum, which Mr. Moore, by mistake, had set for half past three, (instead of four,) went off, as it usually did, with a thundering noise. At this the thieves ran away with all speed, though their work was not half done, and the whole damage which we sustained scarce amounted to six pounds.

An Audience of Forty-seven Persons under Sentence of Death.

Sunday, Dec. 26. I preached the condemned criminals' sermon in Newgate. Forty-seven were under sentence of death. While they were coming in there was something very awful in the clink of their chains. But no sound was heard, either from them or the crowded audience, after the text was named, "There is joy in heaven over one sinner that repenteth, more than over ninety and nine just persons that need not repentance.' The power of the Lord was eminently present, and most of the prisoners were in tears. A few days after twenty of them died at once, five of whom died in peace. I could not but greatly approve of the spirit and behavior of Mr. Villette, the ordinary; and I rejoiced to hear that it was the same on all similar occasions.

Friday, Dec. 31. We had a solemn watch-night, and ushered in the new year with the voice of praise and thanksgiving.

Five Hard Days' Work for the Poor.

Saturday, Jan. 1, 1785. Whether this be the last or no, may it be the best year of my life.

Sunday, Jan. 2. A larger number of people were present this evening at the renewal of our covenant with God than was ever seen before on the occasion.

Tuesday, Jan. 4. At this season we usually distribute coals and bread among the poor of the society. But I now considered they wanted clothes as well as food. So on this and the four following days I walked through the town, and begged two hundred pounds, in order to clothe them that needed it most. But it was hard work, as most of the streets were filled with melting snow, which often lay ankle deep, so that my feet were steeped in snow-water nearly from morning till evening. I held it out pretty well till *Saturday* evening, but I was laid up with a violent flux, which increased every hour, till, at six in the morning, Dr. Whitehead called upon me. His first draught made me quite easy, and three or four more perfected the cure. If he lives some years, I expect he will be one of the most eminent physicians in Europe.

The House of Lords.

Tuesday, Jan. 25. I spent two or three hours in the House of Lords. I had frequently heard that this was the most venerable assembly in England. But how was I disappointed! What is a lord but a sinner, born to die!

The Grain of Mustard-seed.

March. I was now considering how strangely the grain of mustard-seed, planted about fifty years ago, has grown up. It has spread through all Great Britain and Ireland, the Isle of Wight and the Isle of Man, then to America, from the Leeward Islands, through the whole continent into Canada and Newfoundland. And the societies in all these parts walk by one rule, knowing religion is holy tempers, and striving to worship God not in form only, but likewise "in spirit and in truth."

State of the Dublin Society.

April. On *Tuesday* and the three following days I examined the society. I never found it in such a state before ; many of them rejoiced in God their Saviour, and were as plain in their apparel, both men and women, as those in Bristol and London. Many, I verily believe, love God with all their hearts, and the number of these increase daily. The number of the whole society is seven hundred and forty-seven. Above three hundred of these have been added in a few months—a new and unexpected thing! In various places, indeed, we have frequently felt

The o'erwhelming power of saving grace,

which acted almost irresistibly. But such a shower of grace never continued long, and afterward men might resist the Holy Ghost as before. When the general ferment subsides, every one that partook of it has his trial for life, and the higher the flood the lower will be the ebb ; yea, the more swiftly it rose the more swiftly it falls, so that if we see this here we should not be discouraged. We should only use all diligence to encourage as many as possible to press forward in spite of all the refluent tide. Now, especially, we should warn one another not to grow weary or faint in our mind; if haply we may see such another prodigy as the late one at Paulton, near Bath, where there was a very swift work of God, and yet, a year after, out of a hundred converted there was not one backslider!

The number of children that are clearly converted to God is particularly remarkable. Thirteen or fourteen little maidens in one class are rejoicing in God their Saviour, and are as serious and stayed in their whole behavior as if they were thirty or forty years old. I have much hopes that half of them will be steadfast in the grace of God which they now enjoy.

The Baleful Tendency of Riches.

Monday, April 25. Being desired to preach at Ballinasloe, in my way to Aghrim, I stood, about eleven, in the shade of a large house, and preached to a numerous congregation of Papists and Protestants, equally attentive, on "The kingdom of God is at hand." As I entered Aghrim, the Rector, who was waiting at his gate, welcomed me into the country, and desired me to use his church, both now and whenever I pleased. I preached there at six. It was thoroughly filled with well-behaved hearers. But the society here, as well as that at Tyrrell's Pass, is well nigh shrunk into nothing! Such is the baleful influence of riches! The same effect we find in every place. The more men increase in goods (very few excepted) the more they decrease in grace.

Wesley Preaches to Large Congregations in Ireland.

Thursday, April 28. I supposed the house at Portarlington would have more than contained the congregation, but it would scarce contain a third part of them. So I removed to the market-house, and preached on the general judgment. The word was quick and powerful, so that very few appeared to be unaffected. In the evening I preached in the church at Mount Mellick. Perhaps such a congregation was never there before.

Friday, April 29. I preached at our house at Kilkenny to just such another congregation.

Saturday, April 30. I preached at Waterford in the Court-house, one of the largest in the kingdom.

Sunday, May 1. At eight I preached in the Court-house to a larger congregation than before. At four I preached at the head of the Mall to a Moorsfield congregation. All quiet and attentive.

Monday, May 2. The congregation at five in the morning was larger than on *Saturday* evening.

Thursday, May 5. Before I came half way to Cork I was met by about thirty horsemen. We dined at Middleton, and then rode on through a pleasant, well-cultivated country to Cork. In the evening many in the crowded congregation were much comforted.

Death of a Venerable Saint.

Saturday, May 7. On this day that venerable saint, Mr. Perronet, desired his granddaughter, Miss Briggs, who attended him day and night, to go out into the garden and take a little air. He was reading, and hearing her read the three last chapters of Isaiah. When she returned he was in a kind of ecstacy, the tears running down his cheeks from a deep sense of the glorious things which were shortly to come to pass. He continued unspeakably happy that day, and on Sunday was, if possible, happier still. And indeed heaven seemed to be as it were opened to all that were round about him. When he was in bed she went into his room to see if any thing was wanting, and, as she stood at the foot of the bed, he smiled and broke out, "God bless thee, my dear child, and all that belong to thee! Yea, he *will* bless thee!" Which he earnestly repeated many times, till she left the room. When she went in the next morning, *Monday, May* 9, his spirit was returned to God! So ended the holy and happy life of Mr. Vincent Perronet, in the ninety-second year of his age. I follow hard after him in years, being now in the eighty-second year of my age. O that I may follow him in holiness, and that my last end may be like his!

The Happy Little Girl.

Wednesday, May 18. Learning that a little girl had sat up all night and then walked two miles to see me, I took her into the chaise, and was surprised to find her continually rejoicing in God. The person with whom the preachers lodge informed me that she had been two years possessed of his pure love.

Wesley's Views of the Irish Language.

May. In my way from Limerick hither I read and carefully considered Major Vallance's Irish Grammar, allowed to be the best extant. And supposing him to give a true account of the Irish language, it is not only beyond all comparison worse than any ancient language that I know any thing of, but below English, French, German, Italian, Spanish, or any other modern language. The difficulty of reading it is intolerable, occasioned chiefly by the insufferable number of mute letters, both of vowels and consonants, the like of which is not to be found in any language under heaven. The number of pronouns and the irregular formation of the verbs is equally insufferable. But nothing is so insufferable as their poetry, the whole construction of which is so trifling and childish, and yet requires more pains to write than either the modern rhyme or the ancient attention to long and short syllables.

Wesley Preaches Eleven Times in Four Days.

Wednesday, May 25. I preached about ten in the Court-house at Manorhamilton, and then rode over the Black Mountain, now clothed with green, and through a delightful road, to Mount Florence. Here I observed the party-colored gates (as they were some years since) to be painted plain red. The wind was high and piercing cold, yet the multitude of people obliged me to preach in the open air.

Thursday, May 26. I preached in the Assembly-room at Swadlingbar, but not without difficulty, my cold being so increased that I could not sing, nor speak, but just in one key. However, I made shift to preach in the church at Ballyconnel in the evening, though it was very full, and consequently very hot.

Friday, May 27. Feeling myself much as I was eleven years ago, and not knowing how short my time of working might be, I resolved to do a little while I could, so I began at five; and though I could scarce be heard at first, yet the more I spoke the more my voice was strengthened. Before I had half done every one could hear. To God be all the glory!

About ten I preached at Killeshandra to a multitude of people. But my voice was now so strengthened that every one could hear. In the evening, there being no house at Killmore that could contain half the congregation, I was obliged again to preach abroad. There were several sharp showers, but none went away, for it pleased the Lord to send therewith gracious rain on the souls of them that feared him.

Saturday, May 22. At five, though I had not quite recovered my voice, I judged it best to speak as I could. So I preached in Mr. Creighton's barn, and at seven in the ball-room at Cavan. I had designed to go straight from hence to Clones, but, a friend sending me word that Mr. Sanderson was willing I should preach in his church at Ballyhays, I altered my purpose and went thither. Abundance of people were waiting for me, but Mr. Sanderson having changed his mind, I preached in the inn yard to a very well-behaved congregation of rich as well as poor. Hence I went to Clones, where I found such a society as I had hardly seen in Ireland, making it a point of conscience to conform to all our rules, great and small. The new preaching-house was exceeding neat, but far too small to contain the congregation. The first time I preached to-day was with difficulty; the second and third with less; the fourth with none at all.

Wesley Closes his Eighty-second Year!

Tuesday, June 28. By the good providence of God I finished the eighty-second year of my age. Is any thing too hard for God? It is now eleven years since I have felt any such thing as weariness; many times I speak till my voice fails, and I can speak no longer; frequently I walk till my strength fails, and I can walk no further; yet even then I feel no sensation of weariness, but am perfectly easy from head to foot. I dare not impute this to natural causes; it is the will of God.

Wesley Returns from Ireland to London.

Sunday, July 10. I went on board the Prince of Wales, one of the neatest ships I ever was in. We left the work of God increasing in every part of the kingdom, more than it has done for many years. About two in the morning we sailed out of Dublin Bay, and came into Holyhead Bay before one in the afternoon on *Monday*, 11. That evening we went on to Gwendy; *Tuesday*, 12, to Kimmel, one of the pleasantest inns in Wales, surrounded with gardens and stately woods, which their late proprietor must see no more.

Wednesday, July 14. We reached Chester. After preaching there between five and six in the evening I stepped into the stage-coach, which was just setting out, and, traveling day and night, was brought safe to London on *Thursday*, 15, in the afternoon.

Morning Preaching for the Children.

Sunday, July 17. I preached, both morning and evening, on the education of children. I now spoke chiefly to the parents, informing them that I designed to speak to the children at five the next morning.

Monday, July 18. At five not only the morning chapel was filled, but many stood in the large chapel. I trust they did not come in vain.

Seventy Preachers at Conference.

Tuesday, July 26. Our Conference began, at which about seventy preachers were present, whom I had invited by name. One consequence of this was that we had no contention or altercation at all, but every thing proposed was calmly considered, and determined as we judged would be most for the glory of God.

Monday, Aug. 1. Having, with a few select friends, weighed the matter thoroughly, I yielded to their judgment, and set apart three of our well-tried preachers, John Pawson, Thomas Hanby, and Joseph Taylor, to minister in Scotland, and I trust God will bless their ministrations, and show that he has sent them.

Wednesday, Aug. 3. Our peaceful Conference ended, the God of power having presided over all our consultations.

A Preaching-house made of Brass.

Friday, Aug. 26. In the evening I preached in the market-place at St. Ives to almost the whole town. This was the first place in Cornwall where we preached, and where Satan fought fiercely for his kingdom, but all now is peace. I found old John Nance had rested from his labors. Some months since, sitting behind the preacher in the pulpit, he sank down, was carried out, and fell asleep!

Saturday, Aug. 27. About nine I preached at the copper-works, near the Hayle, in the new preaching-house. I suppose such another is not in England, nor in Europe, nor in the world. It is round, and all the walls are brass, that is, brazen slugs. It seems nothing can destroy this till heaven and earth pass away. At two the stewards of all the societies met at Redruth. There is nothing but peace and love among them, and among the societies from whence they came, and yet no great increase! At our love-feast in the evening several of our friends declared how God had saved them from inbred sin with such exactness, both of sentiment and language, as clearly showed they were taught of God.

Wesley's Voice Heard by a Congregation of Thousands in the Open Air!

Sunday, Aug. 28. At half past eight I preached at St. Agnes to the largest congregation I ever saw there. Between one and two I preached in the street at Redruth to thousands upon thousands, and my strength was as my need, yet I was afraid lest I should not be able to make all those hear that assembled in the evening. But, though it was supposed there were two or three thousand more than ever were there before, yet they heard (I was afterward informed) to the very skirts of the congregation, while I applied those solemn words, "One thing is needful."

Wesley Preaches Mr. Fletcher's Funeral Sermon.

Friday, Nov. 4. I returned to London.

Sunday, Nov. 6. I preached a funeral sermon for that great and good man, Mr. Fletcher, and most of the congregation felt that God was in the midst of them. In the afternoon I buried the remains of Judith Perry, a lovely young woman, snatched away at eighteen ; but she was ripe for the Bridegroom, and went to meet him in the full triumph of faith.

Sunday, Nov. 13. I preached at Shoreditch Church. The congregation was very numerous, and the collection unusually large.

A Noble Example.

Monday, Dec. 5, and so the whole week, I spent every hour I could spare, in the unpleasing but necessary work of going through the town and begging for the poor men who had been employed in finishing the new chapel. It is true that I am not obliged to do this, but if I do it not nobody else will.

Tragic Death of Joseph Lee.

Tuesday, Jan. 30, 1786. I had a more particular account of Joseph Lee than ever I had before. When I went first to Newcastle-upon-Tyne I chose him, being a man full of faith and love, to be one of the leaders, steward of the society, and caterer for our family. He discharged his trust with the utmost ability and integrity. He walked humbly and closely with God, and was a pattern to all the town as well as to all the society. But after some time he was persuaded to quit Newcastle and settle at Nottingham. There he fell among Antinomians, and, trusting in his own strength, gradually sucked in their opinion, grew less and less strict, and lost first the power, and then the very form of religion. After he had lived some years openly and avowedly without God in the world, while he was one evening quite merry with his jovial companions, one of them said, "Why, Mr. Lee, you was once very godly ;

you was one of those mad Methodists!" He answered not a word, but leaned his arm on the table and died.

A Cold Sleeping-room.

Sunday, Feb. 26. I took a solemn leave of the congregation at the new chapel, at West-street, and at Brentford.

Monday, Feb. 27. We went on to Newbury, with little interruption from the snow, and I had a comfortable opportunity, with a large and serious congregation. But I have not passed such a night for these forty years, my lodging room being just as cold as the outward air. I could not sleep at all till three in the morning. I rose at four, and set out at five. But the snow which fell in the night lay so deep, it was with much difficulty we reached Chippenham. Taking fresh horses there we pushed on to Bath, and found a larger congregation than could well be expected.

An Army of Sunday-school Children.

Tuesday, April 4. In the evening I preached to a lovely congregation at Stockport.

Friday, April 7. I went on as swiftly as I could through Manchester, Wigan, and Bolton.

Sunday, April 16. (Being *Easter-Day.*) I crossed over to Warrington, where, having read prayers, preached, and administered the Lord's Supper, I hastened back to Bolton. The house was crowded the more, because of five hundred and fifty children who are taught in our Sunday-schools; such an army of them got about me when I came out of the chapel that I could scarce disengage myself from them.

Friday, April 17. I went on to Blackburn, which was sufficiently crowded, it being the fair day. No house could contain the people; so I stood abroad and expounded that awful scripture, "I saw the dead, small and great, stand before God." All were still as night, unless when they sung; then their voices were as the sound of many waters.

Wesley Still Preaching Three and Four Times a Day!

Tuesday, April 18. I preached at Padiham, Burnley, Southfield, and Colne.

Thursday, April 20. I went to Otley, and found God was there both in the evening and morning service.

Friday, April 21. I preached at Yeadon, where the work of God is rapidly going forward. Such a company of loving children I have nowhere seen but at Oldham, near Manchester.

Sunday, April 23. I preached in Haworth Church in the morning, and Bingley Church in the afternoon, but as there were many hundreds that could not get in, Mr. Atmore preached abroad at the same time. In the evening I preached to a huge multitude at Bradford. Surely the people of this town are highly favored, having both a vicar and a curate that preach the truth.

Archdeacon Blackburne.

Tuesday, May 9. I went on to Richmond. I alighted, according to his own desire, at Archdeacon Blackburne's house. How lively and active he was some years ago! I find he is two years younger than me, but he is now a mere old man, being both blind, and deaf, and lame. Who maketh thee to differ?

He durst not ask me to preach in his church, "for fear somebody should be offended." So I preached at the head of the street to a numerous congregation, all of whom stood as still (although it rained all the time) and behaved as well as if we had been in the church.

A Solemn Parting.

Friday, May 12. I preached at Carlisle; and *Saturday*, 13, after a long day's journey, at Glasgow. After spending three days here, fully employed, on *Wednesday*, 17, we went on to Edinburgh. Here likewise I had much and pleasant work. On *Friday*, 19, I went forward to Dundee; and on *Saturday*, 20, to Arbroath, where I spent the Lord's day in the Lord's work.

Monday, May 22. Having a long day's journey before us, we set out at half hour past three; so we came early to Aberdeen.

Wednesday, May 24. We had an exceeding solemn parting, as I reminded them that we could hardly expect to see each other's face any more till we met in Abraham's bosom.

Wesley Preaches Three Times, and Travels Seventy-six Miles in One Day!

Thursday, June 15. I found the work of God at Scarborough more lively than it had been for many years.

Friday, June 16. In the evening I preached, at Bridlington quay, to a numerous congregation.

Saturday, June 17. I found Mr. Parker at Beverley, in a palace. The gentleman that owned it being gone abroad, it was let at a moderate rent. I preached here about twelve, about four at Newlands, and at seven in Hull.

Sunday, June 18. I was invited by the vicar to preach in the High Church, one of the largest parish churches in England. I preached on the Gospel for the day, the story of Dives and Lazarus. Being invited to preach in the afternoon, the church was, if possible, more crowded than before, and I pressed home the prophet's words, " Seek ye the Lord while he may be found ; call ye upon him while he is near." Who would have expected, a few years since, to see me preaching in the High Church at Hull ? I had appointed to preach at Swinfleet, so I went as far as Beverley this evening, and on *Monday*, 19, set out early ; but being vehemently importuned to go round by Malton, I did so, and preached there at nine. Thence I hastened to Pocklington, and, finding the people ready, stepped out of the chaise and preached without delay. We reached Swinfleet between six and seven, having gone in all seventy-six miles. A numerous congregation was assembled under the shade of tall trees. Sufficient for this day was the labor thereof, but still I was no more tired than when I rose in the morning.

Wesley Enters his Eighty-third Year!

Wednesday, June 28. I entered into the eighty-third year of my age. I am a wonder to myself. It is now twelve years since I have felt any such sensation as weariness. I am never tired, (such is the goodness of God!) either with writing, preaching, or traveling. One natural cause undoubtedly is, my continual exercise and change of air. How the latter contributes to health I know not, but certainly it does.

Bristol Conference.

Tuesday, July 25. Our Conference began; about eighty preachers attended. We met every day at six and nine in the morning, and at two in the afternoon. On *Tuesday* and on *Wednesday* morning the characters of the preachers were considered, whether already admitted or not. On *Thursday* in the afternoon we permitted any of the society to be present, and weighed what was said about separating from the Church; but we all determined to continue therein without one dissenting voice, and I doubt not but this determination will stand, at least till I am removed into a better world. On *Friday* and *Saturday* most of our temporal business was settled.

Sunday, July 30. I preached in the room morning and evening; and in the afternoon at Kingswood, where there is rather an increase than a decrease in the work of God.

Monday, July 31. The Conference met again, and concluded on *Tuesday* morning. Great had been the expectations of many that we should have warm debates; but, by the mercy of God, we had none at all; every thing was transacted with great calmness, and we parted, as we met, in peace and love.

Wesley in Holland Again.

Saturday, Aug. 12. Mr. Williams, the minister of the Episcopal Church, and Mr. Scott, minister of the Scotch Church, both welcomed me to Holland, but their kindness involved me in an awkward difficulty.

Mr. Scott had asked the consent of his consistory for me to preach in his church on *Sunday* afternoon; but Mr. Williams had given notice of my preaching in his church both morning and afternoon, and, neither of them being willing to give up his point, I would fain have compromised the matter; but each seemed to apprehend his honor concerned, and would not in any wise give up his point. I saw no possible way to satisfy both but by prolonging my stay in Holland, in order to preach one *Sunday*, morning and afternoon, in the Episcopal, and another in the Scotch Church; and possibly God may have more work for me to do in Holland than I am yet aware of.

Though Mr. Loyal, with whom I lodged when I was at Rotterdam before, was not in town, being gone with a friend to Paris, yet I was quite as at home, and went on in my work without any interruption.

Sunday, Aug. 13. The service began about ten. Mr. Williams read prayers exceedingly well, and I preached on those words in the First Lesson, "How long halt ye between two opinions?" All the congregation gave a serious attention, but I fear they only *heard* but did not *feel;* but many seemed to be much affected in the afternoon while I opened and applied those words, "There hath no temptation taken you but what is common to men." In the evening Mr. Scott called upon me, and informed me that the elders of his Church would not desire me to stay in Holland on purpose to preach, but would dismiss my promise. I then determined to follow my first plan, and (God willing) to return to England in a fortnight.

Wesley busy with his Pen.

Tuesday, Aug. 15. Making the experiment when we took boat, I found I could write as well in the boat as in my study, so from this hour I continued writing whenever I was on board. What mode of traveling is to be compared with this? About noon we called on Professor Roers, at Leyden, a very sensible and conversible man. As he spoke Latin very fluently, I could willingly have spent some hours with him, but I had appointed to be at Amsterdam in the evening.

Writes the Life of Fletcher.

Monday, Sept. 25. We took coach in the afternoon, and on *Tuesday* morning reached London. I now applied myself in earnest to the writing of Mr. Fletcher's Life, having procured the best materials I could. To this I dedicated all the time I could spare till November, from five in the morning till eight at night. These are my studying hours; I cannot write longer in a day without hurting my eyes.

Saturday, Sept. 30. I went to bed at my usual time, half an hour past nine, and, to my own feeling, in perfect health. But just at twelve I was waked by an impetuous flux, which did not suffer me to rest many minutes together. Finding it rather increased than decreased, though (what I never knew before) without its old companion, the cramp, I sent for Dr. Whitehead. He came about four, and, by the blessing of God, in three hours I was as well as ever. Nor did I find the least weakness or faintness, but preached, morning and afternoon, and met the society in the evening without any weariness. Of such a one I would boldly say, with the son of Sirach, "Honor the physician, for God hath appointed him."

Wesley will not Interfere with Church Hours.

Sunday, Oct. 22. I preached at West-street morning and afternoon, and at Allhallow's Church in the evening. It was much crowded, and God gave us so remarkable a blessing as I scarce ever found at that church.

Tuesday, Oct. 24. I met the classes at Deptford, and was vehemently importuned to order the *Sunday* service in our room at the same time with that of the Church. It is easy to see that this would be a formal separation from the Church. We fixed both our morning and evening service all over England, at such hours as not to interfere with the Church ; with this very design, that those of the Church, if they chose it, might attend both the one and the other. But to fix it at the same hour is obliging them to separate either from the Church or us, and this I judge to be not only inexpedient, but totally unlawful for me to do.

Another Martyr to Long and Loud Preaching.

Sunday, Nov. 5. I buried the remains of John Cowmeadow, another martyr to loud and long preaching. To save his life, if possible, when he was half dead, I took him to travel with me. But it was too late ; he revived a little, but soon relapsed, and after a few months died in peace. He had the ornament of a meek and quiet spirit, and was of an exemplary behavior.

Wesley Transcribes the Record of the London Society.

Tuesday, Dec. 5. In the afternoon I took coach again, and returned to London at eight on *Wednesday* morning. All the time I could save to the end of the week I spent in transcribing the society; a dull but necessary work, which I have taken upon myself once a year for near these fifty years.

Prefers St. John's Style.

Friday, Jan. 5, 1787, and in the vacant hours of the following days, I read Dr. Hunter's Lectures. They are very lively and ingenious. The language is good, and the thoughts generally just. But they do not at all suit my taste. I do not admire that florid way of writing. Good sense does not need to be so studiously adorned. I love St. John's style as well as matter.

Begging for the Poor again.

Sunday, Jan. 7. At the desire of many of our friends, we began that solemn work of renewing our covenant with God at three in the afternoon, two hours earlier than usual.

Monday, Jan. 8, and the four following days, I went a begging for the poor. I hoped to be able to provide food and raiment for those of the society who were in pressing want, yet had no weekly allowance; these were about two hundred, but I was much disappointed. Six or seven, indeed, of our brethren gave ten pounds apiece. If forty or fifty had done this I could have carried my design into execution. However, much good was done with two hundred pounds, and many sorrowful hearts made glad.

Wesley Opens the new house at Newark.

Wednesday, Feb. 7. I preached at Brentford, and in the morning; *Thursday* evening at Lambeth. At both places I feund many who promise not to be forgetful hearers but doers of the word. Being earnestly desired by our brethren at Newark, one hundred and twenty-four miles from London, to come and open their new house, I took the mail-coach, *Friday*, 9, in the evening, and reached Newark the next day about four in the afternoon. But having a great cold, and being so hoarse that I could not preach, I desired Mr. Mather to supply my place till I had recovered my voice.

Sunday, Feb. 11. Having partly recovered my voice, I preached in the new house at nine—a lightsome, cheerful building, and gave notice of preaching at five in the afternoon. But it was not long before I received a message from the Mayor, to desire me to begin preaching a little later, that himself and several of the Aldermen might the more conveniently attend. They all came at half an hour past five, and as many people as could possibly squeeze in, and God opened my mouth to speak strong words, and the hearts of many to receive them. Surely God will have a people in this place that will adorn the doctrine of God our Saviour.

Wesley Lifted Over the Seats into the Pulpit.

Sunday, March 4. I began the service at half an hour past nine, and concluded it before one. I suppose such a number of communicants were never seen before at Plymouth Dock, but there was no disorder or hurry at all. There was more difficulty in the evening; the throng was so great that it was impossible for me to get through them to the pulpit; so at length they made shift to lift me over the seats. Again God spoke in his word, I believe to all that could get in; but some could not, and were constrained to go away.

Monday, March 5. The house was well filled again, both above and below; and after a solemn parting we took coach at six, leaving such a flame behind us as was never kindled here before. God grant it may never be put out! We reached Exeter between two and three. In the evening I preached on "By grace are ye saved through faith," to as many as could possibly squeeze into the room. It was a glorious opportunity. God uttered his voice, and that a mighty one. It seemed to break the rocks in pieces, to make the stout-hearted tremble. I know not that I ever saw such an impression made on the people of Exeter before.

An Hour with Mrs. Fletcher.

Saturday, March 10. I had the pleasure of an hour's conversation with Mrs. Fletcher. She appears to be swiftly growing in grace and ripening for a better world. I encouraged her to do all the good she could during her short stay in Bristol. Accordingly she met in the following week as many of the classes as her time and strength would permit, and her words were as fire, conveying both light and heat to the hearts of all that heard her.

Sunday, March 11. We had a solemn season at the room both in the morning and evening; and also in the afternoon at Kingswood, where the work of God revives as well as at Bristol. I strongly warned the people of Bristol of their indolence, through which the preacher had twelve, ten, or five hearers in a morning, and advised them to shake it off. Many of them did so, and I suppose we had three hundred on *Monday* morning, one hundred and fifty on *Saturday*, and between two and three hundred every morning of the week besides.

Gently Sliding into a Better World.

March. In the evening I preached at Congleton to a serious and well-established people. Here I found my co-eval, Mr. ——, two months (I think) younger than me, just as a lamp going out for want of oil, gently sliding into a better world; he sleeps always, only waking now and then just long enough to say, "I am happy."

Ought it to be Suffered in a Christian Church?

Sunday, April 7. (Being *Easter-Day.*) I preached in Bethesda, Mr. Smyth's new chapel. It is very neat, but not gay, and I believe will hold about as many people as West-street chapel. Mr. Smyth read prayers, and gave out the hymns, which were sung by fifteen or twenty fine singers; the rest of the congregation listening with much attention, and as much devotion, as they would have done to an opera. But is this Christian worship? Or ought it ever to be suffered in a Christian church?

Honorable Sinners Accommodated.

April. On *Monday* and *Tuesday* I preached again at Bethesda, and God touched several hearts, even of the rich and great, so that (for the time at least) they were "almost persuaded to be Christians." It seems as if the good providence of God had prepared this place for those rich and honorable sinners who will not deign to receive any message from God but in a genteel way.

An Old Antagonist.

Saturday, May 12. A gentleman invited me to breakfast with my old antagonist, Father O'Leary. I was not at all displeased at being disappointed. He is not the stiff, queer man that I expected, but of an easy, genteel carriage, and seems not to be wanting either in sense or learning. In the afternoon, by appointment, I waited on the Mayor, an upright, sensible man, who is diligently employed from morning to night in doing all the good he can. He has already prevailed upon the corporation to make it a fixed rule that the two hundred a year, which was spent in two entertainments, should for the future be employed in relieving indigent freemen, with their wives and children. He has carefully regulated the House of Industry, and has instituted a Humane Society for the relief of persons seemingly drowned, and he is unwearied in removing abuses of every kind. When will our English Mayors copy after the Mayor of Cork?

The Lions become Lambs.

Wednesday, May 30. A large room, designed for an assembly-room, was filled in the morning, and the poor people appeared to be quite ripe for the highest doctrine of the Gospel; so I exhorted them, leaving the first principles, to "go on unto perfection."

About eleven I preached in the market-house at Enniskillen, formerly a den of lions—but the lions are become lambs. They flocked together from every part, and were all attention. Before I had half done God made bare his arm, and the mountains flowed down at his presence. Many were cut to the heart, and many rejoiced with joy unspeakable. Surely the last shall be first, and poor Enniskillen shall lift up its head above many of the places where the Gospel has been long preached. In the evening I preached to another numerous congregation at Sidare, a large house at the foot of the mountains. One would wonder whence all the people came—they seemed to spring out of the earth. Here, also, there were once many bitter persecutors, but they are vanished away like smoke. Several of them indeed came to a fearful end, and their neighbors took warning by them.

Arrival of Dr. Coke from America.

Tuesday, June 26. We were agreeably surprised with the arrival of Dr. Coke, who came from Philadelphia in nine-and-twenty days, and gave us a pleasing account of the work of God in America.

Thursday, June 28. I had the pleasure of a conversation with Mr. Howard, I think one of the greatest men in Europe. Nothing but the mighty power of God can enable him to go through his difficult and dangerous employments. But what can hurt us if God is on our side?

Saturday, June 30. I desired all our preachers to meet me, and consider the state of our brethren in America, who have been terribly frightened at their shadow, as if the English preachers were just going to enslave them. I believe that fear is now over, and they are more aware of Satan's devices.

Irish House of Commons.

Wednesday, July 4. I spent an hour at the New Dargle, a gentleman's seat four or five miles from Dublin. I have not seen so beautiful a place in the kingdom. It equals the Leasowes in Warwickshire, and it greatly exceeds them in situation—all the walks lying on the side of the mountain, which commands all Dublin Bay, as well as an extensive and finely variegated land prospect. A little river runs through it, which occasions two cascades at a small distance from each other. Although many places may exceed this in grandeur, I believe none can exceed it in beauty. Afterward I saw the Parliament House. The House of Lords far exceeds that at Westminster, and the Lord Lieutenant's throne as far exceeds that miserable throne (so called) of the King in the English House of Lords. The House of Commons is a noble room indeed. It is an octagon, wainscoted round with Irish oak, which shames all mahogany, and galleried all round for the convenience of the ladies. The Speaker's chair is far more grand than the throne of the Lord Lieutenant. But what surprised me above all were the kitchens of the house and the large apparatus for good eating. Tables were placed from one end of a large hall to the other, which, it seems, while the Parliament sits, are daily covered with meat at four or five o'clock for the accommodation of the members. Alas, poor Ireland! Who shall teach thy very Senators wisdom?

Wesley Saved from Shipwreck.

Wednesday, July 11. At five I took an affectionate leave of this loving people, and, having finished all my business here, in the afternoon I went down with my friends, having taken the whole ship, and went on board the Prince of Wales, one of the Parkgate packets. At seven we sailed with a fair, moderate wind. Between nine and ten I lay down as usual and slept till near four, when I was waked by an uncommon noise, and found the ship lay beating upon a large rock about a league from Holyhead. The captain, who had not long lain down, leaped up, and, running upon the deck, when he saw how the ship lay cried out, "Your lives may be saved, but I am undone!" Yet no sailor swore, and no woman cried out. We immediately went to prayer, and presently the ship, I know not how, shot off the rock and pursued her way, without any more damage than the wounding a few of her outside planks. About three in the afternoon we came safe to Parkgate, and in the evening went on to Chester.

Bolton Sunday-school.

Friday, July 27. We went on to Bolton. Here are eight hundred poor children taught in our Sunday-schools by about eighty masters, who receive no pay but what they are to receive from their great Master. About a hundred of them (part boys and part girls) are taught to sing; and they sung so true, that, all singing together, there seemed to be but one voice. The house was thoroughly filled, while I explained and applied the first commandment. What is all morality or religion without this? A mere castle in the air. In the evening, many of the children still hovering round the house, I desired some forty or fifty to come in and sing,

Vital spark of heavenly flame.

Although some of them were silent, not being able to sing for tears, yet the harmony was such as I believe could not be equaled in the King's chapel.

Wesley and Dr. Coke preach alternately.

Saturday, Aug. 11. We went on board the Queen, a small sloop, and sailed eight or nine leagues with a tolerable wind. But it then grew foul and blew a storm, so that we were all glad to put in at Yarmouth harbor. About six Dr. Coke preached in the market-house to a quiet and tolerably attentive congregation. The storm continuing, at eight in the morning, *Sunday,* 12, I preached to a much larger congregation. I had uncommon liberty of speech, and I believe some of them felt that God was there. At eleven we went to church. There was a tolerable congregation, and all remarkably well-behaved. The minister read prayers very seriously, and preached on "Blessed are the poor in spirit." At four I preached again on Luke xix, 42, (part of the second lesson in the morning,) "If thou hadst known, even thou," etc. The market-house was now more than filled, and not a few seemed to hear as for life. In the evening Dr. Coke preached again. We have now delivered our own souls at Yarmouth, and trust God will suffer us to go on to Guernsey.

Resort to Prayer in time of Peril.

Tuesday, Aug. 14. Sailing on with a fair wind, we fully expected to reach Guernsey in the afternoon;

but the wind turning contrary and blowing hard, we found it would be impossible. We then judged it best to put in at the Isle of Alderney, but we were very near being shipwrecked in the bay. When we were in the middle of the rocks, with the sea rippling all round us, the wind totally failed. Had this continued we must have struck upon one or other of the rocks, so we went to prayer, and the wind sprung up instantly. About sunset we landed, and, though we had five beds in the same room, slept in peace. About eight I went down to a convenient spot on the beach, and began giving out a hymn. A woman and two little children joined us immediately. Before the hymn was ended we had a tolerable congregation, all of whom behaved well; part, indeed, continued at forty or fifty yards' distance, but they were all quiet and attentive.

Isle of Guernsey.

Soon after we set sail, and, after a very pleasant passage through little islands on either hand, we came to the venerable castle, standing on a rock, about a quarter of a mile from Guernsey. The isle itself makes a beautiful appearance, spreading as a crescent to the right and left, about seven miles long and five broad, part high land and part low. The town itself is boldly situated, rising higher and higher from the water. The first thing I observed in it was, very narrow streets and exceeding high houses. But we quickly went on to Mr. De Jersey's, hardly a mile from the town. Here I found a most cordial welcome, both from the master of the house and all his family. I preached at seven, in a large room, to as deeply serious a congregation as I ever saw, on "Jesus Christ, of God made unto us wisdom, righteousness sanctification, and redemption."

Wesley in Cornwall again.

Saturday, Sept. 8. Dr. Coke preached at six to as many as the preaching-house would contain. At ten I was obliged to take the field by the multitude of people that flocked together. I found a very uncommon liberty of speech among them, and cannot doubt but the work of God will flourish in this place. In the evening I preached at St. Ives, (but, it being the market-day, I could not stand as usual in the market-place,) in a very convenient field, at the end of the town to a very numerous congregation, I need scarce add, and very serious, for such are all the congregations in the county of Cornwall.

Sunday, Sept. 9. About nine I preached at the Copper Works, three or four miles from St. Ives, to a large congregation gathered from all parts, I believe "with the demonstration of the Spirit." I then met the society in the preaching-house, which is unlike any other in England, both as to its form and materials. It is exactly round, and composed wholly of brazen slags, which I suppose will last as long as the earth. Between one and two, I began in the market-place at Redruth to the largest congregation I ever saw there; they not only filled all the windows, but sat on the tops of the houses. About five I began in the pit at Gwennap. I suppose we had a thousand more than ever were there before; but it was all one, my voice was strengthened accordingly, so that every one could hear distinctly.

A Little Tour through Oxfordshire.

Sunday, Oct. 14. I preached in West-street chapel morning and afternoon, and at St. Swithin's Church in the evening.

Monday, Oct. 15. I began a little tour through Oxfordshire. I preached at Wallingford in the evening, with much enlargement of heart. Mr. Pentycross called upon me in the morning, *Tuesday,* 16. Calvinism and bitterness are fled away together, and we willingly gave each other the right hand of fellowship. About one I preached at Oxford to a very quiet, deeply serious congregation. The house at Witney would nothing near contain the people in the evening—it was well filled at five on *Wednesday* morning. I dearly love this people, they are so simple of heart, and so much alive to God. After dinner we retúrned to Oxford. Half an hour before the hour of preaching a heavy rain began ; by this means the house was filled, and not over filled. I found great liberty of speech in enforcing the first and great commandment, and could not but hope there will be a great work of God here notwithstanding all the wisdom of the world.

Thursday, Oct. 18. We went on to High Wycomb. The work of God is so considerably increased here that, although three galleries are added to the preaching-house, it would scarce contain the people. Even at five in the morning, *Friday,* 19, it was thoroughly filled. Never before was there so fair a prospect of doing good at this place. I dined in London.

Wesley Rides in a Farmer's Cart.

Wednesday, Oct. 31. I preached in the morning on the Woman of Canaan, and in the afternoon I went over to Mr. Hicks, at Wrestlingworth, through such roads as no chaise could pass, so we had the pleasure of riding in a farmer's cart. It was such a motion as I never felt before; but to make amends, the church was so filled as I never had seen it, and I was enabled to speak with unusual plainness. Surely some received the truth in the love thereof.

The Conventicle Act.

Saturday, Nov. 3. I had a long conversation with Mr. Clulow on that execrable act called the Conventicle Act. After consulting the Act of Toleration with that of the fourteenth of Queen Anne, we were both clearly convinced that it was the safest way to license all our chapels, and all our traveling preachers, not as dissenters, but simply as "Preachers of the Gospel;" and that no justice, or bench of justices, has any authority to refuse licensing either the house or the preachers.

Mr. Duff's "Essay on Genius."

Monday, Nov. 5. In my way to Dorkin I read Mr. Duft's "Essay on Genius." It is, beyond all comparison, deeper and more judicious than Dr. G.'s essay on that subject. If the Doctor had seen it, (which one can hardly doubt,) it is a wonder he would publish his Essay. Yet I cannot approve of his method. Why does he not first define his term, that we may know what he is talking about? I doubt, because his own idea of it was not clear; for genius is not imagination, any more than it is invention. If we mean by it a quality of the soul, it is, in its widest acceptation, an extraordinary capacity, either for some particular art or science, or for all; for whatever may be undertaken. So Euclid had a genius for mathematics, Tully for oratory; Aristotle and Lord Bacon had a universal genius, applicable to every thing.

Wesley Still Visits the Classes.

Monday, Nov. 19. I began the unpleasing work of visiting the classes. I continue to do this in London and Bristol, as well as in Cork and Dublin. With the other societies their respective assistants supply my lack of service.

Early to Bed, Early to Rise.

Sunday, Dec. 9. I went down at half hour past five, but found no preacher in the chapel, though we had three or four in the house, so I preached myself. Afterward, inquiring why none of my family attended the morning preaching, they said it was because they sat up too late. I resolved to put a stop to this, and therefore ordered that, 1. Every one under my roof should go to bed at nine; that, 2. Every one might attend the morning preaching, and so they have done ever since.

Crowned Heads of Europe in Wax.

Monday, Dec. 10. I was desired to see the celebrated wax-work at the museum in Spring Gardens; it exhibits most of the crowned heads in Europe, and shows their characters in their countenance. Sense and majesty appear in the King of Spain; dullness and sottishness in the King of France; infernal subtlety in the late King of Prussia, (as well as the skeleton Voltaire;) calmness and humanity in the Emperor, and King of Portugal; exquisite stupidity in the Prince of Orange; and amazing coarseness, with every thing that is unamiable, in the Czarina.

Free Seats Still.

Tuesday, Dec. 18. I retired to Newington, and hid myself for almost three days.

Friday, Dec. 21. The committee proposed to me, 1. That families of men and women should sit together in both chapels; 2. That every one who took a pew should have it as their own; thus overthrowing at one blow the discipline which I have been establishing for fifty years!

Saturday, Dec. 22. I yielded to the importunity of a painter, and sat an hour and a half in all for my picture. I think it was the best that ever was taken; but what is the picture of a man above fourscore?

Monday, Dec. 24. We had another meeting of the committee, who after a calm and loving consultation judged it best, 1. That men and women should sit separate still; and, 2. That none should claim any pew as his own either in the new chapel or in West-street.

Wesley Conscious of Physical Decay.

Saturday, March 1, 1788. I considered, What difference do I find by an increase of years. I find, 1. Less activity; I walk slower, particularly up hill; 2. My memory is not so quick; 3. I cannot read so well by candle-light. But I bless God that all my other powers of body and mind remain just as they were.

Sunday, March 2. I preached at eleven, at half an hour past two, and at half hour past five. The first congregation was large, and so was the second; but the third was far the largest, filling every corner of the house. And the power of God seemed to increase with the number of the people, insomuch that in the evening while I was applying, "To me to live is Christ, and to die is gain," the glory of the Lord seemed to overshadow the congregation in an uncommon manner, and I trust the impression then made upon rich and poor will not soon wear off.

Wesley Preaches on Slavery.

Monday, March 3. I went to Bristol, and having two or three quiet days, finished my sermon upon Conscience. On *Tuesday* I gave notice of my design to preach on *Thursday* evening upon (what is now the general topic) Slavery. In consequence of this, on *Thursday*, the house from end to end was filled with high and low, rich and poor. I preached on that ancient prophecy, "God shall enlarge Japhet. And he shall dwell in the tents of Shem, and Canaan shall be his servant." About the middle of the discourse, while there was on every side attention still as night, a vehement noise arose, none could tell why, and shot like lightning through the whole congregation. The terror and confusion were inexpressible. You might have imagined it was a city taken by storm. The people rushed upon each other with the utmost violence, the benches were broke in pieces, and nine tenths of the congregation appeared to be struck with the same panic. In about six minutes the storm ceased, almost as suddenly as it rose, and, all being calm, I went on without the least interruption. It was the strangest incident of the kind I ever remember, and I believe none can account for it without supposing some preternatural influence. Satan fought lest his kingdom should be delivered up. We set *Friday* apart as a day of fasting and prayer, that God would remember those poor outcasts of men, and (what seems impossible with men, considering the wealth and power of their oppressors) make a way for them to escape, and break their chains in sunder.

Wesley Delighted with the Singing.

Saturday, April 19. We went on to Bolton, where I preached in the evening in one of the most elegant houses in the kingdom, and to one of the liveliest congregations. And this I must avow, there is not such a set of singers in any of the Methodist congregations in the three kingdoms. There cannot be, for we have near a hundred such trebles, boys and girls, selected out of our Sunday-schools, and accurately taught, as are not found together in any chapel, cathedral, or music-room within the four seas. Besides, the spirit with which they all sing, and the beauty of many of them, so suits the melody that I defy any to exceed it, except the singing of angels in our Father's house.

Sunday, April 20. At eight, and at one, the house was thoroughly filled. About three I met between nine hundred and a thousand of the children belonging to our Sunday-schools. I never saw such a sight before.

Wesley in Scotland Again.

May. We set out on *Thursday*, 15, at four, and reached Glasgow, *Friday*, 16, before noon. Much of the country, as we came, is now well improved, and the wilderness become a fruitful field.

Our new preaching-house will, I believe, contain about as many as the chapel at Bath. But O the difference! It has the pulpit on one side, and has exactly the look of a Presbyterian meeting-house. It is the very sister of our house at Brentford. Perhaps an omen of what will be when I am gone. I preached at seven to a tolerably large congregation, and to many of them at five in the morning. At six in the evening they were increased fourfold, but still I could not find the way to their hearts.

Only One Condition.

Sunday, May 18. I preached at eleven on the parable of the sower; at half past two on Psalm i, 23, and in the evening on "Now abideth faith, hope, love; these three." I subjoined a short account of Methodism, particularly insisting on the circumstances. There is no other religious society under heaven which requires nothing of men in order to their admission into it but a desire to save their souls. Look all around you, you cannot be admitted into the Church, or society of the Presbyterians, Anabaptists, Quakers, or any others, unless you hold the same opinions with them, and adhere to the same mode of worship. The Methodists alone do not insist on your holding this or that opinion, but they think and let think. Neither do they impose any particular mode of worship; but you may continue to worship in your former manner be it what it may. Now, I do not know any other religious society, either ancient or modern, wherein such liberty of conscience is now allowed, or has been allowed, since the age of the Apostles. Here is our glorying, and a glorying peculiar to us. What society shares it with us?

The Last Week of Wesley's Eighty-fourth Year—Preaches Seventeen Times!

Thursday, June 19. I went about forty miles out of my way to see my old friends at Malton, and particularly old Mr. Wilson, at whose house I first lodged there. Between eleven and twelve I began preaching on "It is appointed unto men once to die;" and God applied his word, one would almost have thought, to every one under the roof. It was a glorious opportunity. The people were gathered from many miles round, and I think few repented of their labor. As soon as the service was over I hasted away, and reached Beverley (twenty-eight miles) in good time. The house here, though greatly enlarged, was well filled with high and low, rich and poor; and (it being the day of the Archdeacon's visitation) many of the clergy were there. I rejoiced in this, as it might be a means of removing prejudice from many sincere minds.

Friday, June 20. I went on to Hull, and in the evening explained and applied those remarkable words of our Lord, "Whosoever doeth the will of God, the same is my brother, and sister, and mother." The new preaching-house here is nearly as large as the new chapel in London. It is well built and elegantly finished—handsome, but not gaudy.

Saturday, June 21. We had a large congregation at five, larger than even that at Birmingham, which exceeded all the morning congregations I had then seen.

Sunday, June 22. Mr. Clark, the Vicar, inviting me to preach in the High Church, I explained (what occurred in the service of the day) what it is to build our house upon the rock, and applied it as strongly as I could. I dined at the vicarage with Mr. Clark, a friendly, sensible man, and, I believe, truly fearing God. And such, by the peculiar providence of God, are all the three stated ministers in Hull. He said he never saw the church so full before. However, it was still fuller in the afternoon, when, at the desire of Mr. Clark, I preached on St. James's beautiful account of the wisdom which is from above. At six in the evening I preached in our own house, to as many as could get in, (but abundance of people went away,) on Gal. vi, 14.

Monday, June 23. About eight we reached Mr. Stillingfleet's, at Hotham, one of the pleasantest places I have seen. At nine he read prayers, and I preached to a large and serious congregation. At eleven I preached, with much enlargement of heart, in the new chapel at Market Weighton; and at half an hour after one in Pocklington, but the house was like an oven. Between six and seven I began at York on Rom. xiii, 12. The word was as fire, and all that heard it seemed to feel the power thereof.

Tuesday, June 24. Having no other opportunity, I went over to Thirsk, and preached in the evening on 1 Peter i, 24. All the congregation were serious, but two young gentlewomen, who laughed and talked incessantly, till I turned and spoke expressly to them. They then seemed to be ashamed.

Wednesday, June 25. Believing the little flock there wanted encouragement, I took Ripon in my way to York, and gave them a strong discourse on the story of Dives and Lazarus. Many strangers seemed greatly astonished, and I believe they will not soon forget what they heard, for God applied it to their hearts, as he did also the parable of the sower at York, I will hope, to most of the congregation.

Thursday, June 26. The Vicar of Selby having sent me word that I was welcome to preach in his church, I went that way. But before I came he had changed his mind, so I preached in our own chapel, and not without a blessing. In the evening I preached at Thorne to a larger congregation than I ever saw in the house before.

Friday, June 27. At nine I preached in the church at Swinfleet, filled from end to end. About eleven I preached at Crowle to a large congregation, and I am now in hope that there will be a good harvest here also, seeing the almost perpetual jars are now at an end. Thence I came once more (perhaps for the last time) to Epworth, where, by the prudence and diligence of T. Tattershall, the people have now forgot their feuds and are at unity with each other.

Wesley Enters his Eighty-fifth Year

Saturday, June 28. I this day enter on my eighty-fifth year, and what cause have I to praise God, as for a thousand spiritual blessings, so for bodily blessings also! How little have I suffered yet by "the rush of numerous years!" It is true, I am not so agile as I was in times past. I do not run or walk so fast as I did, my sight is a little decayed, my left eye is grown dim, and hardly serves me to read ; I have daily some pain in the ball of my right eye, as also in my right temple, (occasioned by a blow received some months since,) and in my right shoulder and arm, which I impute partly to a sprain and partly to the rheumatism. I find likewise some decay in my memory with regard to names and things lately past, but not at all with regard to what I have read or heard twenty, forty, or sixty years ago ; neither do I find any decay in my hearing, smell, taste, or appetite, (though I want but a third part of the food I did once,) nor do I feel any such thing as weariness, either in traveling or preaching, and I am not conscious of any decay in writing sermons, which I do as readily, and, I believe, as correctly as ever. To what cause can I impute this, that I am as I am ! First, doubtless, to the power of God fitting me for the work to which I am called, as long as he pleases to continue me therein ; and next, subordinately to this, to the prayers of his children. May we not impute it as inferior means, 1. To my constant exercise and change of air ? 2. To my never having lost a night's sleep, sick or well, at land or sea, since I was born ? 3. To my having sleep at command, so that whenever I feel myself almost worn out I call it and it comes, day or night ; 4. To my having constantly, for above sixty years, risen at four in the morning ? 5. To my constant preaching at five in the morning for above fifty years ? 6. To my having had so little pain in my life, and so little sorrow and anxious care ? Even now, though I find pain daily in my eye, or temple, or arm, yet it is never violent, and seldom lasts many minutes at a time. Whether or not this is sent to give me warning that I am shortly to quit this tabernacle, I do not know; but be it one way or the other, I have only to say,

My remnant of days
I spend to his praise,
  Who died the whole world to redeem:
Be they many or few,
My days are his due,
  And they all are devoted to Him!

No Rest this side of Heaven.

Thursday, July 3. I was going to preach at Alford, near the end of the town, but the gentry sent and desired me to preach in the market-place, which I accordingly did to a large and attentive congregation on "It is appointed unto men once to die." Thence we went to Raithby, an earthly paradise! How gladly would I rest here a few days, but it is not my place! I am to be a wanderer upon earth. Only let me find rest in a better world! At six I preached in the church to such a congregation as I never saw here before, but I do not wonder if all the country should flock in hither to a palace in the midst of a paradise.

Age Steals upon Wesley by Gentle Steps.

Monday, Dec. 15. In the evening I preached at Miss Teulon's school in Highgate. I think it was the coldest night I ever remember. The house we were in stood on the edge of the hill, and the east wind set full in the window. I counted eleven, twelve, one, and was then obliged to dress, the cramp growing more and more violent. But in the morning, not only the cramp was gone, but likewise the lameness which used to follow it.

About this time I was reflecting on the gentle steps whereby age steals upon us. Take only one instance. Four years ago my sight was as good as it was at five-and-twenty. I then began to observe that I did not see things quite so clear with my left eye as with my right—all objects appeared a little browner to that eye. I began next to find some difficulty in reading a small print by candle-light. A year after I found it in reading by daylight. In winter, 1786, I could not well read our four-shilling hymn book, unless with a large candle; the next year I could not read letters if wrote with a small or bad hand. Last winter a pearl appeared on my left eye, the sight of which grew exceeding dim. The right eye seems unaltered, only I am a great deal nearer-sighted than ever I was. Thus are "those that look out at the windows darkened"—one of the marks of old age. But I bless God "the grasshopper is" not "a burden." I am still capable of traveling, and my memory is much the same as ever it was, and so I think is my understanding.

Wesley Left no Money in his Will.

Thursday, Jan. 1, 1789. If this is to be the last year of my life, I hope it will be the best. I am not careful about it, but heartily receive the advice of the angel in Milton:

> How well is thine; how long permit to heaven.

Sunday, Jan. 4. Although the extreme severity of the weather kept many tender people away, yet we had a large congregation in the evening to renew covenant with God, and we always find when we avouch him to be our God he avouches us to be his people.

Monday, Jan. 5. At the earnest desire of Mrs. T——, I once more sat for my picture. Mr. Romney is a painter indeed. He struck off an exact likeness at once, and did more in one hour than Sir Joshua did in ten.

Tuesday, Jan. 6. I retired to Highbury Place, and on *Thursday, Jan.* 8, to Peckham. Here, in the evening, I preached to a very serious congregation, although many of them were of the better rank. But rich and poor seemed equally determined to work out their own salvation.

Friday, Jan. 9. I left no money to any one in my will because I had none. But now considering that whenever I am removed money will soon arise by sale of books, I added a few legacies by a codicil, to be paid as soon as may be. But I would fain do a little good while I live, for who can tell what will come after him?

A Day of Rest!

Saturday, March 21. I had a day of rest, only preaching morning and evening.

Sunday, March 22, was appointed for my opening the house at the east end of the town. It would have been crowded above measure but that the friendly rain interposed, so that we had only a moderate congregation. It was otherwise in the evening, when heaps upon heaps were obliged to go away. How white are these fields unto the harvest!

Monday, March 23. The congregation at Dudley pretty well filled the new house, where I preached as I did at London fifty years ago. Thence we hastened to Madeley, where I found Mrs. Fletcher better than she had been for many years, and young Mr. Fletcher much alive to God, and swiftly growing up into the spirit of his uncle. I preached in the evening, after Mr. Horne had read prayers, to a deeply serious congregation; and again at nine in the morning, *Wednesday, March* 24, in the preaching-house she has lately fitted up. Going on to Shrewsbury, at six I preached in the preaching-house on 1 Cor. xiii, 1-3. Several of the gentry and several clergymen were there, and, I believe, not in vain. I had purposed to set out early in the morning, but was persuaded to stay another day, there being now a fairer prospect in Salop than had been before. I preached morning and evening. I have cast my bread upon the waters and hope it will be found again, at least after many days.

Wesley Sails for Ireland.

Thursday, March 26. We set out early, and, taking post-horses at Clowrust, reached Conway between eight and nine o'clock, having traveled seventy-eight miles that day—twenty-eight more than from Chester to Conway.

Friday, March 27. We went on to Holyhead, and at eight in the evening went on board the Claremont packet. The wind stood fair three or four hours; it then turned against us and blew hard. I do not remember I was ever so sick at sea before, but this was little to the cramp, which held most of the night with little intermission. All *Saturday* we were beating to and fro, and gaining little ground, and I was so ill throughout the day as to be fit for nothing ; but I slept well in the night, and about eight in the morning, *Sunday, March* 29, came safe to Dublin quay.

I went straight up to the new room. We had a numerous congregation, and as serious as if we had been at West-street. I preached on the sickness and recovery of King Hezekiah and King George, and great was our rejoicing. I really took knowledge of the change which God has wrought in this congregation within a few years. A great part of them were light and airy, now almost all appear as serious as death.

Monday, March 30. I began preaching at five in the morning, and the congregation, both then and the following mornings, was far larger in proportion than those in London.

Original Design of the Methodists.

Sunday, April 12. (Being *Easter-Day.*) We had a solemn assembly indeed, many hundred communicants in the morning, and in the afternoon far more hearers than our room would contain, though it is now considerably enlarged. Afterward I met the society, and explained to them at large the original design of the Methodists, namely, not to be a distinct party, but to stir up all parties, Christians or Heathens, to worship God in spirit and in truth, but the Church of England in particular, to which they belonged from the beginning. With this view I have uniformly gone on for fifty years, never varying from the doctrine of the Church at all, nor from her discipline of choice, but of necessity; so, in a course of years, necessity was laid upon me, (as I have proved elsewhere,) 1. To preach in the open air. 2. To pray extempore. 3. To form societies. 4. To accept the assistance of Lay Preachers, and, in a few other instances, to use such means as occurred, to prevent or remove evils that we either felt or feared.

The Poor People must have his Blessing.

Sunday, May 24. At seven I preached in the Town-hall at Cavan to a very large and well-behaved congregation. As I went through Ballyhays, the poor people flocked round me on every side, and would not be contented till I came out of the chaise, and spent some time with them in prayer. I expected, being a fair morning, to see a huge congregation at Clones; but while we were at church the rain came on, so all I could do in the evening was to let Joseph Bradford preach to as many as the house would contain, and to administer the Lord's Supper to our own society.

Wesley Enters the Eighty-sixth Year of his Age.

Sunday, June 28. In the conclusion of the morning service we had a remarkable blessing, and the same in the evening, moving the whole congregation as the heart of one man. This day I enter on my eighty-sixth year. I now find I grow old. 1. My sight is decayed, so that I cannot read a small print unless in a strong light. 2. My strength is decayed, so that I walk much slower than I did some years since. 3. My memory of names, whether of persons or places, is decayed, till I stop a little to recollect them. What I should be afraid of is, if I took thought for the morrow, that my body should weigh down my mind, and create either stubbornness by the decrease of my understanding, or peevishness by the increase of bodily infirmities; but thou shalt answer for me, O Lord my God.

The Dublin Conference.

Friday, July 3. Our little Conference began in Dublin, and ended *Tuesday*, 7. On this I observe: 1. I never had between forty and fifty such preachers together in Ireland before; all of them we had reason to hope alive to God, and earnestly devoted to his service. 2. I never saw such a number of preachers before so unanimous in all points, particularly as to leaving the Church, which none of them had the least thought of. It is no wonder that there has been this year so large an increase of the society.

Sunday, July 5. I desired as many as chose it of our society to go to St. Patrick's, being the first Sunday in the month. The Dean preached a serious, useful sermon; and we had such a company of communicants as I suppose scarce had been seen there together for above a hundred years. Our house would not contain them that came in the evening, many of whom being little awakened, I preached on "It is a fearful thing to fall into the hands of the living God." On *Monday* and *Tuesday* we settled the rest of our business, and on *Wednesday* morning we parted in the same love that we met. I had much satisfaction in this Conference, in which, conversing with between forty and fifty traveling preachers, I found such a body of men as I hardly believed could have been found together in Ireland; men of so sound experience, so deep piety, and so strong understanding. I am convinced they are no way inferior to the English Conference except it be in number.

Conference at Leeds.

Sunday, July 26. I preached at noon in Birstal house to as lively a congregation as ever was seen there, and at five preached on the education of children.

Monday, July 27. Being not well able to preach in the morning, through the heat and dryness of my mouth, in the evening I preached on 1 Tim. vi, 20.

Tuesday, July 28. The Conference began, about a hundred preachers were present, and never was our Master more eminently present with us. The case of separation from the Church was largely considered, and we were all unanimous against it.

Saturday, Aug. 1. We considered the case of Dewsbury House, which the self-elected trustees have robbed us of. The point contended for was this: that they should have a right of rejecting any preachers they disproved of. But this, we saw, would destroy itinerancy. So they chose J. A—— for a preacher, who adopted W. E—— for his curate. Nothing remained but to build another preaching-house, toward which we subscribed two hundred and six pounds on the spot.

Sunday, Aug. 2. Knowing the church would not contain half of our congregation added to its own, we began at our room at half an hour past nine. After preaching, with the assistance of three other clergymen I administered the sacrament to fifteen or sixteen hundred persons, I hope all desirous to be inward Christians.

Tuesday, Aug. 4. Having before preached to the people at large, I now spoke directly to the preachers on "If any man speak, let him speak as the oracles of God;" and, I am persuaded, God applied his word to many of their hearts.

Wednesday, Aug. 5. About noon we left Leeds, and that evening went to Newark, about seventy miles.

Thursday, Aug. 6. We set out early, and between four and five reached Hinxworth. I was now pretty well inclined to rest, but a congregation soon getting together I could not disappoint them, but preached on "We love him because he first loved us;" and after preaching, and traveling fourscore miles, I was no more tired than when I set out in the morning.

Another Tour West.

Sunday, Aug. 9. The new chapel was sufficiently crowded, both in the morning and at four in the afternoon. At seven we set out, and about noon on *Monday*, 9, reached Bristol. Finding all things here in a flourishing state, I set out for the West early on *Tuesday* morning, and had an exceeding pleasant journey to Taunton, where we had a full and serious congregation in the evening.

Wednesday, Aug. 10. I had no thought of preaching at Collumpton, though we were to pass through it; but I yielded to importunity, and preached at one to a numerous audience. Thence we went on to Exeter, where the people were in high expectation of seeing the King, who appointed to be there the next day; however, a pretty large congregation assembled, to which I preached at six o'clock. We set out at three on *Thursday*, 13, and reached Plymouth between one and two in the afternoon. I preached to a large audience in the evening; and, although the day was extremely hot, yet I found myself better yesterday and to-day than I have been for some months.

Times Changed in Falmouth.

August. In the afternoon, as we could not pass by the common road, we procured leave to drive round by some fields, and got to Falmouth in good time. The last time I was here, above forty years ago, I was taken prisoner by an immense mob, gaping and roaring like lions; but how is the tide turned! High and low now lined the street from one end of the town to the other, out of stark love and kindness, gaping and staring as if the King were going by. In the evening I preached on the smooth top of the hill, at a small distance from the sea, to the largest congregation I have ever seen in Cornwall, except in or near Redruth. And such a time I have not known before since I returned from Ireland. God moved wonderfully on the hearts of the people, who all seemed to know the day of their visitation.

Wesley Once More in the Amphitheater.

Wednesday, Aug. 19. I preached at noon, in the High-street in Helstone, to the largest and most serious congregation which I ever remember to have seen there.

Thursday, Aug. 20. I went on to St. Just, and

preached in the evening to a lovely congregation, many of whom have not left their first love.

Friday, Aug. 21. About eleven I preached at Newlyn, and in the evening at Penzance; at both places I was obliged to preach abroad.

Saturday, Aug. 22. I crossed over to Redruth, and at six preached to a huge multitude, as usual, from the steps of the market-house. The word seemed to sink deep into every heart. I know not that ever I spent such a week in Cornwall before.

Sunday, Aug. 23. I preached there again in the morning, and in the evening at the amphitheater, I suppose for the last time, for my voice cannot now command the still increasing multitude. It was supposed they were now more than five-and-twenty thousand. I think it scarce possible that all should hear.

A Whole Town Wesley's Hearers.

Thursday, Aug. 27. We set out early, and reached Truro soon after five. I preached at six, to a house full of serious people, on "Awake, thou that sleepest." The congregation seemed to be awake. Thence we hasted forward to Port Isaac. I preached in the evening, in an open part of the town, to almost all the inhabitants of it. How changed [since the time] when he that invited me durst not take me in, for fear his house should be pulled down!

The Request of a Poor Man.

Saturday, Aug. 29. Going through Tavistock, a poor man asked me to preach. I began in about a quarter of an hour, the preaching-house being filled directly, but with so poor a congregation as I have not seen before for twice seven years. In the evening I preached at Plymouth Dock to a very different congregation, but equally serious.

Wesley Returns to Bristol.

Sunday, Sept. 6. I read prayers and preached, and administered the sacrament to many hundred communicants. I preached in the evening as usual, but it was more than I could well do; yet in four-and-twenty hours I was as well as usual. The fair brought abundance of strangers to the preaching on *Monday, Tuesday,* and *Wednesday.*

Fruit After Fifty Years.

Thursday, Sept. 10. I went over to Thornbury, where we preached near fifty years, and hardly saw any fruit; but whom can we despair of? Now at length it seems that God's time is come. A few men of substance in the town have built a neat and commodious preaching-house. It was filled within and without with serious hearers, and they did not hear in vain.

A Good Week's Work.

Sunday, Sept. 13. As Mr. Baddiley assisted me in the morning, I took the opportunity of preaching at Kingswood in the afternoon, and abroad in the evening, and was abundantly better in the evening than in the morning.

Monday, Sept. 14. I spent an agreeable hour with Mr. Ireland and Mr. Romaine at Brislington. I could willingly spend some time here, but I have none to spare.

Tuesday, Sept. 15. In the evening I preached at

Pensford to an uncommon congregation, and with an uncommon blessing.

Wednesday, Sept. 16. I went on to Midsummer Norton. I never saw the church so full before. I preached on that verse in one of the psalms for the day, " Open thy mouth wide, and I will fill it." Many I believe found the promise true. In the evening I preached to our honest, earnest colliers at Coleford, most of whom attended again at five in the morning.

Thursday, Sept. 17. I preached at Frome to a much larger audience, and with much of the presence of God.

Friday, Sept. 18. At noon I preached at Trowbridge, in an open place, to a multitude of people; and in the evening to our old, steady congregation at Bradford, but many of them are gone into a better world. Scarce any of the rich and honorable are left, but it is enough that the Gospel is preached to the poor.

Saturday, Sept. 19. At Bath the scene is changed again. Here we have the rich and honorable in abundance, and yet abundance of them came even in a stormy night, and seemed as attentive as colliers.

Wesley cannot Preach but Twice a Day.

Thursday, Oct. 8. I set out early, and in the afternoon we were brought to London. I am now as well, by the good providence of God, as I am likely to be while I live. My sight is so decayed that I cannot well read by candle-light, but I can write as well as ever, and my strength is much lessened, so that I cannot easily preach above twice a day. But, I bless God, my memory is not much decayed, and my understanding is as clear as it has been these fifty years.

Wesley Preaches at Oxford.

Thursday, Oct. 29. I returned to Oxford; and as notice had been given, though without my knowledge, of me preaching at noon, I did so on "There is one God," to a very serious congregation; but in the evening such a multitude of people pressed in that they hindered one another from hearing. I know not when we have had so noisy a congregation; so that, by their eagerness to hear, they defeated their own purpose.

Friday, Oct. 30. In my way to Wycomb I spent an hour at Mr. Smith's, in Cudsdem. He has ten children, from eighteen to a year or two old, but all under government, so that I met the very picture of my father's family. What a wretched steward was he who influenced Lord H—— to put away such a tenant! In the evening the house at High Wycomb, though full, was still as night.

Saturday, Oct. 31. We came safe and well to London.

The Classes still Share Wesley's Labors.

Monday, Nov. 9. I returned to London, and the four following days I employed in visiting the classes.

Sunday, Nov. 15. We had, as usual, a large congregation, and a solemn opportunity at Spitalfields, and another at Shoreditch Church, where I preached a charity sermon, after the prayers had been read in such a manner as I never heard before. At five I preached in the new chapel and met the society, but it was too much for me.

Wesley Resumes Early Morning Preaching.

Monday, Nov. 16. After an intermission of many weeks, through the dryness of my mouth, I resolved to try if I could not preach at five in the morning, and did so with not much difficulty, and I now hope to hold on a little longer.

Wednesday, Nov. 18. I found much life in the society at Brentford, so little cause have we to despair of any people, though for the present ever so dead!

Thursday, Nov. 19. I preached to a large congregation at Lambeth. On *Friday* and *Saturday* I answered my letters.

He Preaches Away his Hoarseness.

Wednesday, Dec. 16. Being quite hoarse, I could neither sing nor speak; however, I determined to show myself at least where I had appointed to preach. Coming to Sandwich about noon, and finding the congregation was waiting, I trusted in God, and began to speak; the more I spoke the more my voice was strengthened, so that in a few minutes I think all could hear, and many I believe took knowledge that what they heard was not the word of man but of God. I preached again at Margate in the evening, till my voice was near as clear as before I begun. The spirit of God was with us of a truth.

The Tables Turned.

Friday, Dec. 25. (Being *Christmas-Day.*) We began the service in the new chapel at four o'clock as usual, where I preached again in the evening, after having officiated in West-street at the common hour.

Saturday, Dec. 26. We had a very uncommon congregation in the evening, with a very uncommon blessing.

Sunday, Dec. 27. I preached in St. Luke's, our parish church, in the afternoon, to a very numerous congregation, on "The Spirit and the Bride say, Come." So are the tables turned, that I have now more invitations to preach in churches than I can accept of.

An Old Man at Last.

Friday, Jan. 1, 1790. I am now an old man, decayed from head to foot. My eyes are dim, my right hand shakes much, my mouth is hot and dry every morning, I have a lingering fever almost every day, my motion is weak and slow. However, blessed be God, I do not slack my labor. I can preach and write still.

Saturday, Jan. 2. I preached at Snowsfields, to the largest congregation I have seen there this year, on "I am not ashamed of the Gospel of Christ."

Sunday, Jan. 3. I suppose near two thousand met at the new chapel to renew their covenant with God; a scriptural means of grace which is now almost every-where forgotten except among the Methodists.

One More Sermon to Little Children.

Sunday, Feb. 14. I preached a sermon to the children at West-street chapel. They flocked together from every quarter, and truly God was in the midst of them, applying those words, "Come, ye little children, hearken unto me, and I will teach you the fear of the Lord."

Tuesday, Feb. 16. I retired to Balham for a few

days, in order to finish my sermons, and put all my little things in order.

Thursday, Feb. 18. I preached once more at poor Wandsworth.

A Week's Work in Bristol.

Thursday, March 4. I went to Bristol, where I found a people ready prepared for the Lord. The preachers are in earnest, the fruit of which plainly appears in the congregations.

Friday, March 5. Hearing Mr. W——, of Bolton, was dying, I went over and spent an hour with him. His spirit was much comforted, and in a few days he was nearly as well as ever.

Saturday, March 6. I preached in the evening at Temple Church. Mr. Easterbrook has lately been very ill, but God has again lifted up his head to be a father to the poor a little longer.

Sunday, March 7. I preached at the room morning and evening, and about two in the afternoon at Kingswood. Just as I had concluded my sermon in the room a lady came in her carriage in all haste, and, finding the sermon over, earnestly desired to stay at the society. Afterward she importuned me much to call on her at the Hot Wells, where her husband, Governor Johnstone, died two years ago. On *Monday, Tuesday, Wednesday,* and *Thursday* she came to the preaching, and seemed to be much affected. On *Friday* evening I was at Kingswood, and preached to such a congregation as I have not seen there on a week day for forty years, unless it was at a watch-night.

Saturday, March 13. I spent two hours with her

at Granby House, and answered all her questions. She appeared quite willing to know the truth, and to be altogether a Christian, and vehemently desired, if our lives were prolonged, that I would visit her in London. But if we should live, would she then be willing to see me? If she is, it would be a miracle indeed.

This week I visited the classes in Bristol. I wonder we do not increase in number, although many are convinced, many justified, and a few perfected in love. I can impute the want of increase to nothing but want of self-denial. Without this, indeed, whatever other helps they have, no believers can go forward.

Wesley Once More at Birmingham.

Friday, March 19. Coming to Quinton, I found a congregation waiting for me. So that I might not disappoint them, I preached immediately on "We love him because he first loved us," and then went on to Birmingham, which I think is thrice as large as when I saw it fifty years ago. The congregation were well squeezed together, and I think most of them got in. The behavior of the rich and poor is such as does honor to their profession, so decent, so serious, so devout, from the beginning to the end! It was the same the next evening.

Sunday, March 21. The prayers began at the new house about half an hour after ten. It is a little larger than the new house at Brompton, and admirably well constructed. But several hundreds, I suppose, could not get in. I think all who did found that God was there. The great house likewise, in the evening, was utterly insufficient to contain the congregation. But God is able to supply this want also, and his time is best.

Wesley's Eyes now Dim and his Natural Force Abated—but works on!

Wednesday, March 24. We rode to Madeley through a pleasant rain, which did not hinder the church from being thoroughly filled, and I believe all who had spiritual discernment perceived that it was filled with the presence of God.

Thursday, March 25. At nine I preached to a select congregation on the deep things of God, and in the evening on "He is able to save unto the uttermost all them that come unto God through him."

Friday, March 26. I finished my sermon on the Wedding Garment, perhaps the last that I shall write. My eyes are now waxed dim, my natural force is abated. However, while I can I would fain do a little for God before I drop into the dust. In the evening I preached to a crowded audience at Salop on "Acquaint now thyself with him, and be at peace." But I was much ashamed for them. The moment I had done speaking I suppose fifty of them were talking all at once; and no wonder they had neither sense nor good manners—for they were gentlefolks!

Saturday, March 27. I preached in the evening to a sensible and well-behaved congregation at Newcastle-under-Lyne. (Observe, that is the name of the river which runs above the town.)

Sunday, March 28. I preached soon after one in Mr. Myat's yard, at Lane End; the house would not have contained a quarter of the people. At Burslem also I was obliged to preach abroad, such were the multitudes of the people. Surely the people of this place were highly favored. Mercy embraced them on every side.

Monday, March 29. At nine I preached in the new chapel at Tunstal, the most elegant I have seen since I left Bath. My text was, "Let us go on unto perfection," and the people seemed to devour the word. In the evening I preached at Congleton. The minister, the Mayor, and all the heads of the town were present; so, that I might not overshoot them, I preached on Psalm xc, 12, and I believe God applied it to their hearts.

Tuesday, March 30. I went on to Macclesfield, and preached to a crowded audience both this and the following night. On *Thursday* morning one of my horses died. I judged it best to leave the other till I could procure another, and took post-chaise to Stockport. A large congregation was ready at six in the evening. In the morning, on *Good Friday*, we went on to Oldham. The new house would in nowise contain the congregation, but I preached to as many as it would contain on 1 Cor. vi, 19; and at Manchester in the evening, *Saturday, April* 3, on Heb. iv, 14.

Sunday, April 4. (Being *Easter Day.*) I think we had about one thousand six hundred communicants. I preached both morning and evening without weariness, and in the evening lay down in peace.

Wesley in Scotland Again.

Tuesday, May 25. We returned to Aberdeen, and I took a solemn farewell of a crowded audience. If

I should be permitted to see them again, well; if not, I have delivered my own soul.

Wednesday, May 26. Taking the midland road, we spent an hour at Lawrence Kirk, which, from an inconsiderable village, is, by the care and power of Lord Gordon, soon sprung up into a pleasant, neat, and flourishing town. His lordship has also erected a little library here, adjoining to a handsome and well-furnished inn. The country from hence to Brechin is as pleasant as a garden; happy would Scotland be if it had many such gentlemen and noblemen. In the evening I began preaching at Brechin in the Freeman's Lodge, but I was so faint and ill that I was obliged to shorten my discourse.

Thursday, May 27. We went on through Forfar (now a handsome and almost a new town) and Cupar to Auchterarder. Here we expected poor accommodations, but were agreeably disappointed. Food, beds, and every thing else, were as neat and clean as at Aberdeen or Edinburgh.

Friday, May 28. We traveled through a delightful country, by Stirling and Kilsythe, to Glasgow. The congregation was miserably small, verifying what I had often heard before, that the Scots dearly love the word of the Lord on the Lord's day. If I live to come again, I will take care to spend only the Lord's day at Glasgow.

Villainous Tautology.

Tuesday, June 8. I wrote a form for settling the preaching-houses, without any superfluous words, which shall be used for the time to come *verbatim*, for all the houses for which I contribute any thing.

I will no more encourage that villainous tautology of lawyers, which is the scandal of our nation. In the evening I preached to the children of our Sunday-school, six or seven hundred of whom were present.

N. B. None of our masters or mistresses teach for pay; they seek a reward that man cannot give.

Wesley Enters Upon his Eighty-eighth Year!

Friday, June 25. About noon I preached at Beverley to a serious, well-behaved congregation; and in the evening to one equally serious, and far more numerous, at Hull.

Saturday, June 26, was a day of satisfaction. I preached at seven in the morning and at six in the evening to as many as our house could contain, the ground being too wet for the congregation to stand abroad.

Monday, June 28. This day I enter into my eighty-eighth year. For above eighty-six years I found none of the infirmities of old age, my eyes did not wax dim, neither was my natural strength abated, but last August I found almost a sudden change. My eyes were so dim that no glasses would help me. My strength likewise now quite forsook me, and probably will not return in this world. But I feel no pain from head to foot, only it seems nature is exhausted, and, humanly speaking, will sink more and more till

The weary springs of life stand still at last.

Preaches in Epworth Market-place.

Sunday, July 4. I went over to Misterton, where likewise the work of God was exceedingly decayed.

The house being far too small to contain the multitude of people, I stood under a spreading tree, and strongly exhorted them to "strengthen the things that remained" which were "ready to die." Thence I hastened back to Epworth, but I could not reach it till the Church service was begun. It was observed Mr. Gibson read the prayers with unusual solemnity, and I believe he was not displeased to see five times as many at church, and ten times as many at the Lord's table as usual. As soon as the afternoon service ended I began in the market-place to press that awful question, "How shall we escape if we neglect so great salvation?" on such a congregation as was never seen at Epworth before.

A Three Hours' Service.

Sunday, Aug. 29. Mr. Baddiley had gone to the north, and Mr. Collins being engaged elsewhere, I had none to assist in the service, and could not read the prayers myself; so I was obliged to shorten the service, which brought the prayers, sermon, and Lord's Supper within the compass of three hours. I preached in the afternoon near King's Square, and the hearts of the people bowed down before the Lord.

A Vile Custom Ended.

Saturday, Sept. 4. I went on to Bath, and preached in the evening to a serious, but small congregation, for want of notice.

Sunday, Sept. 5. At ten we had a numerous congregation, and more communicants than ever I saw here before. This day I cut off that vile custom, I know not when or how it began, of preaching three times a day by the same preacher to the same congregation; enough to weary out both the bodies and minds of the speaker as well as his hearers.

Wesley's Last Outdoor Sermon.

Thursday, Oct. 7. I went over to that poor skeleton of ancient Winchelsea. It is beautifully situated on the top of a steep hill, and was regularly built in broad streets, crossing each other, and encompassing a very large square, in the midst of which was a large church, now in ruins. I stood under a large tree, on the side of it, and called to most of the inhabitants of the town, "The kingdom of heaven is at hand; repent, and believe the Gospel." It seemed as if all that heard were, for the present, almost persuaded to be Christians.

Cause for Humiliation.

Saturday, Oct. 9. We returned to Lonaon.

Monday, Oct. 11. I went on to Colchester, and still found matter of humiliation. The society was lessened and cold enough; preaching was again discontinued, and the spirit of Methodism quite gone both from the preachers and the people; yet we had a wonderful congregation in the evening, rich and poor, clergy and laity. So we had likewise on *Tuesday* evening. So that I trust God will at length build up the waste places.

An Honorable Man at Last.

Wednesday, Oct. 13. In the evening I preached at Norwich, but the house would in nowise contain the congregation. How wonderfully is the tide turned! I am become an honorable man at Norwich. God has at length made our enemies to be at peace with us; and scarce any but Antinomians open their mouth against us.

The Last Entries in Wesley's Journal.

Thursday, Oct. 14. I went to Yarmouth, and at length found a society in peace and much united together. In the evening the congregation was too large to get into the preaching-house; yet they were far less noisy than usual. After supper a little company went to prayer, and the power of God fell upon us, especially when a young woman broke out into prayer, to the surprise and comfort of us all.

Friday, Oct. 15. I went to Lowestoft to a steady, loving, well-united society. The more strange it is, that they neither increase nor decrease in number.

Saturday, Oct. 16. I preached at Loddon about one, and at six in Norwich,

Sunday, Oct. 17. At seven I administered the Lord's Supper to about one hundred and fifty persons, near twice as many as we had last year. I take knowledge that the last year's preachers were in earnest. Afterward we went to our own parish church; although there was no sermon there, nor at any of the thirty-six churches in the town, save the cathedral and St. Peter's. I preached at two. When I had done Mr. Horne called upon me, who preached at the cathedral in the morning; an agreeable man, both in temper and person, and, I believe, much alive to God. At half an hour after five I preached again to as many as the house would contain, and even those that could not get in stayed more quiet and silent than ever I saw them before. Indeed, they all seemed to know that God was there, and I have no doubt but he will revive his work here also.

Monday, Oct. 18. No coach going out for Lynn to-day, I was obliged to take a post-chaise. But at Dereham no horses were to be had, so we were obliged to take the same horses to Swaffham. A congregation was ready here that filled the house, and seemed quite ready to receive instruction. But here neither could we procure any post-horses, so that we were obliged to take a single horse-chaise. The wind, with mizzling rain, came full in our faces, and we had nothing to screen us from it, so that I was thoroughly chilled from head to foot before I came to Lynn. But I soon forgot this little inconvenience, for which the earnestness of the congregation made me large amends.

Tuesday, Oct. 19. In the evening all the clergymen in the town except one, who was lame, were present at the preaching. They all prejudiced in favor of the Methodists, as indeed are most of the townsmen, who give a fair proof by contributing so much to our Sunday-schools, so that there is near twenty pounds in hand.

Wednesday, Oct. 20. I had appointed to preach at Diss, a town near Scoleton, but the difficulty was where I could preach. The minister was willing I should preach in the church, but feared offending the Bishop, who, going up to London, was within a few miles of the town. But a gentleman asking the Bishop whether he had any objection to it, was answered, "None at all." I think this church is one of the largest in this county. I suppose it has not been so filled these hundred years.

Friday, Oct. 22. We returned to London.

Sunday, Oct. 24. I explained to a numerous congregation, in Spitalfields Church, "the whole armor of God." St. Paul's, Shadwell, was still more crowded in the afternoon while I enforced that important truth, "One thing is needful," and I hope many even then resolved to choose the better part.

Wesley's Final Sickness and Death.

This most interesting record of unparalleled labors "in the Gospel," was for this reason,* it is presumed, discontinued, and closes on Sunday, October 24, 1790, when he states that he preached twice at Spitalfields Church. He continued, however, during the autumn and winter, to visit various places till February, continually praying, "Lord, let me not live to be useless." The following account of his last days is taken from the Memoir prefixed to the edition of his Works by the Rev. Joseph Benson, and is there inserted as a proper close to his Journal:

"He preached, as usual, in different places in London and its vicinity, generally meeting the society after preaching in each place, and exhorting them to love as brethren, to fear God, and honor the king, which he wished them to consider as his last advice. He then usually, if not invariably, concluded with giving out that verse,

'O that, without a lingering groan,
I may the welcome word receive;
My body with my charge lay down,
And cease at once to work and live.'

* Failure of sight.

"He proceeded in this way till the usual time of his leaving London approached, when, with a view to take his accustomed journey through Ireland or Scotland, he sent his chaise and horses before him to Bristol, and took places for himself and his friend in the Bath coach. But his mind, with all its vigor, could no longer uphold his worn-out and sinking body. Its powers ceased, although by slow and almost imperceptible degrees, to perform their sundry offices, until, as he often expressed himself,

'The weary wheels of life stood still at last.'

"Thursday, February 17, 1791, he preached at Lambeth; but on his return seemed much indisposed, and said he had taken cold. The next day, however, he read and wrote as usual; and in the evening preached at Chelsea from "The King's business requires haste," although with some difficulty, having a high degree of fever upon him. Indeed, he was obliged to stop once or twice, informing the people that his cold so affected his voice as to prevent his speaking without those necessary pauses. On Saturday he still persevered in his usual employments, though, to those about him, his complaints seemed evidently increasing. He dined at Islington, and at dinner desired a friend to read him four chapters out of the book of Job, namely, from the fourth to the seventh inclusive. On Sunday he rose early, according to custom, but quite unfit for any of his usual Sabbath day's exercises. At seven o'clock he was obliged to lie down, and slept between three and four hours. When he awoke he said, "I have not had such a comfortable sleep this fortnight past."

In the afternoon he lay down again, and slept an hour or two. Afterward two of his own discourses on our Lord's Sermon on the Mount were read to him, and in the evening he came down to supper.

"Monday, the 21st, he seemed much better; and, though his friends tried to dissuade him from it, he would keep an engagement, made some time before, to dine at Twickenham. In his way thither he called on Lady Mary Fitzgerald; the conversation was truly profitable, and well became a last visit. On Tuesday he went on with his usual work, preached in the evening at the chapel in the City Road, and seemed much better than he had been for some days. On Wednesday he went to Leatherhead, and preached to a small company on "Seek ye the Lord while he may be found; call ye upon him while he is near." This proved to be his last sermon; here ended the public labors of this great minister of Jesus Christ. On Thursday he paid a visit to Mr. Wolff's family at Balham, where he was cheerful, and seemed nearly as well as usual, till Friday, about breakfast time, when he grew very heavy. About eleven o'clock he returned home extremely ill. His friends were struck with the manner of his getting out of the carriage, and still more with his apparent weakness when he went up stairs and sat down in his chair. He now desired to be left alone, and not to be interrupted by any one for half an hour. When that time was expired some mulled wine was brought to him, of which he drank a little. In a few minutes he threw it up, and said, 'I must lie down.' His friends were now alarmed, and Dr. Whitehead was immediately sent for. On his entering the room he said in a cheerful voice, "Doctor, they are more afraid than hurt.' Most of this day he lay in bed, had a quick pulse, with a considerable degree of fever and stupor. And Saturday, the 26th, he continued in much the same state, taking very little either of medicine or nourishment.

"Sunday morning he seemed much better, got up, and took a cup of tea. Sitting in his chair, he looked quite cheerful, and repeated the latter part of the verse, in his brother Charles's Scripture Hymn, on 'Forsake me not when my strength faileth,' namely:

> 'Till glad I lay this body down,
> Thy servant, Lord, attend;
> And, O! my life of mercy crown
> With a triumphant end.'

Soon after, in a most emphatic manner, he said, 'Our friend Lazarus sleepeth.' Exerting himself to converse with some friends, he was soon fatigued, and obliged to lie down. After lying quiet some time, he looked up and said, 'Speak to me, I cannot speak.' On which one of the company said, 'Shall we pray with you, sir?' He earnestly replied, 'Yes.' And while they prayed, his whole soul seemed engaged with God for an answer, and his hearty *Amen* showed that he perfectly understood what was said. About half an hour after he said, 'There is no need of more; when at Bristol my words were,

> 'I the chief of sinners am,
> But Jesus died for me!'

"One said, 'Is this the present language of your heart, and do you now feel as you did then?'

He replied, 'Yes.' When the same person repeated,

> 'Bold I approach the eternal throne,
> And claim the crown, through Christ my own;'

and added, ''Tis enough. He our precious Immanuel has purchased, has promised all;' he earnestly replied, 'He is all! He is all!' After this the fever was very high, and, at times, affected his recollection; but even then, though his head was subject to a temporary derangement, his heart seemed wholly engaged in his Master's work. In the evening he got up again, and, while sitting in his chair, he said, 'How necessary it is for every one to be on the right foundation!

> 'I the chief of sinners am,
> But Jesus died for me!'

"Monday, the 28th, his weakness increased. He slept most of the day, and spoke but little; yet that little testified how much his whole heart was taken up in the care of the societies, the glory of God, and the promotion of the things pertaining to that kingdom to which he was hastening. Once he said, in a low but distinct manner, 'There is no way into the holiest but by the blood of Jesus.' He afterward inquired what the words were from which he had preached a little before at Hampstead. Being told they were these, 'Ye know the grace of our Lord Jesus Christ, that, though he was rich, yet for your sakes he became poor, that ye through his poverty might be rich;' he replied, 'That is the foundation, the only foundation; there is no other.'

"This day Dr. Whitehead desired he might be asked if he would have any other physician called in to attend him; but this he absolutely refused. It is remarkable that he suffered very little pain, never complaining of any during his illness, but once of a pain in his left breast. This was a restless night. Tuesday morning he sung two verses of a hymn; then lying still, as if to recover strength, he called for pen and ink; but when they were brought, he could not write. A person said, 'Let me write for you, sir; tell me what you would say.' He replied, 'Nothing, but that God is with us.' In the forenoon he said, 'I will get up.' While they were preparing his clothes he broke out in a manner which, considering his extreme weakness, astonished all present, in singing,

'I'll praise my Maker while I've breath,
And, when my voice is lost in death,
  Praise shall employ my nobler powers;
My days of praise shall ne'er be past,
While life, and thought, and being last,
  Or immortality endures!'

"Having got him into his chair, they observed him change for death. But he, regardless of his dying body, said, with a weak voice, 'Lord, thou givest strength to those that can speak and to those who cannot. Speak, Lord, to all our hearts. and let them know that thou loosest tongues.' He then sung,

'To Father, Son, and Holy Ghost,
  Who sweetly all agree—'

Here his voice failed.' After gasping for breath, he said, 'Now we have done all.' He was then laid in the bed, from which he rose no more. After resting a little he called to those that were with him to 'pray and praise.' They kneeled down, and the room seemed to be filled with the divine presence. A little after, he said, 'Let me be buried in nothing but what is woolen, and let my corpse be carried into the chapel.' Then, as if he had done with all below, he again begged they would pray and praise. Several friends that were in the house being called up, they all kneeled down again to prayer, at which time his fervor of spirit was manifest to every one present. But in particular parts of the prayer his whole soul seemed to be engaged in a manner which evidently showed how ardently he longed for the full accomplishment of their united desires. And when one of the preachers was praying in a very expressive manner that, if God were about to take away their father to his eternal rest, he would be pleased to continue and increase his blessing upon the doctrine and discipline which he had long made his servant the means of propagating and establishing in the world, such a degree of fervor accompanied his loud *Amen* as was every way expressive of his soul's being engaged in the answer of the petitions. On rising from their knees he took hold of all their hands, and, with the utmost placidness, saluted them, and said, 'Farewell, farewell.'

"A little after, a person coming in, he strove to speak, but could not. Finding they could not understand him, he paused a little, and then, with all the remaining strength he had, cried out, 'The best of all is, God is with us;' and soon after, lifting up his dying arm in token of victory, and raising his feeble voice with a holy triumph not to be expressed, he again repeated the heart-reviving words, 'The best of all is, God is with us.' Being told that his brother's widow was come, he said, 'He giveth his servants rest.' He thanked her as she pressed his hand, and affectionately endeavored to kiss her. On his lips being wetted he said, 'We thank thee, O Lord, for these and all thy mercies; bless the Church and King, and grant us truth and peace, through Jesus Christ our Lord, for ever and ever!' At another time he said, 'He causeth his servants to lie down in peace.' Then pausing a little, he cried, 'The clouds drop fatness!' and soon after, 'The Lord is with us, the God of Jacob is our refuge!' He then called those present to prayer, and, though he was greatly exhausted, he appeared still more fervent in spirit. These exertions were, however, too much for his feeble frame; and most of the night following, though he often attempted to repeat the psalm before mentioned, he could only utter, 'I'll praise—I'll praise—'

"On Wednesday morning the closing scene drew near. Mr. Bradford, his faithful friend, prayed with him, and the last words he was heard to articulate were, 'Farewell!' A few minutes before ten, while several of his friends were kneeling around his bed, without a lingering groan, this man of God, this beloved pastor of thousands, entered into the joy of his Lord.

"He was in the eighty-eighth year of his age, had been sixty-five years in the ministry; and the preceding pages will be a lasting memorial of his uncommon zeal, diligence, and usefulness in his Master's work for more than half a century. His death was an admirable close to so laborious and useful a life.

"At the desire of many of his friends his corpse was placed in the new chapel, and remained there the day before his interment. His face during that time had a heavenly smile upon it, and a beauty which was admired by all that saw it.

"March the 9th was the day appointed for his interment. The preachers then in London requested that Dr. Whitehead should deliver the funeral discourse, and the executors afterward approved of the appointment. The intention was to carry the corpse into the chapel, and place it in a raised situation before the pulpit during the service. But the crowds which came to see the body while it lay in the coffin, both in the private house, and especially in the chapel the day before his funeral, were so great that his friends were apprehensive of a tumult if they should adopt the plan first intended. It was therefore resolved the evening before to bury him between five and six in the morning. Though the time of notice to his friends was short, and the design itself was spoken of with great caution, yet a considerable number of persons attended at that early hour. The late Rev. Mr. Richardson, who now lies with him in the same vault, read the funeral service in a manner that made it peculiarly affecting. When he came to that part of it, 'Forasmuch as it hath pleased Almighty God to take unto himself the soul of our dear *brother*,' etc., he substituted, with the most tender emphasis, the epithet *father* instead of *brother*, which had so powerful an effect on the congregation, that from silent tears they seemed universally to burst out into loud weeping.

"The discourse by Dr. Whitehead was delivered in the chapel at the hour appointed in the forenoon, to an astonishing multitude of people; among whom were many ministers of the Gospel, both of the

Establishment and Dissenters. The audience was still and solemn as night, and all seemed to carry away with them enlarged views of Mr. Wesley's character, and serious impressions of the importance of religion."—*Watson's Wesley*, pp. 285–292.

Extent of Wesley's Ministerial Labors.

"The labors of Mr. Wesley in the work of the ministry for fifty years together were without precedent. During this period he traveled about four thousand five hundred miles every year, one year with another, chiefly on horseback. It had been impossible for him to accomplish this almost incredible degree of exertion without great punctuality and care in the management of his time. He had stated hours for every purpose, and his only relaxation was a change of employment. For fifty-two years or upward he generally delivered two, frequently three or four, sermons in a day. But calculating only two sermons a day, and allowing, as a writer of his life has done, fifty annually for extraordinary occasions, the whole number of sermons he preached during this period will be forty thousand five hundred and sixty. To these must be added an infinite number of exhortations to the societies after preaching, and in other occasional meetings, at which he assisted." —*Watson's Wesley*, page 295.

Number of Preachers and Members at the Time of Wesley's Death.

"Wesley died at the head of a thoroughly organized host of 550 itinerant preachers, and 140,000 members of his societies, in the United Kingdom, British North America, in the United States, and West Indies."—*Stevens's History of Methodism*, vol. iii, page 509.

Tablet in City Road Chapel.

The following is the inscription on the marble tablet erected to his memory in the chapel, City Road:

Sacred to the Memory
OF THE REV. JOHN WESLEY, M. A.,
SOMETIME FELLOW OF LINCOLN COLLEGE, OXFORD;
A Man in Learning and sincere Piety
Scarcely inferior to any;
In Zeal, Ministerial Labours, and extensive Usefulness,
Superior, perhaps, to all Men,
Since the days of ST. PAUL.

Regardless of Fatigue, personal Danger, and Disgrace,
He went out into the highways and hedges
Calling Sinners to Repentance,
And Publishing the GOSPEL of Peace.

He was the Founder of the Methodist Societies,
And the chief Promoter and Patron
Of the Plan of Itinerant Preaching,
Which he extended through GREAT BRITAIN and IRELAND,
The WEST INDIES, and AMERICA,
With unexampled Success.

He was born the 17th of June, 1703;
And died the 2d of March, 1791,
In sure and certain hope of Eternal Life,
Through the Atonement and Mediation of a Crucified Saviour.

He was sixty-five Years in the Ministry,
And fifty-two an Itinerant Preacher:
He lived to see, in these KINGDOMS only,
About three hundred Itinerant,
And one thousand Local Preachers,
Raised up from the midst of his own People;
And eighty thousand Persons in the Societies under his care.

His Name will be ever had in grateful Remembrance
By all who rejoice ln the universal Spread
Of the Gospel of CHRIST.

Soli Deo Gloria.
[Glory to God alone.]

Methodist Membership by Countries—1870.

The following statistics are compiled from the latest reports at hand. Some of them are summaries for 1868.

COUNTRIES.	Trav'ng Preach.	Local Preach.	Memb's.	Total Trav'ng Preach.	Total Memb's
UNITED STATES: M. E. Church, (for 1870)........	9,193	11,404	1,367,144		
M. E. Church, South..........................	2,833	4,753	571,241		
African M. E. Church..........................	1,000	3,000	375,000		
African M. E. Zion Church	391	1,420	172,000		
Evangelical (Methodist) Association..........	475	367	57,226		
Methodist Protestant..........................	423	...	72,000		
The Methodist Church..........................	624	444	49,030		
Wesleyan Methodist............................	250	...	20,000		
Free Methodist................................	109	20	5,766		
Bible Union...................................	...	...	......		
Primitive Methodist...........................	20	...	2,000	15,318	2,691,407
CANADA: Wesleyan Methodist..................	598	250	64,688		
Methodist Episcopal...........................	198	217	20,180		
New Connection Methodist......................	90	...	8,110		
Primitive Methodist...........................	70	290	7,073		
Bible Christians..............................	...	...	......	956	100,051
EASTERN BRITISH AMERICA: Wesleyan Methodist	...	...	......	162	16,287
WEST INDIES: Wesleyans.......................	90	370	43,802		
United Methodist..............................	9	...	1,798	99	45,600
HAYTI: Wesleyan................................	...	...	......	1	200
ENGLAND AND SCOTLAND: Wesleyan Methodist..	1,611	11,980	368,904		
Irish Wesleyan Conference.....................	220	690	20,793		
Primitive Methodist...........................	943	11,169	161,229		
New Connection Methodist......................	170	...	33,095		
United Free Church Methodist..................	288	...	68,092		
Bible Christian Methodist.....................	248	...	26,275		
Lady Huntingdon or Calvinistic Methodist...	...	...	58,577		
Wesleyan Reform Union.........................	21	276	8,659		
Church Methodists in Ireland..................	...	...	9,158	3,501	754,782
FRANCE: French Wesleyan Methodist...........	36	...	2,216		
Wesleyan Missions.............................	...	...	111		
Methodist Episcopal...........................	1	...	62	37	2,389
GERMANY AND SWITZERLAND: M. E. Church....	45	29	6,956		
Wesleyan......................................	...	...	1,584		
Evangelical Association.......................	17	...	4,774	62	13,314
SPAIN AND MALTA: Wesleyan Methodist.........	...	...	......	2	51
ITALY: Wesleyan Methodist.....................	...	...	......	3	70
DENMARK, SWEDEN, AND NORWAY: Meth. Epis'l.	...	...	......	17	763
INDIA AND CEYLON: Wesleyan Missions..........	33	...	662		
Methodist Episcopal Missions..................	29	32	737		
Wesleyan Missions, North and South Ceylon..	31	...	1,993	93	3,392
CHINA: Wesleyan Methodist Missions...........	9	...	58		
Methodist Episcopal Missions..................	14	...	1,514		
Methodist Episcopal Church, South, Missions.	...	...	......		
United Methodist Free Church Missions......	12	...	612		
New Connection Methodist Missions..........	12	...	147	47	2,331
AFRICA: Wesleyan Missions.....................	84	...	37,751		
Liberia Conference Meth. Episcopal Church..	18	32	1,830		
United Methodist Free Church................	3	...	2,612	105	42,193
AUSTRALIA AND POLYNESIA: Wesl'n Conferences	282	3,000	65,647		
Primitive Methodist...........................	25	...	1,904		
United Methodist Free Church................	12	...	612		
New Connection Methodist.....................	12	...	147	331	68,310
SOUTH AMERICA..................................	...	...	......	8	171
TURKEY...	...	...	......	2	....
Grand Total....................................				20,744	3,741,317

www.ingramcontent.com/pod-product-compliance
Lightning Source LLC
LaVergne TN
LVHW090545110826
845146LV00001B/24
9781425551988